Africa in Transition: Witness to Change

Godfrey Mwakikagile

Copyright (c) 2018 Godfrey Mwakikagile
All rights reserved.

Africa in Transition: Witness to Change

First Edition

ISBN-13: 978-9987-16-008-2

New Africa Press
Dar es Salaam, Tanzania

Introduction

ONE of the most momentous events in the history of Africa was the end of colonial rule.

The transition from colonial rule to independence took place mostly in the sixties. Almost all countries on the continent had won independence by 1968. It was a transition that shaped the destiny of the continent.

Another fundamental change took place in the 1990s when most African countries gradually moved from authoritarian rule to democracy. It was a major transition but with pitfalls. Genuine democracy remains elusive in many countries across Africa.

This work, which is autobiographical and biographical, is intended to shed some light on some of the events I witnessed or closely followed through the years since the fifties.

I hope it complements the works of others on some of the most critical events in the history of our continent.

Witness to Change

Godfrey Mwakikagile was born in the town of Kigoma in western Tanganyika – what is now mainland Tanzania – on 4 October 1949.

He was baptised Godfrey on Christmas day, 25 December 1949, as a member of the Church Missionary Society (CMS) among whose supporters was Scottish explorer and missionary-doctor, David Livingstone, of the London Missionary Society.[1]

Dr. Livingstone campaigned against slavery and the slave trade but also helped pave the way for the colonisation of Africa.[2]

Missionaries from Europe were some of the earliest trail blazers of the colonial enterprise. As Jomo Kenyatta said:

> The white man came and asked us to shut our eyes and pray. When we opened our eyes it was too late - our land was gone. – (Jomo Kenyatta, quoted by Godfrey Mwakikagile, *Africa in The Sixties*, New Africa Press, 2014, p. 130; G. Mwakikagile, *Africa After Independence: Realities of Nationhood*, 2009, p. 51; G. Mwakikagile, *Africa 1960 - 1970: Chronicle and Analysis*, p. 134; G. Mwakikagile, *Africa and The West*, 2000, p. 5. This witticism is attributed to Jomo Kenyatta by various sources including Kenyan Professor Ali Mazrui in his book, *The Africans: A Triple Heritage*, 1986, p. 108, among other works).

According to his autobiography, Godfrey Mwakikagile was born at Kilimani Hospital and lived with his parents in one of the government houses for government employees in Mwanga, on a street with the same name, in the town of Kigoma when his father worked as a medical assistant at the same hospital.

He later moved to Ujiji with his parents where his sister Maria was born at a Roman Catholic hospital. The rest of his siblings were also born in different parts of the country: Morogoro, Mbeya, and Tukuyu.

He was named Godfrey by his aunt, Isabella, one of his father's younger sisters.

He was, according to his birth certificate, baptised by Reverend Frank McGorlick (from Victoria, Australia), a Scottish minister of the Church Missionary Society in Kigoma his parents belonged to. But he was brought up as a member of the Moravian Church at Kyimbila, three miles south of the town of Tukuyu, in Rungwe District in what was then the Southern Highlands Province in colonial Tanganyika, as he has stated in his books, *Life in Tanganyika in The Fifties* and *My Life as an African: Autobiographical Writings*.

The church was built by the Germans in 1912 and ministered by them. It was built in an area where they also established a tea estate in 1904 which did not become fully operational on commercial basis until 1926.

The first Moravian Church in Rungwe District was established near Mount Rungwe in 1891. According to the history of Moravian missions:

> The Berlin Missionary Society was already at work in German East Africa; with that Society the Moravian Church did not want to compete and, therefore, to prevent friction or overlapping,...the two Societies, working side by side, will found stations north of Lake Nyassa....
>
> In 1891 the campaign began. For twenty-three years the chief leader and superintendent of the work in German Nyassaland was Theodore Meyer, son of Henry Meyer, the pioneer in Hlubiland. One of his colleagues was a Swiss, Theophilus Richard, and these two, pushing north from Lake Nyassa, discovered, at the foot of Mt.

Rungwe, a spur of the Livingstone Hills, a splendid sight for the first station. The date was August 21st.

The two men had never beheld a more gorgeous scene. On the north-west rose Mt. Rungwe; on the west lay a dense forest; on the south-east lay the teeming dales of Kondeland; and gazing southwards towards Lake Nyassa....

Rungwe seemed an ideal site for a mission-station. The land was high, the water pure, and the air clear and bracing. – (Joseph E. Hutton, "A History of Moravian Missions," Internet Archive).

The founding of the Moravian Church near Mount Rungwe was followed by the establishment of two missions at Lutengano and Ipyana in 1894.

Lutengano Moravian Church is three miles southwest of Kyimbila. Godfrey Mwakikagile had a second baptism at age 14 at Lutengano Moravian Church under Reverend Mwatonoka in June 1964 when he was on holidays for one month from boarding school at Mpuguso Middle School. He was in Standard Eight and in his last year at Mpuguso.

Other mission stations were established by the Moravians in Rungwe District and beyond in about fifteen years, some of them in neighbouring Mbeya District:

In 1903 they opened a Training College for Evangelists, and in 1910 they opened a Normal School, and thus Rungwe (mission near at the foot of Rungwe Mountain) became the centre of widespread evangelistic and educational activity.

For twenty years the Brethren were engaged, not merely in building a model Christian village at Rungwe, but in attempting to christianize the whole surrounding neighbourhood. In this work they employed twenty missionaries, fifty-three native helpers, thirty-seven native evangelists, and twenty-seven volunteer assistants. And in each of the five districts mentioned, strong stations, surrounded by many preaching places, were founded.

In Kondeland, besides Rungwe, they founded Rutenganiot (1894), Ipiana (1894), Mueia (1907), and Kyimbila (1912); in Bundah, Isoko (1900); in Nyika, Mbozi (1900); in Usafwa, Utengulet (1895); and in Mawanda, Ileya (1906).

In addition, however, to these head stations, the Brethren had also thirty-five out-stations and one thousand and eighty-one preaching places. The number of converts rose to 1,955; the number of schools was 144; and the number of scholars attending them, 4,949....

The missionaries..., in some cases,...introduced entirely new forms of industry. At Rungwe there was a carpenters' shop and woodworking establishment; there sixteen large saws could be seen working at once; and the natives learned to manufacture beams, joists, boards, doors, cupboards and chairs, and other articles of domestic furniture. At Utengule there was a large boot factory. At Kyimbila there was a rubber plantation.

Some of the missionaries introduced Muscat donkeys, said to be able, unlike horses, to resist the attacks of the tsetse fly; others planted rice in the lowlands and potatoes in the hilly districts; others introduced sheep and a new and hardier breed of cattle; others cultivated coffee and tea; and others, with varying success, introduced strawberries, gooseberries, plums, peaches, apricots, oranges, lemons, grapes, and other fruits previously unknown to the natives....

Formerly the natives had few implements; now they became experts in the use of hoes, knives and axes. At the head stations the Church as such generally owned a large tract of land...and the natives preferred to live near a station...partly because they felt sure that their children would be well educated. – (Ibid.).

About a quarter of mile north of Kyimbila Moravian Church, which was in the midst of a large tea plantation, was Kyimbila Primary School.

The pastor of Kyimbila Moravian Church was Godfrey Mwakikagile's great uncle (grand uncle), Asegelile Mwankemwa, who was the younger brother of his maternal grandmother Tungapesyaga (Tunga) Mapunga Mwankemwa; they were the only siblings.[3] He was the first African pastor of the church.

Godfrey Mwakikagile's mother, Syabumi Mwambapa (her maiden name), was brought up by her uncle Asegelile Mwankemwa and by her mother Tungapesyaga. She lived with him after her parents died. She was almost 14 years old when her mother died.

Her mother went to live with her brother Asegelile Mwankemwa after her husband Mwambapa died in 1929. Her mother died in 1943 and was buried on her brother's family compound in Katusyo about five miles southeast of Tukuyu. That is also where Syabumi was born, on 8

November 1929, in the same year her father died.

She was brought up on the same compound together with her first cousins, the children of Asegelile Mwankemwa, and with her brothers and sisters. One of Syabumi's cousins, Lugano Mwankemwa who was born on 25 November 1933, married a childhood friend of her husband. Their husbands came from the same area the two cousins came from.

Syabumi and her cousins attended Kyimbila Girls' School headed by the British feminist educator Mary Hancock. Hancock was also a friend of Julius Nyerere and his family since the 1950s before Nyerere became prime minister and then president of Tanganyika:

> Maureen Cowan and March Hancock have told me about Tabora Girls' School, of which both have been headmistresses. Miss Hancock is a devoted friend of the Nyerere family; while Julius and Maria Nyerere were struggling with financial difficulties, two of their children lived with her. – (Judith Listowel, *The Making of Tanganyika*, London: Chatto & Windus, 1965, p. 428).

And as William Edgett Smith stated in his book, *We Must Run While Others Walk: A Portrait of Africa's Julius Nyerere*:

> Miss Mary Hancock, a peppery little Englishwoman who had come to Tanganyika in 1940 'to help the black people, as we called them then, has recalled, 'Oh, that man, how he thinks! The civil servants in Musoma couldn't see why I remained his friend after he declared for Uhuru. We civil servants had to be careful, you know --- we couldn't attend political meetings. I would say, 'He's my friend. If you can'r differentiate, I can. Well! You should have seen the civil servants change when it became clear that he was winning. – (William Edgett Smith, *We Must Run While Others Walk: A Portrait of Africa's Julius Nyerere*, New York: Random House, 1972, p. 84; W. E. Smith, *Nyerere of Tanzania*, Faraday Close, Worthing, UK: Littlehampton Book Services, 1973, p. 65; The New Yorker, Volume 47, Issues 27 - 35, 1971, p. 84).

Mary Hancock was the District Education Officer in

Musoma in the 1950s when she first met Nyerere and his family. Musoma was Nyerere's home district. – (Pat Holden, Oxford Development Records Project, 1985, *Women Administrative Officers in Colonial Africa 1944 - 1960*, p. 194; Mary Hancock, Wikipedia).

She later, in the late fifties, became a Provincial Education Officer for the Lake Province and was based in Mwanza, the provincial capital.

Mary Hancock played a major role in the education of girls in colonial Tanganyika and after independence.

She was born in 1910 in England and went to Tanganyika in 1940 to work as a volunteer teacher. She became headmistress of Tabora Girls' School in the Western Province.

She also taught at Kyimbila Girls' School three miles south of the town of Tukuyu in Rungwe District in the Southern Highlands Province in the 1940s and founded Loleza Girls' School in the town of Mbeya in the same province during the same period.

She became a citizen of Tanzania and a senior education inspector. She was elected member of parliament in 1970. Fondly known as Mama Hancock, she died in October 1977.

Godfrey Mwakikagile remembers his mother Syabumi talking about Mary Hancock – as a devoted teacher and very strict disciplinarian – during her days as a student at Kyimbila Girls' School in the 1940s, the same area where her uncle Asegelile Mwankemwa served as a pastor of the Moravian Church.

Later in the fifties, Godfrey Mwakikagile also went to school at Kyimbila, a primary school for boys and girls. One of his teachers there, Eslie Mwakyambiki, was later elected member of parliament. He then became Deputy Minister of Defence and National Service appointed by President Nyerere.

The sons of the Kyimbila Moravian Church pastor Asegelile Mwankemwa also used another family name,

Mwaiseje, as their surname; for example, Itika Mwaiseje, the last-born child, about whom Godfrey Mwakikagile has written in some of his writings stating that he was one of the last two relatives to bid him farewell when he left Tanzania for the United States. He took a taxi to the airport to see Mwakikagile less than an hour before the plane left Dar es Salaam and had a farewell drink (Tanzanian beer) with him.

The other one was Godfrey Mwakikagile's first cousin Tunga Mwambapa, daughter of Johan Chonde Mwambapa, who worked at Dar es Salaam's international airport as a ground hostess and later married a general in the Tanzanian army whose career had striking parallels with that of her elder brother who was also in the army and had the same rank.

Itika's first cousin Syabumi, Godfrey Mwakikagile's mother, was also brought up by her elder brother Johan Chonde Mwambapa, a teacher, who was almost thirteen years older than she was. He was born in 1917. She was the youngest in their family and lived with him until she got married. She later followed in her uncle's footsteps and became involved in church activities teaching Sunday school.

One of her brothers, Amos Mwambapa, a teacher and World War II veteran born in 1914, also became involved in church activities serving as a deacon of the Moravian church in their area.

Another brother, Benjamin Mwambapa born in 1922, pursued a career in law enforcement. He became head of the criminal investigation department (CID) in the ministry of home affairs in the government of newly independent Tanganyika in the early sixties in the town of Tukuyu serving Rungwe District.

Syabumi had another elder brother, Andengenye Mwambapa, an active member of the Moravian Church who also became an elder of the church and whose son, Brown Mwambapa, became a Seventh-Day Adventist

(SDA) pastor in Tanzania. And her daughter Maria Kasuka, Godfrey Mwakikagile's sister, married a Seventh-Day Adventist pastor Anyitike Mwaipopo.

She also had two elder sisters, Mbage and Nyambilila. Born in 1925 and the immediate elder sibling of Syabumi, Nyambilila also became an active member of the Moravian Church in her area and got involved in church activities in varying degrees.

And one of their cousins, Mbutolwe, a daughter of their uncle Asegelile Mwankemwa, became deeply involved in church activities as a missionary worker and an itinerant preacher spreading the Gospel.

Their brother Johan Mwambapa, simply known as Chonde or Chonde Mwambapa, was also the father of Brigadier-General Owen Rhodfrey Mwambapa who was the head of the Tanzania Military Academy, an army officers' training school at Monduli in Arusha Region in the northeastern part of the country, whose alumni include army officers from South Africa, Uganda, Kenya, Zambia, Seychelles, Rwanda, Lesotho and other countries. It is one of the leading military academies on the continent.

Born in 1945, Owen Mwambapa graduated as an army officer (lieutenant) from Sandhurst, a royal military academy in the United Kingdom, in the sixties.

Godfrey's younger brother, Lawrence Anyambilile Mwakikagile, was also a lieutenant in the national army, the Tanzania People's Defence Forces (TPDF), and participated in the Uganda-Tanzania War, also known as the Kagera War, which started on 30 October 1978 and ended on 11 April 1979. He retired with the rank of captain in 1996. And their younger sister, Gwangu Kasuka, was married to a sea captain, John Mwakibete.

The patriarch of the family, Asegelile Mwankemwa, died in September 1983.

Godfrey's father, Elijah Mwakikagile, attended Malangali Secondary School, one of the top schools in colonial Tanganyika. His classmates at Malangali, where he was head prefect, included Jeremiah Kasambala who became a cabinet member under President Julius Nyerere after Tanganyika won independence from Britain, and John Mwakangale who, during the struggle for independence in the 1950s, became one of the leaders of the independence movement in Tanganyika. Elijah's maternal uncle, Eliakim Simeon Mwaibanje who was the younger brother of his mother Laheli Kasuka Mwaibanje, paid for his education.

The parents of Laheli Kasuka and Eliakim Simeon Mwaibanje were Kasofu Mwamwaja and Mary Iseke. They had other children all of whom, together with Laheli and Eliakim, were born in Mpata village in the ward of Kabula in Selya in the eastern part of Rungwe District.

Another maternal uncle of Elijah Mwakikagile, Jotham Mwaibanje, was the father of Oscar Mwamwaja, one of Tanzania's first commercial airline pilots. Oscar was named after his grandfather Kasofu Mwamwaja whose other children with Mary Iseke were Kilabo Ndaga, Amos, Jane, and Anyegile. Kasofu Mwamwaja and Mary Iseke were Godfrey Mwakikagile's great-grandparents.

Oscar Mwamwaja was the co-pilot of an Air Tanzania plane, a Boeing, 737, that was hijacked on 26 February 1982 and forced to fly from Mwanza, Tanzania, to London Stansted Airport in the United Kingdom. The aircraft was on a domestic flight.

The pilot was Deo Mazula, elder brother of George Mazula who, together with his brother, was also among the first commercial airline pilots in Tanzania. George was also a classmate of Godfrey Mwakikagile at Tambaza High School in Dar es Salaam. Another classmate was Mohamed Chande Othman, also known as Othman Chande, who became chief justice of Tanzania appointed by President Jakaya Kikwete.

The hijacked plane had 99 passengers. The pilot and co-pilot were assisted by a crew of three. After stopping in Dar es Salaam, Deo Mazula was forced to fly the plane to Nairobi in Kenya, Jedda in Saudi Arabia, Athens in Greece, and finally the United Kingdom where he landed at Stansted about 30 miles northeast of London.

A British defence ministry spokesman said "there are contingency plans involving military units" at Stansted. The hijackers threatened to blow up the plane if security forces attempted to storm in.

The police refrained from storming the plane fearing they would endanger the passengers. But anti-terrorist units were already in position ready for an assault on February 27th, one day after the plane was hijacked in Tanzania and flown to the UK.

The hijackers said they wanted to see Britain's foreign secretary, Lord Carrington, and Tanzania'a high commissioner (ambassador) to Britain, Amon Nsekela. Carrington was then on an official visit to Kenya.

They also demanded to speak to Oscar Kambona, Tanzania's former minister of foreign affairs who had fallen out with President Nyerere and who was then living in exile in London.

A crackled radio message from the pilot, Deo Mazula, to the controllers at Stansted international airport that was later broadcast on BBC, said:

> We have a request. Would like the following persons to meet the aircraft on arrival: The Tanzanian high commissioner in London and the British foreign minister and Mr. Oscar Kambona. – ("Hijacked Jetliner Arrives in Britain," *The New York Times*, 28 February 1982).

But negotiators ended the ordeal before Kambona arrived on the scene. His younger brother Mattiya, also living in exile in London and who was a fierce opponent of Nyerere like his brother, said in a radio interview that he did not believe his elder brother would meet the hijackers.

The hijackers, all in their early twenties, wanted President Nyerere to resign. They claimed to be members of a movement which their leader alternatively described as the "Tanzania Youth Democratic Movement" and the "Tanzania Youth Revolutionary Movement." There was no such movement or political organisation in or outside Tanzania demanding change in the country.

Their level of education was low, between primary school and secondary school, from standard 7 to standard 12.

The hijacking ended when the hijackers surrendered on February 28th. There were five hijackers, all related through birth and marriage. There were two pairs of brothers and one a brother-in-law. His sisters were married to the eldest brother in each pair:

> A 48-hour hijacking drama that began in East Africa ended tonight...with the surrender of...(the) young terrorists and the release of more than 90 hostages....
>
> Security sources here said that explosives were found wired to the aircraft doors and placed in a toilet. The hijackers had threatened to blow up the plane, a Boeing 737, at 10:30 Saturday night. 'Please Bring 100 Coffins.'
>
> 'We are going to blow the plane,' one terrorist said in talks with airport officials. "We are going to die now. Please bring 100 coffins at once.'
>
> The only known casualty was the co-pilot, who was injured when he was...shot...in the waist just before the plane arrived in Athens. The hijackers, who were taken into custody this evening, were armed with knives, pistols, submachine guns and grenades. However, some of the arms were said to have been made of wood or plastic.
>
> According to the police, the terrorists were seeking the overthrow of the President of Tanzania, Julius K. Nyerere. They were identified as members of a left-wing group that describes Mr. Nyerere as a traitor who has suborned Marxist ideology.
>
> The drama was brought to an end by the intervention of Oscar Kambona....Once Mr. Kambona arrived at Stansted, which is in the county of Essex, about midway between London and Cambridge, the terrorists began to release the hostages. Later on Saturday night they freed a pregnant mother and her 5-year-old son. At noon today (Sunday, 28 February) four women, a man and a baby girl were freed.
>
> Then at 2:30 P.M., seven men and three women were set free. The injured co-pilot was released at 3:15 P.M. and 41 passengers were

allowed to leave at 4. P.M. About an hour later the rest of the hostages walked down the ramp and the hijackers surrendered.

Robert Bunyard, the Chief Constable of Essex, said all of the hijackers were in their early 20's. 'The people are all safe,' he said. – (R.W. Apple, Jr., reporting from Bishop's Stortford, England, 28 February 1982, Special to *The New York Times*, "4 Tanzanian Hijackers Surrender; 90 Hostages Are Freed in Britain," published in *The New York Times*, 1 March 1982. See also "A Hijacking of a Tanzanian Aircraft," *Tanzanian Affairs*, 1 July 1982; "Former Hijacker Arrested," *Tanzanian Affairs*, 1 January 1991).

The co-pilot, Oscar Mwamwaja, was shot by the leader of the hijackers. He underwent an operation at a hospital in the UK to remove a bullet from his body and returned to Tanzania.

Years later, one of the hijackers was arrested when he returned to Tanzania after serving eight years in prison in the United Kingdom:

Musa Membar, who took a free ride to Britain aboard an Air Tanzania Boeing 737 which he hijacked with four other youths in 1982, was arrested on September 14th 1990 when he crossed the Kenya-Tanzania border. He had been jailed in Britain for eight years. After his release he became a founder member of the Tanzania Youth Democratic Movement under the umbrella of a Tanzanian opposition front headed by Oscar Kambona, former Foreign Minister who has been in exile in Britain since 1967.

Speaking in a BBC interview the other day, Mr Kambona denied any prior knowledge of Member's departure from London. 'He did not bid any of us farewell' he said.

In a letter from the Ukonga maximum security prison, where he is being held, Member said 'I returned to Tanzania ... to lead a peaceful campaign for multi-party democracy....' (*Business Times*, 19 October 1990). – "Former Hijacker Arrested," *Tanzanian Affairs*, 1 January 1991).

Oscar Mwamwaja, who was Elijah Mwakikagile's first cousin, later became a commercial pilot training instructor at the Nigerian College of Aviation Technology in Zaria, northern Nigeria.

A former American Peace Corps teacher, Leonard

Levitt – author of *An African Season*, the first book ever written by a Peace Corps – who taught Oscar Mwamwaja and Godfrey Mwakikagile at Mpuguso Middle School (1963 - 1964) wrote about his former students and his experiences in Tanzania in his article, "Tanzania: A Dream Deferred," published in *The New York Times Magazine* on 14 November 1982.

Other alumni of Mpuguso Middle School who went there in the late 1950s a few years before Godfrey Mwakikagile (1961 – 1964) and Oscar Mwamwaja (1962 – 1965) did include Brigadier-General Owen Rhodfrey Mwambapa, Godfrey's first cousin; and David Mwakyusa, President Nyerere's last personal physician who was with the Tanzanian leader until his last days when he died at a hospital in London, United Kingdom, in October 1999.

The headmaster of Mpuguso Middle School in 1961, the year Godfrey Mwakikagile first went there and enrolled in Standard Five, Moses Mwakibete who was also his math teacher, years later became the Registrar of the High Court of Tanzania. He was appointed Judge of the High Court by President Nyerere in 1972.

Geoffrey Sawaya, Director of Tanzania's Criminal Investigation Department (CID) who presented evidence against the coup plotters in the 1970 treason trial at the High Court of Tanzania also was once headmaster of Mpuguso Middle School before he was later appointed CID Director by President Nyerere. As Leonard Levitt stated in his article about Mpuguso, one of the leading schools in what was then the Southern Highlands Province (later divided into Mbeya and Iringa Regions), and about Tanzania in general:

> I first arrived in Tanzania in 1963, as a teacher in the Peace Corps, in the heady days just after independence from Britain. The school I was assigned to was in the southern highlands, in blue mountains shadowed by clouds and mist. It was a setting as pristine as the ideals that had brought me there.

The school was named Mpuguso, after the surrounding village of mud huts and shambas, small plots where farmers kept cattle and chickens and where they planted banana trees and tea and coffee shrubs. Mpuguso was an upper primary school - that is, it included grades 5 to 8, and the students' ages ranged from 10 to 20; proper birth records had not been kept. The school consisted of a complex of brick buildings: classrooms, dormitories, a dining hall and teachers' houses. Below the dining hall lay a large soccer field, the grass cut short by cattle the villagers led there to graze.

My students, nearly all of them boys, were as bright and hard working as any I'd ever known. Many walked 10 or 15 miles each day from their villages to Mpuguso. During the masika, or long rains, when we wouldn't see the sun for days or weeks, they'd arrive each morning, barefoot and sopping wet in their white school uniforms, with long, green banana leaves over their heads. The boarders - those whose fathers owned enough cows to sell in order to pay the 150 shillings, or $20-a-year fees -studied in their classrooms until midnight by a kerosene lamp hung from a rafter. Hunched over their desks, they squinted and scribbled as the light became fainter and fainter.

The goal of each student was to pass his exam for secondary school, where there were places for only a quarter of them. Passing the exam was the first step necessary to leaving their villages and entering the modern world of the 20th century, which to them meant a world where everyone wore new clothes and shoes, listened to transistor radios and rode in cars and airplanes. To my students, this was the promise of uhuru, or independence from British rule.

Uhuru had been won by the young and charismatic President Julius K. Nyerere, who so eloquently urged a new and better life for Tanzania and for Africa. The son of an illiterate tribal chief from a village not unlike Mpuguso, Nyerere had been a teacher himself -hence his Swahili title of Mwalimu. Educated in Britain, he had translated Shakespeare's *Julius Caesar* into Swahili. More important, Nyerere had persuaded the British to quit Tanzania without firing a shot. Among Western liberals and intellectuals, he came to be regarded as a kind of African philosopher-king. He was perceived as a selfless leader, a man who disdained violence; a nonracist who offered Tanzanian citizenship to any European or Asian who wished to remain; a benevolent socialist who wished to rid Tanzania, indeed all Africa, of its triple plagues - ignorance, poverty and disease.

In retrospect, there was an almost touching naivete about all he sought to accomplish and about American eagerness to believe and support him. We Americans were certain that we could help transform Tanzania, quickly and painlessly, into a modern nation - one that would incorporate the best aspects of Western culture without sacrificing its own African identity.

And we were not alone. Tanzania came to be viewed as a model developing country. Billions of dollars and thousands of volunteers poured into Tanzania, not only from America, but also from Europe, Canada, Israel, the Soviet Union, China, Japan and even other undeveloped nations such as Brazil. Tanzania became the second largest recipient nation, on a per capita basis, of foreign aid in the world.

Despite the money and the hopes - and, to an extent, because of them - Tanzania today is a tragedy. Nyerere's political party - the only party in the country - now controls the Government, the military, the press. His ideals have atrophied into an ideology, called 'African Socialism,' that seems to combine the worst features of East and West. Business and industry have been nationalized and have become dependent on foreign subsidies. Corruption is epidemic. There are no goods in the stores, and no foreign currency to purchase spare parts when machines break down. If, outside Tanzania, the Mwalimu is still regarded as the eloquent champion of African and third-world aspirations, his own people are now poorer in almost every way than they were before independence.

In September 1981, 18 years after I first arrived in Tanzania, I returned to find my students, and from them, perhaps, to learn something of what had happened to the country. They were all as delighted to see me as I was to see them, and to my surprise they remembered even the most obscure details about our time together - words I'd spoken, lessons I'd taught, books I'd given them.

On the surface many members of this first generation of uhuru's beneficiaries appeared to have prospered. Of the 10 I saw, half had studied abroad; nearly all held Government jobs. Yet there was a quality of despair and desperation about all of them. They were, without exception, disillusioned in some way: frustrated in their careers, disappointed in their lives, unfulfilled in their expectations. They seemed not to understand why the dreams they had been told were rightfully theirs had not been realized. For them, as for Tanzania, the road from the village to the 20th century had proved more tortuous than they or I had imagined.

Tanzania is not unique in any of this. Many, if not most, of the African nations that a generation ago gained their independence in a rush of self-confidence and optimism today resemble defeated nations, countries where prosperity now appears to be farther out of reach than ever, where basic freedoms have never been granted, where the participation of the people in the governments that rule them seem as remote as it was during the days of colonialism. Tanzania's decay is evident as soon as one arrives. I drive from the airport to Dar es Salaam in a sagging, unpainted airport bus whose rear door bangs open in the wind. It is a Sunday evening, and a gasoline shortage and a ban on Sunday driving have emptied the streets of cars. Green-leafed banana trees and mud-brown huts with corrugated roofs line the road, while barefoot children in unwashed shorts wander down dirt-filled side streets. In the dusk, once-white buildings appear yellow and brown, stained with dirt and neglect. Windows are broken, panes of glass missing. Downtown, along Independence Avenue, near the harbor, storefronts are bare of goods. There are, I learn, shortages of all staples - sugar, salt, butter, rice, soap, light bulbs. Each day a line of people winds around the block from a bakery, waiting for bread.

I am staying at the Kilimanjaro Hotel, which is said to be the best hotel in Dar es Salaam. It is nine stories high, with a balcony outside each room, and with a swimming pool. In this tropical city of two-and three-story buildings, it seems out of place. The hotel was built by the Israelis in the mid-1960's, and managed by them until Nyerere broke relations after the 1973 October War. Now it is managed by a Dutchman. Over the last six years, the Dutch have provided Tanzania with more than $300 million in aid.

My window overlooks the harbor to the Indian Ocean, where huge Soviet and Yugoslav ships lie at anchor while tiny wooden dhows of another age sail past them. Though the temperature and humidity in Dar both approach 100 degrees, the hotel's air-conditioning barely functions. At night, with my balcony doors open, the stench of the harbor at low tide floods my room. Some mornings there is no hot water. A valve has broken, the hotel operator explains, and there are no spare parts. A few months earlier, I learn, the water came out the taps mud-brown because the city's water system had run out of aluminum-sulphate purifier.

In the lobby of the Kilimanjaro I meet one of my former students, whom I will refer to here as Rashid. I remember him as a small, light-complexioned boy, younger than the others. Now, though he is still short, his color has darkened and he has gained weight, giving him the portly appearance of prosperity.

'So, Mr. Levitt. How are you?' he says to me, standing in the lobby. He is wearing slacks and an open-neck sport shirt, the dress of the urban Tanzanian. He smiles. 'How are things?'

This colloquialism reminds me of the fine linguist Rashid was. Remarkably, at Mpuguso, he learned to speak English with barely an accent.

'Do you remember the book you gave me, Mr. Levitt, when you left Mpuguso?' he says. 'Inside you wrote, 'To Rashid, you have been a pleasure to teach. I am sure one day you will study in the United

States.' Well, Mr. Levitt, I have not yet been to the United States, but I have studied in Europe.'

We walk upstairs to the hotel lounge and order two Kilimanjaro beers (which, when available, cost 20 shillings, or $2.50, a bottle) while Rashid begins telling me about himself. 'As I am sure you know, Mr. Levitt, I passed my exam for secondary school. After secondary school, I passed Form V and Form VI on my own and was accepted at the University of Dar es Salaam, where I received a degree with honors in international marketing. I am now,' he says proudly, 'the manager of a small, private tourist company. So you see, Mr. Levitt, I am doing very well.'

A few days later, I visit Rashid at his office. It is in an Indian, or 'Asian' - as Indians are called - section of the city, and consists of a small room off the sidewalk. The room is filled with old men in Muslim skull caps and long white gowns.

Perhaps to explain why his small tourist company is smaller than he indicated, perhaps because he decided he would rather confide in me than attempt to impress me, Rashid begins speaking in a rapid voice. 'You see, Mr. Levitt, with my degree in international marketing, I became an assistant manager with the T.T.C.,' he said, referring to the Government-run Tanzania Tourist Corporation, which has taken over most segments of Tanzania's once-lucrative tourist industry. 'I did very well there. I was sent to Sweden for a year's course of study. And I received a scholarship to study in France and was studying French in preparation.'

He pauses. 'Mr. Levitt, my superior was jealous of me. I was better educated than he, and he resented my success. A year ago, a woman tourist made a complaint against me, and my superior dismissed me. I was in Sweden at the time and was recalled. My scholarship to France was canceled. I was out of work for nine months. I was married to a young girl, and we had two small children. I had no money and the poor girl was so upset she ran away. I had to send the children back to my mother near Mpuguso.'

He waits for my reaction, but I can say nothing. I am thinking of what those nine months must have been like for him - no job, no money, abandoned by his wife, left with the two small children. It would have been difficult for any man. For an African accustomed to traditional family roles, one can only imagine the pain.

'Mr. Levitt, life is not good here in Tanzania,' he says, now in a whisper. 'There is no longer opportunity here. The Government controls everything, and now that I no longer work for them they do not care about me anymore. I want to leave Tanzania. I want to move to Nairobi, to Zambia, even to Botswana, but without sponsorship they will not let me. When I lost my scholarship, I wrote to the French

Government, but they said without Government sponsorship they could not give me one. Perhaps you know of some way I could go to the United States. Perhaps I could get a scholarship. There is nothing here for me anymore.'

There are two ways to travel overland to Mpuguso. A new tarmac road built by the Americans runs from Dar southwest to Mbeya, the regional capital of the southern highlands; from Mbeya, another new tarmac road, built by the Germans, runs south past Mpuguso, 50 miles away, and continues down to the Malawi border. The problem with these roads - all of which are foreign built - is that they are not maintained. Sections are filled with potholes; bridges are collapsing. Some are already impassable, so that now it takes more time to travel from, say, Dar to Arusha in the north than it did 20 years ago.

There is also the Tazara Railway, built by the Chinese, which runs from Dar to Mbeya, and then southwest into Zambia. Completed in 1976, it, too, has deteriorated - as I discover when I take it. The cars are dirty; toilets do not flush. The Tanzanians have not maintained the tracks and trains are out of service for days and weeks at a time.

I share my compartment with two Asians, a father and son. The father says he is a retired schoolteacher who owns a duka, or small shop, outside Mbeya. He has just returned from Canada, where two other sons have emigrated, and he says he and this son will soon be going there, too. Echoing Rashid he tells me, 'There is nothing here for us in Tanzania anymore.'

Unlike Uganda, where Idi Amin confiscated their businesses and then expelled them, Tanzania originally permitted Asians to live in relative calm and prosperity as its merchant class. Then, in 1977, Nyerere began abolishing the village dukas, virtually all of which were owned by Asians. Nonracist that he professes to be, Nyerere claimed the measure was not directed against the Asians but was, rather, in keeping with the philosophy of "African Socialism," a first step in nationalizing all business in Tanzania. For the Asians, the effect was little different from Uganda.

We arrive in Mbeya, about 50 miles from Mpuguso, early the next morning. I remember it as having been a lovely place set in the mountains, with purple jacaranda trees and Asian dukas lining its two main streets. In its center was the British settlers' Mbeya Club, with a bar, squash court and nine-hole golf course with 'greens' of black tar, and which only the year before uhuru began accepting African and Asian members. But now, as the train pulls into Mbeya, nothing seems familiar. The land is bare and dusty. A haze covers the mountains. We arrive at a white-brick station on the town's outskirts that had not existed when I was there. Later, when I walk through the town, I see many of the dukas have been shuttered. The windows of others are bare of goods. What does remain is the Mbeya Club. Its door is unlocked. Its brick walls have holes in them. Through its cracked rear window, I can look down the hill that had been the first hole of the golf course and that is now filled with half-completed mud-brick houses.

The Mbeya Hotel also remains, a relic of the colonial past where visiting Tanzanian dignitaries from Dar es Salaam are now put up and where, at night, at the bar, the elite of Mbeya's officials congregate. The hotel is seedy with age. The windows are broken or missing panes of glass, and its flowers have been destroyed by a herd of goats that grazes on the front lawn.

I introduce myself to the young African at the front desk, but I am unprepared for his reply. 'Are you the Mr. Levitt from Mpuguso school?' he asks. He introduces himself as Azim A. Mwinyimvua, though he prefers to be called Bwana Simba, or, in English, Mr. Lion. Bwana Simba remembers me, he says, because as a schoolboy he visited Mpuguso for a track meet and attended the Friday night debates when I was debate master. We had debated topics of the students' choosing, such as 'Resolved: It Is Better to Marry an Educated Girl Than an Uneducated Girl,' or 'Resolved: It Is Better to Have One Wife Than Many Wives.'

Bwana Simba, it turns out, is the manager of the Mbeya Hotel. He apologizes for the state into which it has fallen, explaining that although he studied hotel management in Nairobi and in Italy, there is no money and no trained staff to maintain its former standards. He does his best for me, however. He places me in the hotel's deluxe suite, which consists of a bedroom, sitting room and bathroom with a light bulb, and a chandalua, or mosquito net, with a hole the size of my fist. In the corners of the room, a stream of red ants eats away at the unbaked brick walls, which, in a few more years, I fear, will no longer exist. At meals, I am offered the finest carvings of goat meat, which come from the herd on the front lawn. Bwana Simba assigns special staff members to clean my room and serve my meals.

Yet sometimes at meals there is no meat, no bread, no milk, no sugar. Sometimes in the bar there is no beer, and Bwana Simba is forever using his ingenuity to procure these items. Each Saturday night he acts as a host at a disco and charges 30 shillings a head, then uses the money to purchase such items as curtains. Other money goes for soap or light bulbs, or for such minor luxuries as Coca-Cola or Fanta orange soda, which are smuggled in over the Zambian border or purchased, with a bribe, from the Government-run corporations that supply them. What he cannot purchase are new panes of glass; the materials no longer exist in Tanzania.

While I am at the hotel, Bwana Simba tells me he has received

Government permission to attend a two-week course in hotel management in England. He awaits only the final call to proceed to Dar es Salaam. But the call never comes. When I leave the hotel and return to Dar es Salaam, he is still waiting. There is a group of Swedes living at the hotel. They are part of a Scandinavian aid program that from 1976 to 1980 provided Tanzania with more than $600 million. In Mbeya, the Swedes have built three factories to produce sweaters, wooden clogs and plastic toys. It is as ridiculous a project as can be imagined, for the raw materials are purchased abroad and the finished products are too costly to sell effectively on the export market. As for the Tanzanians themselves, they have little need for sweaters, clogs or plastic toys.

The factories have been operating since mid-1981, but because of the lack of water, electricity, diesel fuel and generator maintenance and breaking of the cooling pipes, they are operating at one-third capacity.

'Recently a Swedish aid official visited Mbeya,' says Thomas Gotting, the Swedish manager of the sweater factory. 'But he visited our factory for only five minutes, then gave a lunch at the Mbeya Hotel for the Africans where they all made speeches praising each other. You see, the Swedish Government gives 1 percent of its gross national product away in foreign aid. And the bureaucrats care only about giving it away, not if it does any good. The man who came here made no attempt to find anything of the kind.'

'In Sweden, people don't understand how much time it takes to learn,' adds Anders Otterstram, the Swedish technical adviser to the plastic toy factory. 'In Sweden it took us generations, with many mistakes. When I was home last year, I tried to explain this to people, but they do not listen. When I tell them things are not working in Tanzania, they call me -what is the English word? -they call me a racist.'

There is also a Peace Corps worker in Mbeya. The Peace Corps was dismissed in the late 1960's by Nyerere, ostensibly in protest against the United States' involvement in Vietnam. Meanwhile, in the villages, the Government spread rumors that Peace Corps workers were spies. Ten years later, in the late 1970's, Nyerere was feted at the White House by President Carter. Subsequently, he proposed that the Peace Corps return.

In keeping with its new image of pragmatism and practicality, as opposed to my generation's unskilled idealism, the Peace Corps worker in Mbeya is a forestry specialist. Her job is to plant trees, as the Tanzanians have denuded their hillsides by cutting down too many for firewood. The problem, she explains, is that the Tanzanians insist on planting European pine and cypress, which mature faster than the indigenous eucalyptus. But the pine and cypress do not retain the soil's moisture as well as eucalyptus does. Thus the topography is changing and the land is becoming dusty and bare.

In Mbeya I find one of my students, whom I will refer to as Henry, and who is now a teacher. Like Rashid, he was one of my brightest and most hard-working pupils. He was gifted in all subjects, but was especially interested in English and history.

He has grown a beard but I recognize him immediately. And he recognizes me. 'Levitt! Is it really you?' he shouts as I arrive at his school. He tells me he is not teaching English or history, as I'd imagined, but science. 'At secondary school my headmaster encouraged me to pursue a degree in agriculture,' he explains. 'I received a scholarship to study abroad - a six-year course in the Soviet Union.'

He was there three years, he tells me, but returned home. 'I became sick there, Mr. Levitt. I could not work. I could not concentrate on my studies. I was laughing, and crying. I do not know why. I was sent back to my village and remained there an entire year. When I became better, I took this job.'

He tells me he does not enjoy teaching science and has applied to the university in Tanzania to complete his degree in agriculture, so that he can go abroad again. 'I want to travel. I want to go to the West, to Europe, to America. Then, after some years, I will return to Tanzania.' But without his degree, he says, he will be unable to leave Tanzania. 'Mr. Levitt, if I am not accepted at the university, I do not know what I will do.'

He also tells me he married last year. His wife is a teacher and she is three months pregnant. But he is not pleased about becoming a father as most Africans would be. He is afraid. 'When my wife has the baby and stops working, it will be very hard for us. It is very expensive here in Mbeya. I do not know how we will live.'

Listening to him, my former student who is now a man, who has traveled abroad and suffered a breakdown, who is married and is soon to become a father, I find myself thinking back 18 years to when he was a young boy in a white Mpuguso school uniform. Hard as he had worked, hard as he had studied, in retrospect his life seemed simple then. He had had a goal. He had succeeded. He had passed his exam, graduated from secondary school and gone on to study abroad. Yet something had gone wrong. He had achieved his goal, but his success had created other, unforeseen problems.

No longer was he content to be a teacher, to have a wife and children, as he might have a generation before. Now he wanted something else - to travel to the West -something, I feared, that now lay beyond his grasp. I imagine him waiting, like Bwana Simba, for a call from Dar es Salaam, a call that, like Bwana Simba's, may never come.

Afterward, I invite Henry and his wife to the Mbeya Hotel for tea or Cokes. It is a treat for them, he tells me, as they can afford such luxuries only once a month. His wife, a lovely young woman of 23, wears her best clothes - perhaps her only dress clothes -a dungaree skirt and white blouse. Though she understands English, she is too shy to speak it. As they prepare to leave, he says to me, 'Mr. Levitt, I beg you not to write about me. I am ashamed of my life. I do not want people knowing about me.' I tell him I will change his name. I am to travel to Mpuguso the next day, so we agree to have lunch together when I return to discuss it further. But he never appears. I never see him again.

Mpuguso has also changed. It is no longer an upper primary school; instead, refresher courses for school teachers are now given there. One of Tanzania's proudest boasts is that it has provided free primary education for all school-age children. In each village I pass on the way to Mpuguso, a primary school stands by the side of the road. But while school children roam outside, most of the classrooms are empty.

At Mpuguso, I walk along dirt paths I remember, past rows of brick houses where we teachers lived, past my own brick house, where two African women sit in the doorway. A new row of classrooms has been built alongside our old ones, but when I look into the windows, they, too, are empty. Where are the students who worked until midnight by the light of a kerosene lamp? Where are the students who walked 10 to 15 miles to school each day? I remain in Mpuguso less than an hour, struggling to recapture something that, for me, is lost forever.

Before I return to Dar es Salaam, Bwana Simba takes me to a political rally. The rally is to be held in the stadium across from the hotel. It is organized by Nyrere's Revolutionary Party and is to celebrate the women of the region. And all that morning, the road into Mbeya is filled with dilapidated buses and open-backed trucks carrying loads of women from the outlying villages.

The rally's organizers have arranged a series of races for the women - 100-yard dashes, quarter- and half-mile runs and relays - and, as the women run, their kangas (colorful cotton material wrapped as a skirt or a dress) flap wildly around their legs. The crowd laughs and shouts in delight. Each winner is then brought to the podium and awarded a prize - a bar of soap, which, like so many items, is unobtainable in the stores.

When the races end, the speeches begin. The crowd has heard them all before and quickly grows restless. The women begin moving toward the stadium's two large gates, which have been locked to prevent their premature departure. Watching it all, my eyes travel upward to the green billboards emblazoned with Swahill slogans, political jargon of a long-forgotten age. 'Kazi Ndiyo Msingi Wa Maendeleo' - 'Work Is the Foundation of Progress.' 'Nchi Maskini Haiwezi Kuendelea Kwa Msingi Wa Fedha' - 'A Poor Country Will Not Progress If It Depends On Aid (Will not Develop Depending on Money).' 'Nchi Maskini Haiwezi Kujitawala Kama Inategemea Misaada Toka Nje" - 'A Poor Country Cannot Rule Itself If It Relies on Foreign Help.'

Reading these slogans, rendered absurd by the direction Tanzania has taken, I imagine a more apt one: 'Njia Ya Jehanum Inatengenezwa Kwa Nia Njema' - 'The Road to Hell Is Paved With Good Intentions.'

The reasons why Tanzania has become a mockery of its own slogans are, of course, complex. Some - such as the rising price of oil and turbulence in the world economy -were clearly beyond the small nation's control. Tanzania had always been a poor country, with few natural resources. Nyerere's well-meaning but authoritarian attempts to redistribute among the country's 18 million people what little wealth there was only led to a decline in production, to endemic corruption and, finally, to the withdrawal of thousands of citizens from the official economy and their return to the subsistence farming of their ancestors. Finally, Nyerere's Government has become as oppressive and out of touch with its own people as the colonial system he sought to replace.

Back in Dar es Salaam I meet with my student George. He is a communications officer for the meteorological department at the airport, an imposing-sounding title. He'd been an excellent student, with a gift for mathematics. He was older than most of the boys and he had a steadiness and maturity beyond that. He'd wanted to become an engineer. I expected much from him.

'Mr. Levitt,' he begins, 'you will be very disappointed in me when I tell you about my life.' He tells me that he passed his exam at Mpuguso and was accepted at Tusamaganga secondary school, one of the best-known in the country. But in 1967, his second year, he contracted a severe case of malaria. 'I was in Iringa Hospital five months,' he says. 'When I came out, I found I could not concentrate on my studies. And I especially could not concentrate on mathematics. I failed my exams. Mr. Levitt, you will not believe this, but I failed mathematics.'

So George dropped engineering and instead joined the meteorological department. 'But I am only a communications officer. Not a meteorological officer. I simply push papers. When I try to concentrate, to use my brain, I cannot.'

I meet a Canadian psychologist, Dr. Morris Block, at Dar es Salaam's Muhimbili Hospital. When I mention George to him, he offers to see him. Afterward, Dr. Bloch tells me George's symptoms suggest a mental disorder peculiar to educated Africans that has been reported in psychiatric journals He and Dr. William Lucieer, a Dutch psychiatrist at Muhimbili, explain there is no organic reason why one should be unable to concentrate as a result of malaria. Rather, Block and Lucieer say, for reasons doctors cannot explain, a surprisingly large number of educated Africans suddenly become depressed, unable to sleep or concentrate. The disorder, they say, usually occurs after emotional shocks or disappointments - in George's case, probably set off by the malaria.

Of all my former students, the most successful turns out to be Oscar Mwamwaja, who has become a pilot for Air Tanzania. It is a prestigious job, for there are few qualified African pilots. Of the 40-odd pilots at Air Tanzania, half are foreigners.

We meet on a Saturday evening in the lounge of Dar es Salaam's Kilimanjaro Hotel. Little Oscar - who was smaller than the other boys - is now tall and thin, a few inches taller than I. He is wearing his navy-blue Air Tanzania uniform and he walks with jaunty confidence, in the manner of pilots everywhere.

'I was in the States, you know,' he says. 'I trained for two years in Texas. I've also been to Europe and to India, where I trained to fly the 737's.' Watching him so poised, listening to him speak so casually of being a pilot, it is difficult to remember Oscar had once been a 'day boy' at Mpuguso school, living in a mud hut outside Tukuyu, walking six miles each day to and from school.

'Life is not good here in Tanzania now, Mr. Levitt,' he says, leaning toward me and lowering his voice. 'Our salaries have been cut. The best pilots are leaving the country.'

As he speaks, a young African plunks himself down at our table and sits staring off into space. Gradually, he joins our conversation. When he leaves, Oscar looks at me. 'Do you know him?' he asks. I shake my head. 'A stranger sits down at our table,' he says. 'Who is he? Maybe he is a spy. You know, Mr. Levitt, there are spies at all the hotels. They are there to spy on foreigners, like yourself.'

Although I was not to see Oscar again, I was to hear of him. Last February, after I'd left Tanzania, an Air Tanzania 737 on a domestic flight was hijacked by three men and forced to fly to London. There, the hijackers surrendered, released their passengers and read a proclamation demanding the resignation of President Nyerere.

A few weeks later, I received a letter from Rashid in Dar es Salaam. 'You will get a shock to learn that the Air Tanzania plane which was hijacked to London was being manned by Oscar Mwamaja as copilot,' he wrote.

Then last month, I received a letter from Oscar himself. He was in Nigeria. 'This surely will be a surprise for you,' he began, 'especially to hear from me being in Nigeria. ... Maybe you know I was involved in the hijacking which happened in Tanzania in February. That was a terrible experience.' He went on to say he had been shot in the back, but no major organs had been touched and in London the bullet had been removed. He said he had resigned from Air Tanzania and left the country 'for my peace of mind.'

He told me he was now working as a flying instructor in Nigeria, and that he hoped to go to the United States. He asked me to write him a recommendation to a university in California. He gave no indication that he had any intention of ever returning to Tanzania.

Even Oscar, the most successful of the young Africans I had known, no longer saw a future for himself in Tanzania. 'At the moment, I don't miss home much,' he wrote. 'I have a lot to do here and life isn't that difficult.'" – (Leonard Levitt, "Tanzania: A Dream Deferred," *The New York Times Magazine*, 14 November 1982).

Besides Oscar Mwamwaja, another first cousin of Elijah Mwakikagile was Absalom Mwaibanje. He was the son of Eliakim Simeon Mwaibanje and attended Malangali Secondary School after Elijah did.

He was among the first civil servants in the government of newly independent Tanganyika from a school which – together with Tabora Boys, Tanga School and Old Moshi – produced a large number of people who went on to fill government positions, especially in the civil service, in the early years of independence when the country did not have many educated people.

Secondary school graduates formed the backbone of the civil service in Tanganyika, later Tanzania, during the post-colonial era. Among the alumni of Malangali – of other schools as well – were some of the people who played a major role in the struggle for independence in Tanganyika and in the new nation after it emerged from colonial rule.

Another alumnus of Malangali Secondary School was Amon Nsekela from Lupepo in Rungwe District. His contemporaries at Malangali included Elijah Mwakikagile,

Brown Ngwilulupi, Jeremiah Kasambala and John Mwakangale. He also went to Tabora Boys.

Amon Nsekela later became a prominent figure in the government under President Nyerere. He served as permanent secretary in the ministry of foreign affairs soon after independence and held the same position in three other ministries at different times including the ministry of finance.

He was also the first chairman and director of the country's largest bank, the National Bank of Commerce, appointed by President Nyerere. He assumed the post in 1967only a few years after independence and served in that capacity for many years. He was also the first chairman of the Council of the University of Dar es Salaam and later served as high commissioner (ambassador) to Britain. He held many other high-level positions in Tanzania through the years from the 1960s to the 1990s.

A college, Dr. Amon J. Nsekela Bankers' Academy in the town of Iringa in the Southern Highlands, was named after him.

Before being actively involved in politics, Elijah Mwakikagile's classmate at Malangali Secondary School, Jeremiah Kasambala, was the head of the Rungwe Cooperative Union in Rungwe District in the Southern Highlands Province, a position which thrust him into national prominence because of the major role cooperative unions - of farmers - across the country played in the struggle for independence. He was elected member of parliament representing Rungwe District and was appointed by President Nyerere as minister of trade and cooperatives, a portfolio that reflected his background as a leader of the cooperative union in Rungwe, one of the largest farmers' unions in Tanganyika. He also served as minister of industries, minerals and energy among other posts.

Besides being one of the leading figures in the

independence struggle in Tanganyika, another Malangali alumnus, John Mwakangale, was also one of the leaders of the Pan-African Freedom Movement for East and Central Africa (PAFMECA) founded in the port town of Mwanza on the shores of Lake Victoria,Tanganyika, in September 1958 under the leadership of Julius Nyerere.

PAFMECA mobilised forces and coordinated the struggle for independence in Tanganyika, Kenya, Zanzibar, Uganda, Nyasaland (renamed Malawi), Northern Rhodesia (now Zambia), and Southern Rhodesia (renamed Zimbabwe).

It was renamed the Pan-African Freedom Movement for East, Central and Southern Africa (PAFMECSA) after it was expanded to include the countries of southern Africa: apartheid South Africa, Bechuanaland (now Botswana), South West Africa (renamed Namibia), Basutoland (renamed Lesotho), and Swaziland.

John Mwakangale remained a prominent leader in the larger freedom movement which also played a major role in the formation of the Organisation of African Unity (OAU) in Addis Ababa, Ethiopia, in May 1963. The OAU was renamed the African Union (AU) in July 2002.

In 1958, John Mwakangale was one of the few African leaders who were elected to the Legislative Council (LEGCO), a colonial parliament of Tanganyika dominated by the British colonial rulers led by the British governor.

Members of LEGCO were elected on a tripartite system representing three racial categories: Europeans, mostly British settlers; Asians, mostly Tanganyikans of Indian and Pakistani origin, a category which also included Arabs in terms of racial separation; and Africans, or blacks, who constituted the overwhelming majority of the population of Tanganyika but whose numerical preponderance did not overshadow racial minorities. Collectively, non-blacks were a significant minority.

Africans in Tanganyika – as in other British colonies including neighbouring Kenya, Uganda, Zanzibar,

Northern Rhodesia and Nyasaland – were also subjected to indignities of colour bar similar to apartheid in South Africa, although not as rigid, yet equally humiliating. There were signs designating racial categories. Toilets were labelled "Europeans," "Asians" and "Africans." Some hotels and bars were labelled "Europeans." Facilities for Africans were the worst. There were separate schools for Europeans, Asians and Africans.

The school Godfrey Mwakikagile attended in Dar es Salaam, Tambaza High School, was predominantly Asian. It was in an upper middle-class area of Upanga. The head of the school during that period, Bori Lira, was the school's first African headmaster.

The students at the school were mostly Tanzanians of Indian and Pakistani origin even ten years after independence. It was once known as H.H. The Aga Khan High School, almost exclusively for Asian students, and changed its name to Tambaza after independence when the government decided to integrate all schools including Christian schools to enable Muslims and other non-Christians to enroll as students. Integration was mandatory.

Godfrey Mwakikagile was among the first African students to integrate the former H.H. The Aga Khan High School. And the hostel where some students stayed, known as H.H. The Aga Khan Hostel only a few yards from the school, was also overwhelmingly Asian. Mwakikagile was one of the few African students who stayed there.

It was a socially and racially stratified society. As Trevor Grundy, a British journalist who worked in Tanzania on the same newspaper where Godfrey Mwakikagile also worked as a news reporter and during the same period, stated:

I worked in Dar es Salaam (1968 - 1972) for one of the English papers....

Between 1933 and World War II there was next to no development in Tanganyika. Hitler wanted his colonies back and the various British politicians thought it a good idea to return them - an act of appeasement to the German leader. So why spend money on something you're sooner or later give away?

After 1918, Tanganyika became a mandated territory under the League of Nations.

In African eyes, the British were no more popular than the Germans. The British turned Tanganyika into an undeclared apartheid state that was socially divided between divided Africans, Europeans and Asians....

(It was) British-style apartheid – their secret was never to give racial segregation a name. – (Trevor Grundy, "Julius Nyerere Reconsidered," 4 May 2015, africaunauthorised.com).

Godfrey Mwakikagile lived under this system of racial segregation when he was growing up in Tanganyika in the fifties and wrote about it in his books, *Life in Tanganyika in The Fifties*, *My Life as an African*, *Africa and The West* and other works including *Nyerere and Africa: End of an Era* and *Tanzania under Mwalimu Nyerere: Reflections on an African Statesman*. For example, he vividly remembers the public toilet he and other Africans had to use at the bus station in the town of Mbeya in the Southern Highlands Province where he came from. It was labelled "Africans" and was filthy. The label on the toilet was still there even after independence, a chilling reminder of an inglorious past.

He remembers using the toilet during holidays when he was a student, going to and from Songea Secondary School, a boarding school in southern Tanzania he attended from 1965 to 1968.

The bus station in Mbeya was also the only one in town in those days. The buses were owned by the East African Railways and Harbours Corporation (EAR&H) serving the three African countries of Kenya, Uganda and Tanganyika (later Tanzania) founded by the British colonial rulers.

There was also, in the town of Mbeya, the Mbeya Club

exclusively for whites before independence; Mbeya School for white children, mostly of British settlers; and a residential area and houses for whites, again mostly British.

Godfrey Mwakikagile also spent a part of his childhood in Mbeya from 1954 to 1955.

He has written about the "complex" race relations between Africans and the British settlers in those days in his book, *Life in Tanganyika in The Fifties*:

> What makes this account particularly compelling is that he is an African whose own family experienced life under colonial rule. Interviewing many surviving actors, this book offers compelling primary evidence on the state of race relations at this delicate time before independence. – (British Empire Books, Authors, Bibliography, Historiography and Library:
> http://www.britishempire.co.uk/library/library.htm).

The book has had favourable reviews. A reviewer on amazon.com who lived in Tanganyika in those days stated the following:

> I grew up in Tanzania, and this book really takes me back home. The man tells how things were without hiding the bad times of the colonial era. But, I must say, he is NOT bitter and angry at the British like many other African writers. This story has its boring moments of course because life is like that. I found it very realistic and refreshing." - (Steve VN, An African Growing up in Tanzania in the 1950s and 1960s, amazon.com, August 18, 2016, https://www.amazon.com/Life-Tanganyika-Fifties-Godfrey-Mwakikagile/dp/9987160123 #customerReviews).

Another reviewer, also on amazon.com, wrote the following about the same book:

> I was there. What a beautiful country! Wonderful days, wonderful memories. The best of times. Brought tears to my eyes. I have yet to read a better book on Tanganyika in those days." - (Keith, Tanganyika

in the fifties - a decade to remember, amazon.com, July 7, 2006, https://www.amazon.com/Life-Tanganyika-Fifties-Godfrey-Mwakikagile/dp/9987160123#customerReviews).

It was an era of delicate and sometimes tense race relations, with Africans confined to a subordinate status, being on the lowest rung of the racial hierarchy.

African leaders, including Julius Nyerere, campaigning for independence were subjected to the same indignities which continued even after the end of colonial rule, especially during the early years, but drew a swift response from the new government which was predominantly black and multi-racial. As Mwakikagile stated in *Nyerere and Africa: End of an Era*:

> Mwalimu himself had experienced racial discrimination, what we in East Africa – and elsewhere including southern Africa – also call colour bar. As Colin Legum states in a book he edited with Tanzanian Professor Geoffrey Mmari, *Mwalimu: The Influence of Nyerere*:
>
> 'I was privileged to meet Nyerere while he was still a young teacher in short trousers at the very beginning of his political career, and to engage in private conversations with him since the early 1950s.
>
> My very first encounter in 1953 taught me something about his calm authority in the face of racism in colonial Tanganyika. I had arranged a meeting with four leaders of the nascent nationalist movement at the Old Africa Hotel in Dar es Salaam. We sat at a table on the pavement and ordered five beers, but before we could lift our glasses an African waiter rushed up and whipped away all the glasses except mine.
>
> I rose to protest to the white manager, but Nyerere restrained me. 'I am glad it happened,' he said, 'now you can go and tell your friend Sir Edward Twining [the governor at the time] how things are in this country.'
>
> His manner was light and amusing, with no hint of anger.'
>
> Simple, yet profound. For, beneath the surface lay a steely character with a deep passion for justice across the colour line and an uncompromising commitment to the egalitarian ideals he espoused and implemented throughout his political career, favouring none.
>
> Years later his son, Andrew Nyerere, told me about an incident

that also took place in the capital Dar es Salaam (near the school he and I attended and where we also stayed from 1969 - 1970) shortly after Tanganyika won independence in 1961. Like the incident earlier when Julius Nyerere was humiliated at the Old Africa Hotel back in 1953, this one also involved race. As Andrew stated in a letter to me in 2002 when I was writing this book:

'As you remember, Sheikh Amri Abeid was the first mayor of Dar es Salaam. Soon after independence, the mayor went to Palm Beach Hotel (near our high school, Tambaza, on United Nations Road in Upanga). There was a sign at the hotel which clearly stated: 'No Africans and dogs allowed inside.' He was blocked from entering the hotel, and said in protest, 'But I am the Mayor.' Still he was told, 'You will not get in.' Shortly thereafter, the owner of the hotel was given 48 hours to leave the country. When the nationalization exercise began, that hotel was the first to be nationalized.'

Such insults were the last thing that could be tolerated in newly independent Tanganyika. And President Nyerere, probably more than any other African leader, would not have tolerated, and did not tolerate, seeing even the humblest of peasants being insulted and humiliated by anyone including fellow countrymen. – (Godfrey Mwakikagile, *Nyerere and Africa: End of an Era*, New Africa Press, 2010, pp. 501 – 502).

It was also at the Palm Beach Hotel where Stokely Carmichael (Kwame Ture) stayed when he went to Tanzania in November 1967; he was interviewed by the *Sunday News* and *The Nationalist*, Dar es Salaam, 5 – 6 November.

He gave a fiery speech at the University of Dar es Salaam in early 1968 denouncing racism which he himself would have experienced at the Palm Beach Hotel had he gone there before or soon after independence, as did the first African mayor of Dar es Salaam, Sheikh Amri Abeid, who assumed the post not long after Tanganyika attained sovereign status.

Professor Terence Ranger (1929 – 2015), a renowned British historian who specialised in African history and who taught at the University College of Rhodesia and Nyasaland (now the University of Zimbabwe) in Salisbury (renamed Harare in 1982) from 1957 until 1963 when he was deported in March by the white minority regime for supporting Africans in their quest for racial equality – he went to teach at the University of Dar es Salaam after he was deported – recalled the day Stokely Carmichael spoke at Tanzania's leading academic institution. As he stated in his book, *Writing Revolt: An Engagement with African Nationalism, 1957 – 67*:

> Early in 1968 Stokely Carmichael [Trinidadian-American civil rights activist] visited the College to give a lecture under the auspices of the Student Revolutionary Front. As the frogs croaked loudly in the pool outside, Stokely held his audience spellbound inside. A master orator, he could do more with a whisper than anyone else with a shout.
>
> He had three messages. The first was that African students were the true proletariat and that they, guns in hand, must spearhead the revolution.
>
> The second was that the major liberation movements could not be trusted. He attacked particularly the so-called 'authentic' movements, recognized as such by Soviet Russia - ZAPU, FRELIMO, and the MPLA. He offered to chair a debate between their representatives and spokesmen of the rival parties, ZANU included. (Wisely none of them took up the challenge). Giovanni Arrighi, now teaching in Dar and a strong supporter of ZAPU, was incandescent with rage, hissing to me that Stokely must be an agent of the CIA.
>
> The third message was that it was necessary, but hard, to hate the whites. It was easy to hate Asians, he said, but whites were so much admired and so dominant that one had to work really hard to hate them.
>
> At one stage he was interrupted while students came up and mopped his brow with a large handkerchief.
>
> A history student sitting next to me was shouting 'I do hate the whites, I do hate the whites,' pausing to whisper to me, 'I don't mean you, Professor Ranger.'
>
> Stokely's then wife, Miriam Makeba, sang 'Nkosi Sikelel' iAfrika,' a moment of true emotion.
>
> It was the only meeting I have ever been to at which it was impossible for me to raise a question or to make an objection.
>
> The next day I visited the Refugee School, where the teachers thought their students would be interested to hear about 1896 (when blacks fought white settlers in Zimbabwe and lost). I took *Revolt* with me.

It turned out that Stokely had been there the day before. He had told the students that he was pleased they were passing exams but they must not take this white knowledge seriously. They must always be suspicious of whatever whites told them, and be most suspicious when a white told them something they liked to hear. They must always ask themselves what the motive was. So I encountered a very critical audience.

The first questioner told me that he had understood what I had said but that what he wanted to know was the function of it. Fortunately for me, he gave an example by adding:

'I think you have told us about 1896 because the Africans were defeated in the end and you want to discourage us.'

I determined not to knuckle under and fought back, grasping a convenient hammer which was lying on the desk. I asked whether Nyerere talked of Maji Maji because it had been defeated in the end and he wanted to discourage Tanzanians.

When they refused to believe that some Africans served on the white side in 1896, I showed them photos in the book (*Revolt*). 'But who took the photos?' they asked.

Would that all audiences were so critical!

A very different repudiation of the book came when I arrived at UCLA in 1969. As I entered the elevator in the Bunche building, Donald Abraham wheeled himself out. 'I hold you personally responsible for the death of spirit mediums in Mozambique,' he said in passing.

Nor were the academic reviews all positive. Robert Rotberg wrote a particularly disobliging one for *African Historical Studies*. – (Terence Ranger, *Writing Revolt: An Engagement with African Nationalism, 1957 - 67*, Woodbridge, Suffolk, UK: James Currey; Harare, Zimbabwe: Weaver Press, 2013, pp. 178 - 170).

Stokely Carmichael's message had universal appeal in terms of struggle against racism, especially in the context of southern Africa where white minority regimes were in control during that period, with Tanzania being the headquarters of all the African liberation movements.

It was also a message that resonated with his audience at the University of Dar es Salaam and at the school for young refugees (Kurasini International Education Centre on the outskirts of Dar es Salaam) from southern Africa in a country where incidents of racism were nothing new, blacks being the main victims during colonial times and even after independence at the hands of other non-blacks as well, not just whites.

Godfrey Mwakikagile's home region, the Southern Highlands Province, was one of the areas of Tanganyika which had a significant number of white settlers, mostly British, during the colonial period and in the early years of independence.

Incidents of racial discrimination in the province were not uncommon, including some involving his father in the town of Tukuyu, as he explained in his book *Life in Tanganyika in The Fifties*. He has, in the same book, written about other incidents when he himself was a victim of racism; incidents which he has also narrated in his other work, *Tanzania under Mwalimu Nyerere: Reflections on an African Statesman*.

It was also in the town of Tukuyu where the first meeting of the leaders of the white settlers met in October 1925 to discuss formation of a giant federation covering East and Central Africa – Kenya, Uganda, Tanganyika, Nyasaland, Northern Rhodesia and Southern Rhodesia – to consolidate imperial rule.

The conference was called by Lord Delamere, the leader of the British settlers in Kenya. Godfrey Mwakikagile wrote about that in his books, *Africa and the West* and *Africa After Independence: Realities of Nationhood*. As he stated in *Africa and the West*:

> In 1920, the protectorate of British East Africa became Kenya Colony...a fundamental transition...intended to consolidate the power of the white settlers.
>
> In London the Secretary of State for the Colonies, Winston Churchill, speaking at an East African dinner...in January 1922...said the democratic principles of Europe were 'by no means suited to the development of Asiatic and African people.'
>
> According to *The Times*, London, 28 January 1922, he stated that the intention was to enable British settlers in Kenya to have their own

government, a situation similar to what led to the consolidation of white power in Southern Rhodesia and...to the eruption of guerrilla warfare years later by black nationalists in both countries....

Had such self-government been granted,...it would eventually have led to a declaration of independence by whites, making Kenya an independent 'white' nation like apartheid South Africa, Australia and New Zealand, and as Rhodesia attempted to do when it declared independence in November 1965, had black people in Kenya not unleashed Mau Mau.

There was such a determined attempt to consolidate white power that even a giant federation of all the British territories in East and Central Africa was considered. Settler leaders from the British colonies in the region met for the first time in October 1925 at Tukuyu, in the southwestern highlands of Tanganyika, to consider the proposal with the blessings of the British government. As George Bennett states:

'In Kenya Delamere was ready for (Governor Edward) Grigg's federation plans...(and) called a conference, at Tukuyu in southern Tanganyika, of settler leaders from the whole area from Kenya to Nyasaland and Northern Rhodesia. This was succeeded by others, at Livingstone (Northern Rhodesia) in 1926 and Nairobi in 1927.'

However, after the British Conservative Government fell in June 1929, hopes for any federation of East and Central African territories were also dashed....

Yet the Hilton Young Commission of the British government which issued a report on the failure of the proposed federation was condescending towards Africans, and its recommendations were endorsed by successive governments. As Bennett states:

'The Report itself describes (Africans as) 'the backward races' twenty centuries (2,000 years) behind the Europeans.'

That was tantamount to saying the interests of the indigenous people could never be considered equal to those of the members of the 'advanced' race. According to the Hilton Young Report:

'(Waiting) till the backward races have reached their (white settlers') standard is an impossible proposition which no virile and governing race could be expected to acquiesce in'....

Continued mistreatment of Africans led to increased political agitation...during the late 1920s and thereafter. – (Godfrey

Mwakikagile, *Africa and the West*, Huntington, New York: Nova Science Publishers, Inc., 2000, pp. 88 – 89).

In his work, *Sidney Webb and East Africa: Labour's Experiment with the Doctrine of Native Paramountcy*, Professor Robert G. Gregory provided another perspective on Lord Delamere and the meeting of the white settler leaders he convened at Tukuyu:

> The idea of a federation in East and Central Africa was not new; it was almost as old as white settlement in Kenya....By 1925, when Griggs became Governor, Delamere had decided that federation was inevitable.
>
> In October 1925, with characteristic zeal, he organized an unofficial conference. At Tukuyu, a remote outpost in southern Tanganyika, he met with twelve influential settlers from Kenya, Tanganyika, Nyasaland, and Northern Rhodesia to discuss closer union. He fed them canned food and champagne and by the end of the week had convinced them of the advantages of a federation. ...Sir Herbert Stanley, Governor of Northern Rhodesia, delivered the opening address, and Delamere as chairman presided over the other sessions.
>
> But although Delamere at this time gained much prestige and was hailed as 'the Rhodes of East Africa,' he did not succeed in bringing the delegates to any agreement. Representatives from the Rhodesias (Northern and Southern Rhodesia) feared amalgamation with the 'Black North.' – (Robert G. Gregory, *Sidney Webb and East Africa: Labour's Experiment with the Doctrine of Native Paramountcy*, Berkeley: University of California Press, 1962, pp. 64 - 65).

In the late 1920s and 1930s and even thereafter, British settlers, especially in Kenya, continued to campaign for a federation of the three East African countries – Kenya, Uganda and Tanganyika – they knew they would dominate. Nairobi, Kenya's capital, had, in the 1920s, virtually become the capital of the British East African colonies. The proposed federation was strongly opposed by African leaders who saw it as an instrument of domination to perpetuate imperial rule.

The Central African Federation, also known as the

Federation of Rhodesia and Nyasaland (Northern Rhodesia, Southern Rhodesia and Nyasaland), collapsed for the same reason. Formed in August 1953 and dominated by Southern Rhodesia which had the largest number of white settlers among the three countries, it was dissolved in December 1963 because of strong opposition by African nationalists.

Founded in 1900 by the German colonial rulers and named Neu Langenburg, the town of Tukuyu where the leaders of the white settlers met to formulate plans on how to turn the entire region into a white dominion was and still is the headquarters of Rungwe District in the Southern Highlands. It was partly destroyed by an earthquake in 1919:

> During May and June, 1919, very severe seismic disturbances were experienced in the south-western portion of the Territory, which wrecked the Government station and several mission buildings in the Rungwe (former Langenburg) district and caused much damage at Songea....
> At Tukuyu, (formerly Neu Langenburg) the shocks occurred almost hourly till the end of the month, and at Songea 72 separate shocks were recorded. They appeared to emanate from the Livingstone Mountains and to travel in a north-easterly or north-westerly direction. All earth tremors were accompanied by heavy rumblings, whilst rumblings were frequently heard though no shock was felt. – (*Report on Tanganyika Territory, Covering the Period from the Conclusion of the Armistice to the End of 1920*, H.M. Stationery Office, Dar es Salaam, Tanganyika, 1921, p. 10; and Gerald Fleming Sayers, *The Handbook of Tanganyika*, London: MacMillan and Co., 1930, p. 28).

A hilly plateau with abundant rain (more than 100 inches every year) at an elevation of 3,000 - 5,000 feet above sea level with mountain ranges which form the walls of the Great Rift Valley reaching up to 8,000 – 10,000 feet or more in the peaks of the eastern range (Livingstone Mountains also known as the Kipengere Range), Rungwe District has very fertile soil and temperatures ranging from 40°F – 80°F; before climate change, temperatures were sometimes in the 30s and frost was common. The district is prone to earthquakes like other parts of the Southern Highlands.

John Mwakangale represented the Southern Highlands Province in the colonial legislature (LEGCO) where, together with his colleagues, he continued to campaign for independence.

The Southern Highlands Province in the southwest bordering Northern Rhodesia (now Zambia) and Nyasaland (now Malawi) was one of seven provinces of colonial Tanganyika.

The provinces were Western Province which was the largest; Lake Province, Northern Province, Central Province, Coast Province, Southern Province, and the Southern Highlands Province which was simply known as the Southern Highlands. The provinces were divided into smaller administrative units called regions in 1963.

After Tanganyika won independence in December 1961, John Mwakangale continued to be a member of parliament. He was appointed Regional Commissioner of the Southern Highlands in 1962 after serving as TANU provincial secretary for the same province.

Others who were appointed regional commissioners in the same year – and who had also served as TANU provincial secretaries of other provinces – were Richard Wambura, Samuel Luangisa, John Nzunda, S.J. Kitundu and J. Abdallah. S.A. Mtaki and S. P. Muro, who once served as TANU provincial chairmen, were also appointed regional commissioners.

During colonial rule, heads of provinces – all British – were known as provincial commissioners (PCs). Led by Nyerere, TANU – Tanganyika African National Union – was the nationalist movement that won independence for Tanganyika.

John Mwakangale was also the first leader of Tanganyika whom Nelson Mandela met in January 1962 when Mandela secretly left South Africa to seek assistance from other African countries in the struggle against white minority rule in his home country.

Tanganyika was the first country in the region to win independence; it was also the first independent African country Mandela visited after he left South Africa for the first time on 11 January 1962.

He met John Mwakangale in Mbeya, the capital of the Southern Highlands Province. Mwakangale had been assigned to receive Mandela in Mbeya on behalf of the government of Tanganyika. After meeting Mwakangale, Mandela flew to Dar es Salaam the next day where he met Julius Nyerere.

Nyerere was the first leader of an independent African country Mandela met. In his autobiography, *Long Walk to Freedom*, Mandela recalled his meeting with John Mwakangale in the town of Mbeya and how, for the first time in his life, he felt free and proud to be in an independent African country:

> Early the next morning we left (Bechuanaland, now Botswana) for Mbeya, a town near the Northern Rhodesian border....
> (In Mbeya) we booked in a local hotel and found a crowd of blacks and whites sitting on the veranda making polite conversation. Never before had I been in a public place or hotel where there was no color bar.
> We were waiting for Mr. John Mwakangale of the Tanganyika African National Union, a member of Parliament and unbeknown to us he had already called looking for us.
> An African guest approached the white receptionist. 'Madam, did a Mr. Mwakangale inquire after these two gentlemen?' he asked, pointing to us. 'I am sorry, sir,' she replied. 'He did but I forgot to tell them.' 'Please be careful, madam,' he said in a polite but firm tone. 'These men are our guests and we would like them to receive proper attention.'
> I then truly realized that I was in a country ruled by Africans. For the first time in my life, I was a free man. Though I was a fugitive and wanted in my own land, I felt the burden of oppression lifting from my shoulders. Everywhere I went in Tanganyika my skin color was automatically accepted rather than instantly reviled. I was being judged for the first time not by the color of my skin by the measure of

my mind and character. Although I was often homesick during my travels, I nevertheless felt as though I were truly home for the first time....

We arrived in Dar es Salaam the next day and I met with Julius Nyerere, the newly independent country's first president. We talked at his house, which was not at all grand, and I recall that he drove himself in a simple car, a little Austin. This impressed me, for it suggested that he was a man of the people. Class, Nyerere always insisted, was alien to Africa; socialism indigenous. – (Nelson Mandela, *Long Walk to Freedom: The Autobiography of Nelson Mandela*, Little, Brown and Co., New York, 1994, p. 538).

Besides John Mwakangale and Jeremiah Kasambala, Brown Ngwilulupi, who was one of the founders and leaders of the main opposition party in Tanzania, Chadema, was also a classmate of Elijah Mwakikagile. He served as vice chairman of Chadema when the party was founded in 1992. Edwin Mtei was the party's chairman.

Mtei also wrote a book, *From Goatherd to Governor*, an autobiographical account of his rise from humble roots and poverty to the corridors of power in Tanzania, also in the regional context of East Africa and in the international arena.

Edwin Mtei worked with President Nyerere for many years. He was the first governor of the Bank of Tanzania, appointed by Nyerere in 1966, and later served as minister of finance. After he differed with Nyerere on economic policies, he left the cabinet and went to work at the World Bank in Washington, D.C., on Nyerere's recommendation. He supported structural adjustment programmes (SAPs) and other austerity measures including currency devaluation recommended by the International Monetary Fund (IMF) and which were to be imposed on Tanzania as a mandatory condition for financial aid to rejuvenate the country's economy.

Nyerere was strenuously opposed to that. He saw the measures as a deliberate attempt by the United States and other Western powers who dominate the IMF and the

World Bank to reverse his socialist policies and force the country to mortgage its independence in order to get assistance from the world's financial institutions. He also said the draconian IMF measures would hurt the poor. He went on to say that IMF imposition of ready-made prescriptions on poor countries for their ailing economies as a condition for aid was unacceptable:

> Any serious Third World government will ask serious questions. I cannot sign an agreement (with the IMF) and then have riots on the streets. You may be the economic experts but I am the political expert - allow me at least to say how much the people can take. – (Julius Nyerere at a press conference in Dar es Salaam, Tanzania, 22 November 1984, quoted by Godfrey Mwakikagile, *Economic Development in Africa*, Commack, New York: Nova Science Publishers, Inc., 1999, pp. 63 and 66; and in *Mwenge*, Tanzania Embassy Newsletter, Washington, D.C., November 1984. On the hardship on the poor caused by IMF conditions imposed on African countries, see also Joe Mensah, quoted by Colleen Lowe Morna, "Surviving Structural Adjustment," *Africa Report*, September-October 1989, p. 48, and by G. Mwakikagile, *Economic Development in Africa*, op. cit., p. 68; and Chinua Achebe, "Africa is People," in his Presidential Fellow Lecture to the World Bank Group, Washington, D.C., 1998).

The heavy-handed approach taken by the IMF ostensibly to fuel economic growth and alleviate the plight of the poor in developing countries prompted Nyerere to ask what came to be a famous question:

> When did the IMF become an International Ministry of Finance? When did nations agree to surrender to it their power of decision-making? – (Julius Nyerere, quoted in "NO to IMF Meddling," *Daily News*, Dar es Salaam, Tanzania, 2 January 1980, quoted by Lawrence E.K. Lupalo, *Nyerere and Nkrumah: Shared Vision*, CreateSpace, Scotts Valley, California, USA, 2016, p. 41).

Nyerere also contended that IMF conditions for aid had not only made life worse for the poor but had not been helpful in improving the overall condition of developing countries. As he stated:

> I was in Washington last year (1997). At the World Bank the first question they asked me was 'how did you fail?' I responded that we took over a country with 85 per cent of its adult population illiterate. The British ruled us for 43 years. When they left, there were 2 trained engineers and 12 doctors. This is the country we inherited.
> When I stepped down there was 91-per-cent literacy and nearly every child was in school. We trained thousands of engineers and doctors and teachers.
> In 1988 Tanzania's per-capita income was $280. Now, in 1998, it is $140. So I asked the World Bank people what went wrong. Because for the last ten years Tanzania has been signing on the dotted line and doing everything the IMF and the World Bank wanted. Enrolment in school has plummeted to 63 per cent and conditions in health and other social services have deteriorated.
> I asked them again: 'What went wrong'? These people just sat there looking at me. Then they asked what could they do? I told them have some humility. Humility - they are so arrogant!....
> It seems that independence of the former colonies has suited the interests of the industrial world for bigger profits at less cost. Independence made it cheaper for them to exploit us. We became neo-colonies. Some African leaders argued against Kwame (Nkrumah)'s idea of neocolonialism.
> The majority of countries in Africa and the rest of the South are hamstrung by debt, by the IMF. We have too much debt now. It is a heavy burden, a trap. It is debilitating. We must have a new chance. If we doubled our production and debt-servicing capabilities we would still have no money for anything extra like education or development. It is immoral. It is an affront. The conditions and policies of the World Bank and the IMF are to enable countries to pay debt not to develop.
> – (Julius Nyerere, in an interview with Ikaweba Bunting, "The Heart of Africa: Interview with Julius Nyerere on Anti-Colonialism," *New Internationalist*, Oxford, UK, January-February 1999; and in G. Mwakikagile, *Nyerere and Africa: End of an Era*, op. cit., p. 582).

Paying debts is an enormous burden African countries and others in the developing world continue to bear, prompting Nyerere in 1986 to ask:

"Must we starve our children to pay our debt?"

Although Mtei had fundamental differences with Nyerere on economic policy, he did not alienate Tanzania's founding father and remained on very good terms with him. That is why Nyerere recommended him for the IMF position as Africa's representative – director of IMF's African Department – after he left the cabinet; it was Tanzania's turn to choose one and Nyerere chose Mtei.

And when Mtei founded the opposition party Chadema, Nyerere predicted then (proved correct years later) that it was the only party - among all the new parties formed in the early 1990s - which had a clear programme and which would become the main opposition party in the country. Many of its founding members had been senior government officials and politicians who decided to leave the ruling party and provide a credible challenge to it in the political arena and chart a new course for the country.

Nyerere also advised the leaders of the opposition parties to unite and form one major party with a nationwide base of support to challenge the ruling party if they were to have a chance at winning elections instead of pursuing the goal as a divided opposition. It is an advice that has gone unheeded through the years, thus helping the ruling party – in stewardship of the nation for decades – to perpetuate itself in power.

Even Mtei, as the leader of the main opposition party in the country, did not seek unity with the other leaders – nor did they – to form one broadly-based national party, not an alliance of parties – to challenge the ruling party whose dominance on the political landscape and hegemonic control of the country tilted the balance in its favour in every election even without rigging electoral contests.

Mtei also once served as secretary-general of the East African Community (EAC) and was one of the most prominent Tanzanians in the nation's post-colonial history when he founded Chadema with Brown Ngwilulupi and other leading figures including Bob Nyanga Makani, the first secretary-general of Chadema and former deputy governor of the Bank of Tanzania. Makani also once served as Tanzania's deputy attorney general. He was later elected chairman of Chadema after Mtei stepped down.

The leadership of Chadema, when the party was formed, was nationally representative. Chairman Mtei came from the northeastern part of the country. Vice chairman Ngwilulupi came from the southwest, and secretary-general Makani from the lake zone comprising regions around Lake Victoria. There were also high-ranking officials representing western, central and coastal regions including the former island nation of Zanzibar, now semi-autonomous.

Brown Ngwilulupi (his father was Ngwilulupi Mwasakafyuka) who came from Rungwe District in the southern highlands was also a childhood friend of Elijah Mwakikagile. They came from the same village of Mpumbuli in the area of Kyimbila four miles south of the town of Tukuyu. John Mwakangale's home village was about five miles north of theirs near Tukuyu.

They were, together with John Mwakangale, classmates all the way from Tukuyu Primary School (in the town of Tukuyu) to Malangali Secondary School in Iringa District (then a part of the Southern Highlands Province) and later became relatives-in-law. Brown Ngwilulupi's wife, Lugano Mwankemwa, and Elijah Mwakikagile's wife, Syabumi Mwambapa, were first cousins.

Brown Ngwilulupi also went to Tabora Government School (in Western Province), also known as Tabora Boys, another highly-rated academic institution in colonial Tanganyika which Professor Julian Huxley described as "the Eton of Africa," patterned after the British school.

He attended Tabora School together with Amon Nsekela; Oscar Kambona who became Tanganyika's minister of defence and foreign affairs after the country won independence; and Kanyama Chiume who also became minister of foreign affairs in his home country of Malawi after independence. Both Kambona and Chiume held other ministerial posts at different times in their respective countries in the sixties.

Kanyama Chiume left Nyasaland in 1937 and went to Tanganyika to live with his uncle in what is now Morogoro Region in the eastern part of the country. He was about eight years old.

He grew up in Tanganyika where he attended primary school and secondary school before going to Makerere University College in Uganda. After he graduated from Makerere, he returned to Tanganyika where he became a secondary school teacher.

He spoke perfect Swahili and became one of the most eloquent "native" speakers of the language. He lived in Tanzania (and Tanganyika) longer – for decades since his childhood – than he did in Malawi (and Nyasaland) and was in that sense more Tanzanian than Malawian.

His classmates at Dar es Salaam Central School included Rashidi Kawawa who later became prime minister and vice president of Tanzania; Abdul Sykes and Ali Sykes who became some of the leading members of the nationalist movement in the struggle for independence; and Hamza Aziz who became the second indigenous Inspector General of Police since 1961 and later ambassador to the United States among other posts; he was buried with full military honours when he died in 2004. As Chiume stated in an interview with Benjamin Lawrence of the Hoover Institution, Stanford University, on 13 November 1998:

> I was born on the 22nd of November in 1929...at Usisya, which is my home village,...in Nkhata Bay District, Nyasaland. I had my primary education in Tanzania, Tanganyika as it was then, because up to the death of my mother in 1937 when I was about eight years old, my uncle, who himself had been very much helpful to me and my mother...took me to Tanganyika where he was working as a head clerk under the district commissioner in Kiberege in the then Eastern

Province.

And from there I went to Dar es salaam Central School where I had the rare privilege of going to the same class, same dormitory, for five years, with Rashidi Mfaume Kawawa, among many others, who later on became...the vice president and prime minister of Tanzania.

From Dar es Salaam, in 1946, after I had skipped one class, Standard Eight, I was selected as the only student from that school to go to Tabora Secondary School which was then the senior territorial secondary school in Tanzania (Tanganyika) for those who came from eight government junior secondary schools. This is the school to which Nyerere himself went. He was not a student at the time when I was there but he was teaching in a Catholic School (St. Mary's) just about a mile or so from Tabora (School).

And from there in 1949 after I had passed...Makerere College Entrance Examination – we also did Cambridge School Certificate Examination, we were the first people in that government school to sit for the Cambridge School Certificate Examination – I went to Makerere as a science student.

Kanyama Chiume also played a major role as one of the main leaders of the independence movement in Nyasaland (Malawi). After he and other cabinet members fell out with Malawi's President Hastings Kamuzu Banda in 1964, he returned to Tanzania where he lived for 30 years in Dar es Salaam before going back to Malawi in 1994.

During his years of exile in Tanzania, Kanyama Chiume worked as a features writer and editor at *The Nationalist*, the ruling party's daily newspaper, together with Benjamin Mkapa who was the managing editor before President Nyerere appointed Mkapa editor of the *Daily News*. Chiume also worked with the *Daily News* during that period.

Before joining the opposition, Brown Ngwilulupi was a member of the ruling party, TANU, renamed CCM, and served for many years as secretary-general of the country's largest farmers' union, the Cooperative Union of Tanganyika (CUT), appointed by President Nyerere. His younger brother, Weidi Ngwilulupi Mwasakafyuka, a former ambassador, also left the ruling party and joined one of Tanzania's opposition parties in the early 1990s and served as head of its foreign affairs division.

Godfrey Mwakikagile stated in his autobiographical works that he moved to Rungwe District in 1955 with his parents when he was 5 years old after living in different parts of Tanganyika – Kigoma, Ujiji, Kilosa, Morogoro, and Mbeya – where his father worked as a medical assistant for the British colonial government.

They also stayed in what is now Kyela District for many months in 1955 before moving to Rungwe District in the same year.

His father was one of the few medical assistants in colonial Tanganyika. In a country with an acute shortage of doctors, medical assistants played a critical role in the provision of vital medical services.

Well-trained, they were, in many cases, a substitute for doctors during colonial rule and even after Tanganyika won independence. In fact, when Tanganyika won independence from Britain on 9 December 1961, it had only 12 doctors. As Professor John Iliffe of the University of Cambridge stated in his book, *East African Doctors: A History of the Modern Profession*:

> Medical assistants, normally with three years of medical training, and often much practical experience, had become the core of colonial medical systems....(In Tanganyika)...the Medical School opened (in 1963) but...by the mid-1960s it was realised that medical assistants were still needed and their training resumed in 1968. - (John Illife, *East African Doctors: A History of the Modern Profession*, Cambridge University Press, 1998, p. 128).

They were few in colonial Tanganyika, a vast expanse of territory of about 365,000 square miles with millions of people to serve. According to John Illife, there were only about 300 medical assistants in January 1961, in the whole country, the same year Tanganyika won independence. Tanganyika had a population of 12 million during that time.

Godfrey Mwakikagile stated in his autobiography that his father also worked at Amani Research Institute in Muheza District.

During German colonial rule, Amani Research Institute was world-renowned for its research in a number of areas including tropical medicine (for malaria and other vector-borne diseases among others), as well as biological and agricultural sciences and had highly trained scientists. It excelled in high-quality research and retained its international reputation under British rule after Germany lost its colony (Deutsch-Ostafrika – German East Africa – renamed Tanganyika) in World War I.

His father also worked in Handeni and then in Tanga before moving to Kigoma four months before Godfrey Mwakikagile was born. Coincidentally, it was also in what is now Tanga Region where Godfrey's paternal grandfather, Kasisika Molesi Mwakikagile, died.

Born and brought up in Mwaja, Kyela, in what is now Mbeya Region, his grandfather went to work in Tanga and Muheza and worked there for a number of years. He died in 1937 and was buried at Power Station, Muheza, in the northern part of what was then known as the Coast Province.

His younger brother, Lamusi Mwakalinga (Mwakikagile), the only sibling he had, who was also born in Mwaja, lived almost his entire life in Kasumulu, Kyela.

Godfrey Mwakikagile states in some of writings that when he and his siblings were growing up, and before he went to boarding school in 1963, their paternal grand uncle Lamusi Mwakalinga used to visit them and their parents in Kyimbila, travelling on the bus from Kyela, a distance of about 30 miles.

Godfrey's father Elijah Mwakikagile was also born in what is now Kyela District in an area called Lwangwa in the ward of Busale but grew up in Kyimbila near the town of Tukuyu in Rungwe District. He was born on 25 October 1924.

His son Elijah Mwakikagile was also born (25 October 1924) in what is now Kyela District in an area called Lwangwa in the ward of Busale but grew up in Kyimbila near the town of Tukuyu in Rungwe District.

Rungwe was the home district of Godfrey Mwakikagile's parents. Both were born and brought up in Rungwe District and were members of an ethnic group indigenous to that part of Tanzania.[4]

Rungwe District, ringed by misty blue mountains, is close to the border with Malawi and is located in the Great Rift Valley north of Lake Nyasa. And what is now Kyela District bordering Malawi was once a part of Rungwe District.

Godfrey Mwakikagile went to school in Tanzania and in the United States.

Tanganyika united with Zanzibar in 1964 to form Tanzania.

Early years

Godfrey Mwakikagile attended Kyimbila Primary School (up to Standard 4) two miles south of the town of Tukuyu and Mpuguso Middle School (up to Standard 8) seven miles southwest of Tukuyu in Rungwe District in Mbeya Region in the Southern Highlands; Songea Secondary School (up to Standard 12 or Form Four) near the town of Songea in Ruvuma Region, and Tambaza High School (up to Standard 14 or Form Six) in the nation's capital Dar es Salaam.[5]

The headmaster of Songea Secondary School, Paul Mhaiki, when Godfrey Mwakikagile was a student there from 1965 to 1968, later in the early 1970s Director of Adult Education at the Ministry of National Education, appointed by President Nyerere. He later became Director of UNESCO's Division of Literacy, Adult Education, and Rural Development.

After finishing high school at Tambaza in November 1970, he joined the National Service in January 1971, which was mandatory for all those who had completed secondary school, high school, college and university.

He underwent training, which included basic military training, at Ruvu National Service camp in the Coast Region. After that, he went to another national service camp in Bukoba on the shores of Lake Victoria in the North-West Region bordering Uganda.

The region was later renamed Kagera Region. Ugandan military ruler, Idi Amin, attempted to annex the region when he invaded Tanzania in October 1978.

Godfrey Mwakikagile once worked as a news reporter at the *Standard*, which was later renamed *Daily News*, and as an information officer at the Ministry of Information and Broadcasting in Tanzania's capital Dar es Salaam before going to school in the United States in November 1972.[6]

He left Tanzania on November 3rd and arrived in the United States on November 4th, three days before the US presidential election on November 7th the incumbent, Richard Nixon, a Republican, won against his Democratic opponent George McGovern in one of the biggest landslide victories in the nation's modern history.

He first joined the editorial staff of the *Standard* as a junior reporter when he was still in high school, in Form Five (Standard 13), in 1969.[7]

Coincidentally, his editor at the *Daily News*, Benjamin Mkapa, who also helped him to go to school in the United States, years later became president of Tanzania and served two five-year terms (1995–2005).[8]

He was the third president in the nation's history since the country won independence from Britain in 1961. Before then, Benjamin Mkapa served as Tanzania's minister of foreign affairs, among other ministerial posts, and as high commissioner (ambassador) to Nigeria and Canada, and as ambassador to the United States.

He also served as press secretary to President Julius Nyerere and was later appointed minister of information and broadcasting before assuming other cabinet posts in the following years.

The president of Tanzania during that period, Julius Nyerere who led the country from 1961 to 1985, was the editor-in-chief of the *Daily News*. But his role was only ceremonial rather than functional.

Mkapa was preceded by Sammy Mdee as managing editor of the *Daily News*. Godfrey Mwakikagile joined the editorial staff when Mdee was the editor. After he was replaced by Mkapa, Mdee became Director of Information Service at the Ministry of Information and Broadcasting, appointed by President Nyerere, and later served as Nyerere's press secretary and, after that, as a diplomat.

Godfrey Mwakikagile graduated from Wayne State University in Detroit in the state of Michigan, USA, in 1975 and was president of the African Students Union at that school.[9]

He also attended Aquinas College in Grand Rapids, Michigan, in 1976.

One of his professors of economics at Aquinas College was Kenneth Marin who once worked in Tanzania.[10]

It was just a coincidence that he went to Aquinas College where he ended up being taught by someone who had worked in Tanzania years before. He did not know anything about Professor Marin before then and met him at Aquinas College for the first time.

Here is another coincidence: Kenneth Marin worked in the multi-storey Co-operative Building on Lumumba Street, in Dar es Salaam, where Brown Ngwilulupi also worked as secretary-general of the country's farmers' union. The two knew each other well and used to have lively exchanges on a number of issues, as Professor Marin said in an economics class he taught at Aquinas College when he recalled his days working in Tanzania.

Godfrey Mwakikagile was in that class, one of four

African students and the only one from Tanzania; three were Nigerian.

Professor Marin was a great admirer of President Nyerere as a leader and as an intellectual and said he used to go to the same church he did in Oyster Bay, Dar es salaam. They were Roman Catholic. He called him a world leader, not just an African leader, as Mwakikagile stated in his book, *Nyerere and Africa: End of an Era*.

He even read Nyerere's writings in class when he lectured on development economics and other Third World subjects. He also said Nyerere was an excellent writer and had thorough command of the English language. He also said the following about Nyerere in one of his lectures at Aquinas College: "He is one of the best world leaders we have today."

Professor Marin worked as an economist for the government of Tanzania in the late sixties and early seventies. He went to Tanzania in 1968 and served as an adviser to the government on capital mobilisation and utilisation. Before then, he worked as an economist for the United States federal government. He was appointed by President Lyndon B. Johnson to serve on Wage and Price Control during the mid-sixties. President Johnson appointed Professor Kenneth Marin as a member of the White House Consumer Advisory Council.[11]

In 1966, Professor Marin was a member of a U.S. State Department evaluation team that was assigned to review various performances in the economic and political arena in six South American countries.[12]

Years later, one of his students, Godfrey Mwakikagile, also ended up writing about economics, among other subjects, mostly about Africa. And coincidentally, Mwakikagile's first book, *Economic Development in Africa*, was also about economics.[13]

Writings

Godfrey Mwakikagile came into prominence in Tanzania and elsewhere after he wrote a major book about Julius Nyerere not long after the former Tanzanian president died.[14]

He is considered by many people, including those who have reviewed his books about President Nyerere in different newspapers, magazines and academic journals in a number of countries, to be an authority on Nyerere and one of his most prominent biographers.[15]

One scholar who cited Godfrey Mwakikagile as an authoritative source on President Nyerere was Professor David Simon, a specialist in development studies at the University of London and Director of the Centre for Development Areas Research at Royal Holloway College at the university. Professor Simon published excerpts from Godfrey Mwakikagile's book on Nyerere in his compiled study, *Fifty Key Thinkers on Development*, published in 2005.[16]

During that time and thereafter, Professor David Simon was also the editor of the scholarly *Journal of Southern African Studies* and was on the editorial staff of another academic publication, the *Review of African Political Economy*.

Godfrey Mwakikagile's works have been getting serious attention among many people including academics in many countries who have also reviewed some of his books in scholarly journals.

His first book, *Economic Development in Africa*, was published in June 1999 and he has maintained a steady pace since then, writing books, as demonstrated by the number of titles he has on the market. He is one of Tanzania's most well-known authors and one of Africa's most prolific.

He has written more than 40 books (since 1999) mostly about Africa during the post-colonial period, and has been described as a political scientist although his works defy classification.

He has written about history, politics, economics, as well as contemporary and international affairs from an African and Third World perspective and is known for such works as *Nyerere and Africa: End of an Era*, and *Africa and the West*.[17]

Both have been favourably reviewed in a number of publications including the highly influential *West Africa* magazine (founded in 1917 and based in London) which reviewed two of his books in the same year; a rare accomplishment in such a major publication.

The books were reviewed by *West Africa* magazine editor Kofi Akosah-Sarpong, a Ghanaian who also once was a visiting lecturer and scholar-in-residence at the University of Botswana. They were excellent reviews.

Godfrey Mwakikagile's book, *Nyerere and Africa: End of an Era*, his magnum opus and probably his most well-known title, was reviewed by *West Africa* magazine in 2002 three years after Nyerere died of leukemia in October 1999 at the age of 77.[18]

It was also reviewed by a prominent Tanzanian journalist and political analyst, Fumbuka Ng'wanakilala of the *Daily News*, Dar es Salaam, Tanzania, in October 2002 and is seen as a comprehensive work, in scope and depth, on Nyerere.[19]

Others who have reviewed the book include Professor A.B. Assensoh, a Ghanaian teaching at Indiana University in Bloomington, Indiana, in the United States. He reviewed the first edition of *Nyerere and Africa: End of an Era* in the *African Studies Review*, an academic journal of the African Studies Association, in 2003.

The same book was also reviewed by Professor Roger Southall of the University of the Witwatersrand (Wits), formerly of Rhodes University, South Africa, in the biannual interdisciplinary publication, the *Journal of Contemporary African Studies* (Taylor & Francis Group), 22, No. 3, in 2004. Professor Southall was also the editor of the journal during that period.

The first edition of *Nyerere and Africa: End of an Era* was published in November 2002, and the second, an expanded edition, in January 2005. The third edition, also an expanded version, was published in November 2006. The fourth edition, also expanded, was published in December 2008. And the fifth edition was published in 2010.

The book has also been cited by a number of African leaders including South African Vice President Phumzile Mlambo-Ngcuka in one of her speeches about African leadership and development in which she quoted the author.[20]

She was the main speaker at a conference of African leaders, diplomats and scholars at the University of the Western Cape in South Africa in September 2006 when she gave her speech.

Although his books have been able to get the attention of some African leaders, it is impossible to know if they have had any influence on any of them. But the mere fact that they are cited by them shows that he is taken seriously as an author, not only in Tanzania but in other African countries and elsewhere.

One of Godfrey Mwakikagile's books, *Africa and the West*, which is a sweeping survey of the continent before the advent of colonial rule and during the colonial era as well as after independence, was also reviewed by *West Africa* magazine in its edition of 21–27 January 2002.[21]

The book, which was published in 2000, has been described as an appeal to Africans to respect their cultures, values and traditions and take a firm stand against alien ideas which pollute African minds and undermine Africa. It is also a philosophical text used in a number of colleges and universities in the study of African identity, philosophy and history. It is also a strong condemnation of the conquest of Africa by the imperial powers.

West Africa magazine, in its January 2002 edition, also described Godfrey Mwakikagile as an author who articulates the position of African Renaissance thinkers.

But in spite of his passionate defence of Africa, past and present, Godfrey Mwakikagile is also highly critical of some Afrocentric scholars who propagate myths about Africa's past and even reinvent the past just to glorify the continent, claiming spectacular achievements in the precolonial era in some areas where there were hardly any or none; for example, in advanced science, technology and medicine. They also inflate achievements in some areas.

He contends that "true scholarship requires rigorous intellectual discipline and entails objective enquiry and analysis of facts and evidence including admitting failures and shortcomings"; a position he forcefully articulates in his books *Africa and The West* and *Africa is in A Mess: What Went Wrong and What Should be Done*, among other works.

It is a position that led one renowned Afrocentric Ghanaian political analyst and columnist, Francis Kwarteng, to describe Godfrey Mwakikagile as a "Eurocentric Africanist" in his article, "End of the Dilemma: The Tower of Babel," on GhanaWeb, 28 September 2013, in which he discussed the role and the question of race, religion, and ethnicity in Ghana's politics and, by extension, in a Pan-African context including the African diaspora; which is a wrong characterisation of Mwakikagile since all his works are written from a purely African, not a Eurocentric, perspective.

In his article, Francis Kwarteng also cited one of Godfrey Mwakikagile's books, *Ethnic Politics in Kenya and Nigeria*, in his analysis of the role of ethnicity in national politics in Africa:

Wole Soyinka...rightly admits in *Of Africa* that if America, a racist country at that, can elect a person of African ancestry, a black man of Luo ethnicity, president, then, he sees no reason Kenya shouldn't learn from that—that precedent....

Soyinka believes Kenya's democratic process must allow enough political space for the accommodation of ethnic diversification, so that qualified minorities can also partake in leadership positions, principally the presidency....But Soyinka's Nigeria has its own fair share of problems, a cornucopia of them. A truism flies across Nigeria's social and political landscape that Hausas are born natural rulers....

Yet Nigeria has about 250 ethnic groups. So, what defines the criteria for Nigeria's multiethnic exclusivism from the presidential pie?....

This is not unique to Nigeria, however. The same thing happened in Ghana and Uganda, producing the likes of Idi Amin. This phenomenon is captured in the Eurocentric Africanist Godfrey Mwakikagile's *Ethnic Politics in Kenya and Nigeria.*

In another article on GhanaWeb, 15 October 2013, Francis Kwarteng also stated:

We all know how Western material culture and unholy spiritualism are destroying Africa. Corruption in Africa is proliferating like cancerous cells in the body politic. Corrupt African politicians collaborate with Western banking officials to secrete the people's money in Western banks, monies, which, however you look at it, either fortunately for the West or unfortunately for Africa, are reinvested in Western national economies. So, in the long run Africa becomes positively poorer and the West negatively wealthier. Analytically, this runs counter to the central thesis of Rodney's *How Europe Underdeveloped Africa.* In fact, it's what the Eurocentric Africanist Godfrey Mwakikagile calls 'Africa in a Mess.' This inverse relationship of economic bilateralism is unhealthy and must be critically addressed by Africa.

It is a case of Africans themselves, especially the leaders, contributing to the underdevelopment of Africa. Bad leadership including corruption in African countries is one of the subjects Godfrey Mwakikagile has addressed extensively in his books, especially in *Africa is in A Mess: What Went Wrong and What Should be Done, The Modern*

African State: Quest for Transformation, Africa After Independence: Realities of Nationhood, Africa at the End of the Twentieth Century: What Lies Ahead, and *Statecraft and Nation Building in Africa: A Post-colonial Study.*

He contends that bad leadership is the biggest problem most African countries have faced since independence, and everything else revolves around it.

Africans of all ideological stripes agree corruption is one of the biggest problems African countries face. It is even acknowledged by some leaders. And a number of African scholars including Godfrey Mwakikagile have addressed the problem, proposing solutions to a seemingly intractable problem. As Francis Kwarteng stated in "A Political Coin of Three Sides: What Do We Actually Want?," GhanaWeb, 8 November 2013:

> Today's leadership has failed to show moral and social leadership in the face of mounting national crisis. Indeed corruption threatens the very future of the youth....President Mahama's book (*My First Coup D'état*) must be read in tandem with Wole Soyinka's *The Open Sore of a Continent*, Ali Mazrui's *The African Condition: A Political Diagnosis*, Molefi Kete Asante's *Rooming in the Master's House*, and Godfrey Mwakikagile's *Africa is in A Mess: What Went Wrong and What Should Be Done* and *Africa After Independence: Realities of Nationhood*. In fact, these bibliographies must be included in every secondary school curriculum as well as the curricula of teacher training institutions across the country. We may then use them as bibliographical platforms to ask students to come up with comprehensive solutions to our myriad national problems.

He stated in another article, "Africa Must Practice Its Own Democracy: A Moral Necessity," GhanaWeb, 17 October 2013:

> We were not the first to raise this question; others had before us!
> Celebrated prescient leaders like Kwame Nkrumah made this philosophical mantra part of their political platform, so were others — Patrice Lumumba, Amilcar Cabral, etc. Literacy scholars like Chinua Achebe, and Ngugi wa Thiong'o; international economists like

Dambisa Moyo and Yaw Nyarko; political scientists like Ali Mazrui, Godfrey Mwakikagile, and Mahmood Mamdani; legal experts like Shadrack Gutto and Randall Robinson; world-renowned anthropologists and linguists like Cheikh Anta Diop and Théophile Obenga; and Afrocentrists like Molefi Kete Asante, Chinweizu, Maulana Karenga, and Ama Mazama had made similar arguments in the past few decades—via their prolific scholarship, organizations, and political activism.

One of the problems Africa faces in nation building is how to achieve unity in diversity in countries composed of different ethnic groups and threatened by ethno-regional loyalties and rivalries. It is one of the subjects Godfrey Mwakikagile has addressed in his books.

He has written extensively about ethnicity and politics in Africa in the post-colonial era and how the two phenomena are inextricably linked in the African political context. He has used case studies in different analyses of the subject in different parts of the continent.

One of his books, *Ethnicity and National Identity in Uganda*, has been described by Tierney Tully as "a great book, but very dense." A reviewer on amazon, UK, has described Godfrey Mwakikagile's work, *Uganda: The Land and Its People*, as a "very studious book about Uganda's history, politics, ethnic groups and social structure."

His other books on the subject include *Identity Politics and Ethnic Conflicts in Rwanda and Burundi: A Comparative Study*; *Burundi: The Hutu and The Tutsi: Cauldron of Conflict and Quest for Dynamic Compromise*; *Civil Wars in Rwanda and Burundi: Conflict Resolution in Africa*; *Ethnic Diversity and Integration in The Gambia*; *The People of Ghana: Ethnic Diversity and National Unity*, and *Belize and Its Identity: A Multicultural Perspective*, a scholarly work on the Central American nation founded by the British colonial rulers and African slaves as British Honduras and which, culturally and historically, is considered to be an integral part of the

Afro-Caribbean region, hence of the African diaspora. Although written by an African, the book is an important part of Afro-Caribbean literature.

One American journalist who interviewed Godfrey Mwakikagile described him as an independent scholar who was also a widely read and highly regarded author.

Godfrey Mwakikagile responded by saying that he was just an ordinary African, like tens of millions of others, deeply concerned about the plight of his continent.

But there is no question that he is a serious writer whose writings are widely read even if he considers himself to be just an ordinary African like millions of his brethren across the continent and elsewhere.

In his book, *African Political Thought* (Palgrave Macmillan, 2012), Professor Guy Martin has described Godfrey Mwakikagile as one of Africa's leading populist scholars who refuse to operate and function within the limits and confines of Western ideologies – or any other external parameters – and who exhort fellow Africans to find solutions to African problems within Africa itself and fight the syndrome of dependency in all areas and create a "new African."

He goes on to state that all these African-populist thinkers are academics and deal strictly with ideas, without being directly involved in politics, although most of them are political scientists.

Professor Martin states in his book that some of the most prominent African-populist scholars include Senegalese scientist, historian and Egyptologist Cheikh Anta Diop (1923 – 1986), Nigerian political scientist Calude Ake (1939 – 1996), Burkinabé historian Joseph Ki-Zerbo (1922 – 2006), Tanzanian scholar Godfrey Mwakikagile, Kenyan political science professor, Mueni wa Muiu, and Daniel T. Osabu-Kle, a professor of politicial science from Ghana.

He goes on to state that all these scholars are also ardent Pan-Africanists and, for reasons explained in the book, he has devoted chapter eight exclusively to the thoughts, concepts and ideas of only four scholars: Mwakikagile, Ake, Osabu-Kle and Muiu. As he states in Chapter Eight, "The Africanist-Populist Ideology: Popular Democracy and Development in Africa," which he starts with a quotation from President Julius Nyerere:

> *Africa...is isolated. Therefore to develop, it will have to depend upon its own resources basically, internal resources, nationally, and Africa will have to depend upon Africa. The leadership of the future will have to devise, try to carry out policies of maximum national self-reliance and maximum collective self-reliance. They have no other choice. Hamna! [There is none!]* – Julius K. Nyerere, *"Reflections," quoted in John S. Saul, The Next Liberation Struggle, 159.*

As we saw in Chapter 7, Frantz Fanon's warning to African people, leaders, and scholars was that for popular democracy and development to succeed in Africa, they must stop blindly following the West: they must stop aping Western culture, traditions, ideas, and institutions; they must think 'outside of the box'; and, above all, they must be bold and innovative and develop their own ideas, concepts, and institutions based on African values, culture, and traditions. This alternative path to Western liberal democracy and capitalist development is precisely the line of thinking of an emerging African scholarship, exemplified by the four African scholars whose political ideas are examined in this chapter.

More specifically, this chapter reviews the ideas and values for a new, free, and self-reliant Africa put forth by African scholars who have the best interest of the African people at heart and thus advocate a popular type of democracy and development. However, unlike the populist-socialist scholars, the Africanist-populist scholars refuse to operate within the parameters of Western ideologies - whether of the socialist, Marxist-Leninist, or liberal-democratic persuasion - and call on all Africans to become the initiators and agents of their own development, with the ultimate goal of creating a 'new African.' – (Guy Martin, *African Political Thought*, New York: Palgrave Macmillan, 2012, pp. 129 - 130).

Professor Guy Martin is also the author of *Africa in World Politics: A Pan-African Perspective* (2002); co-editor, with Chris Alden, of *South Africa and France:*

Towards a New Engagement in Africa (2003); and, with Mueni wa Muiu, co-author of *A New Paradigm of the African State: Fundi wa Afrika* (2009). As Edmond J. Keller, professor of political science and former Director of the UCLA Globalization Research Center- Africa and of the James S. Coleman African Studies Center at the University of California-Los Angeles, stated in his review of Professor Guy Martin's book, *African Political Thought*, in one of the leading academic journals on African research and studies, *Africa Today*, Volume 60, Number 2, Winter 2013, published by Indiana University Press:

> The work is an ambitious survey. Martin is encyclopedic in his treatment of the subject of African political thinking. He demonstrates a comprehensive knowledge of African political thought throughout history. He has succeeded in his efforts to produce what is arguably the first real attempt to synthesize African political thought into a single thematic volume....
>
> Martin begins his analysis by focusing on indigenous political thought dating back to ancient times (Kush/Nubia, sixth century BCE). He then brings his study up to the present...He systematically introduces the reader to the ideas of specific theorists and their biographies. He situates these thinkers in the context of their times.
>
> Some were political activists, such as Amílcar Cabral, Samora Machel, Kwame Nkrumah, Julius Nyerere, and Steve Biko. Others were public intellectuals and academic theorists, such as Claude Ake, Godfrey Mwakikagile, Daniel Tetteh Osabu-Kle, and Mueni wa Muiu.
>
> For the amount of ground covered in *African Political Thought*, this is quite a slim colume. The comprehensiveness of the book is its greatest strength. It touches upon most of the major African political thinkers....
>
> It is interesting that the political thought of Meles Zenawi, the now-deceased political leader of Ethiopia, is not considered. Debate is currently raging as to whether or not, despite his views on Marxism, he was an original thinker.

Godfrey Mwakikagile is also featured as a major African author and scholar in the *Dictonary of African Biography, Volume 6* (Oxford University Press, 2011), edited by Harvard University professors, Emmanuel K.

Akyeampong and Henry Louis Gates, Jr. As Professor Ryan Ronnenberg who wrote a profile of Mwakikagile in the *Dictionary of African Biography* (pp. 365–366) states:

Godfrey Mwakikagile's childhood in the closing stages of Tanzania's colonial period made a significant impression on him. He witnessed colonial oppression firsthand, and the racist ideology that upheld it....

Indeed, the ideas of Pan-Africanism embraced by the early Nyerere government would resonate with Mwakikagile deeply, as he early on came to possess a deep and abiding respect for Africans and African Americans who preserved their culture in the face of racist ideology and institutions.

In his introduction to *Africa and the West* (2000), he wrote, 'Much as the conquest of Africa led to the denigration of the African personality, leading many Africans to hate themselves by despising their heritage; an equally intense but opposite reaction was caused by this very invasion and conquest of our continent.'

Mwakikagile embraced Tanzania's independence, and the independence of the African continent as a whole, with fierce pride. 'I was too young to play a role in the independence movement, but old enough to know what Mau Mau in neighboring Kenya was all about, and who our leaders were: from Kwame Nkrumah in Ghana to Julius Nyerere in Tanganyika; from Nnamdi Azikiwe in Nigeria to Jomo Kenyatta in Kenya and Patrice Lumumba in Belgian Congo' (*Africa and the West*, 2000)

His experience also inspired his thinking regarding Africa and its relationship to the Western world, which led to several academic works dedicated to the subject.

Mwakikagile's early works focused on pressing issues in African studies, particularly the theory and realization of development in Africa. *Economic Development in Africa*, published in 1999, uses the rich case study of Tanzania's transition from socialism to free-market capitalism as a foundation for broader conclusions concerning the continent's development failures.

Mwakikagile writes about Africa as a whole in such a way as to suggest that he possesses not only a keen understanding of the way things are, but also a deep understanding of the way they should be.

The arcebically titled *Africa Is in a Mess: What Went Wrong and What Should Be Done* reflects on the decades since independence with pragmatism and regret, observing the loss of both leadership and ingenuity as the continent's intellectual elite settle abroad, while suggesting how this process might be reversed.

In fact, as the years have passed, and as those early optimistic moments after independence have slipped away, Mwakikagile has taken it upon himself to write about why Africa has fallen short of its vision.

Mwakikagile has translated his experience as a youth in colonial East Africa and his adulthood in postcolonial Tanzania into provocative scholarship concerning topics vitally important to African studies.

Deeply invested in the ideas of Pan-Africanism that guided the Nyerere government, Mwakikagile has brought this perspective to bear upon a variety of crucial areas of scholarship, including postcolonial development, the African diaspora, and the late Julius Nyerere's career. – (Ryan Ronnenberg, "Godfrey Mwakikagile," in Emmanuel K. Akyeampong and Henry Louis Gates, Jr., eds., *Dictonary of African Biography, Volume 6*, New York: Oxford University Press, 2011, pp. 365 – 366).

Kofi Mensah, one of the people who reviewed Godfrey Mwakikagile's book *Africa is in A Mess: What Went Wrong and What Should Be Done* on amazon.com wrote the following about Godfrey Mwakikagile:

He was one of the most promising intellectuals of our generation, and one of the most inspiring, to emerge out of the seventies, when he graduated from university.

In one of his lectures, Professor Abdul Karim Bangura of Howard University, a Sierra Leonean, cited Godfrey Mwakikagile as one of the major African thinkers. He used Godfrey Mwakikagile's book, *The Modern African State: Quest for Transformation*, among other works by different scholars, in his lecture, "The Democratic Project and the Human Condition across the African Continent" in January 2013 at Howard University and stated that his lecture was "based on the analyses of major African thinkers" including Godfrey Mwakikagile.

Godfrey Mwakikagile has also been invited to give lectures at different universities because of the books he has written. And his role as a public intellectual has been demonstrated in other ways. For example, he has been sought for interviews by BBC, PBS (America's public television network), and byVoice of America (VOA), among other media outlets. This is documented in the interview he had with the American journalist.

The interview, which focused on Julius Nyerere as a leader and on other subjects about Africa, is reprinted in its entirety in one of Godfrey Mwakikagile's books, *Nyerere and Africa: End of an Era.*

Although he has been exposed to Western cultures, was educated in the Western intellectual tradition and even lived in the United States for many years, his perspectives and philosophical conceptions have undoubtedly been shaped by his African upbringing and are deeply rooted in African cultures and traditions. And he rejects the notion that Africa was a blank slate until Europeans came to write on it.

He passionately argues that the history written about Africa by Europeans when they first went to Africa and even during colonial rule as well as after independence is not African history but the history of Europeans in Africa and how they see Africa and Africans from their European perspective or perspectives.

He also contends that traditional Africa has produced philosophers and other original thinkers whose knowledge and ideas – including ideas at a high level of abstraction – can match and even surpass the best in the West and elsewhere in the world. He forcefully articulates that position in his book, *Africa and The West.*[22]

And although he sees Africa as an indivisible whole, he also argues that all nations, include those in Africa, have different national characters. He looks at the concept of national character in the African context in one of his books, *Kenya: Identity of A Nation*, and makes a compelling case for this idea which is sometimes highly controversial.

The work is, among other subjects, a study of comparative analysis in which the author looks at the national characters of Kenya and Tanzania, thus demonstrating that nations do indeed have different national characters and have been that way throughout history.

Kenyans themselves have had to grapple with questions of identity, ethnic versus national, and how to reconcile the two for the sake of national unity, peace and prosperity. As Dr. George Nyabuga, a lecturer at Nairobi University, stated about Godfrey Mwakikagile's book, *Kenya: Identity of a Nation*, in his article, "Politics of East Africa," in *Oxford Bibliographies*, 29 November 2011:

> Ethnicity, identity, conflict, power, democracy, corruption, and governance are often mentioned as issues of interest when examining not only African but also East African politics. Sometimes these issues make it difficult for people within the countries of East Africa to develop appropriate characteristics with which to identify themselves. This is perhaps the issue that Mwakikagile tries to examine as many nation-states grapple with their multiple identities. However, in most instances many people identify with their ethnic groups whose consequences for politics in Africa are sometimes deleterious. In Kenya, ethnicity has been the cause of numerous conflicts, most recently the post-election violence of late 2007 and early 2008.

Tanzania is one of the few countries on the continent which have been spared the agony and scourge of ethnic conflicts, unlike Kenya which Godfrey Mwakikagile has used for comparative analysis in looking at the identities of the two neighbouring countries.

In his books, including *Nyerere and Africa: End of an Era*, he has also explained how Tanzania has been able to contain and even neutralise tribalism unlike other countries on the continent. As Keith Richburg, who travelled and reported on many African countries when he was *The Washington Post* bureau chief based in Nairobi in the 1990s, stated in his book, *Out of America: A Black Man Confronts Africa*:

One of my earliest trips was to Tanzania, and there I found a country that had actually managed to purge itself of the evil of tribalism. Under Julius Nyerere..., the government was able to imbue a true sense of nationalism that transcended the country's natural ethnic divisions.... Tanzania is one place that has succeeded in removing the linguistic barrier that separates so many of Africa's warring factions. But after three years traveling the continent, I've found that Tanzania is the exception, not the rule. In Africa..., it *is* all about tribes.

One of Africa's most prominent political analysts, Kenyan columnist Philip Ochieng, articulated the same position. As he stated in his article, "Mwalimu Nyerere's Bequest to Mkapa a Tall Order," in one of Kenya's main newspapers, the *Daily Nation*, Nairobi, 16 October 1999:

Tanzania (is) the most united country in Africa. This unity and sharp national consciousness was contributed to by (the) life-works of the Teacher (Mwalimu Nyerere).... He insisted on uniform Kiswahili throughout the Republic. During the three years that I worked in Dar es salaam I rarely heard any tribal language spoken.

He also stated in another article, "Africa's Greatest Leader," in *The East African*, Nairobi, 19 October 1999:

(Under President Nyerere) Tanzania became the African country with the highest degree of national self-consciousness and has almost annihilated the bane of Kenya that we call tribalism.... At a time when Nairobi was drowning in crude elite grabbing, Dar es Salaam was a Mecca of the world's national liberation movements, and a hotbed of global intellectual thought.... Mwalimu Julius Kambarage Nyerere is the most successful leader that Africa has ever produced since the European colonial regime collapsed 50 years ago.

One Kenyan reviewer of *There Was a Country*, a book about Biafra by Chinua Achebe who considered Nyerere to be the role model for African leaders, stated on amazon.com:

Nyerere succeeded in creating the only non-tribal country in Africa where there is no tribalism..... I have seen... tribalism in Kenya and know how it works. And surely enough, we also have violence in almost every election we have because of tribalism.

President Ellen Johnson-Sirleaf of Liberia also said in a television interview that Nyerere was her role model. Wole Soyinka also considered Nyerere to be a role model other African leaders should emulate.

Godfrey Mwakikagile has written extensively about tribalism and contends that it is one of the biggest problems Africa faces and is the source of instability in many countries on the continent, including civil wars.

He undoubtedly has strong convictions but does not neatly fit into any ideological category. He expresses strong Pan-Africanist views in his writings and sees Africa as a collective entity and one organic body and has strongly been influenced by staunch Pan-Africanist leaders such as Kwame Nkrumah, Julius Nyerere, Ahmed Sekou Toure and Patrice Lumumba whom he also strongly admires.[23]

He says Africa does not have leaders of that kind anymore.

He also strongly admires Thomas Sankara as a man of the people like Nyerere and contends that among the new breed of African leaders, Sankara – who has been described as the African Che Guevara – showed great promise but was eliminated by some of his so-called compatriots working for France and other Western powers before he could realise his full potential the same way Lumumba was, eliminated by the United States and Belgium.

Godfrey Mwakikagile has written about Thomas Sankara in his book *Military Coups in West Africa Since The Sixties* and in *African Countries* among other works.

But some of his critics contend that he overlooks or glosses over the shortcomings of these leaders precisely because they are liberation icons and played a leading role in the struggle for independence and against white minority rule in Southern Africa.²⁴

He also seems to be "trapped" in the past, in liberation days, especially in the seventies when the struggle against white minority rule was most intense. But that may be for understandable reasons.²⁵

He was a part of that generation when the liberation struggle was going on and some of his views have unquestionably been shaped by what happened during those days as his admiration for Robert Mugabe, for example, as a liberation icon clearly shows; although he also admits in his book, *Nyerere and Africa: End of an Era*, that the land reform programme in Zimbabwe could have been implemented in an orderly fashion and in a peaceful way and without disrupting the economy.

But his admiration for Mugabe as a true African nationalist and Pan-Africanist remains intact; a position that does not sit well with some of his critics although he does not condone despotic rule as he clearly states in his writings.

He admires Mugabe mostly as a freedom fighter and liberation hero who freed his people from colonial rule and racial oppression and exploitation, and as a strong leader who has taken a firm and an uncompromising stand against Western domination of Africa.

And by remarkable contrast, his contempt for African leaders whom he sees as whites with a black skin also remains intact. He mentions Dr. Hastings Kamuzu Banda as a typical example of those leaders.

He has written about Dr. Banda and other African leaders, among other subjects, in his book, *Africa After Independence: Realities of Nationhood*.²⁶

Godfrey Mwakikagile also contends that only a few African leaders – Kwame Nkrumah, Julius Nyerere, Ahmed Sekou Toure, Gamal Abdel Nasser, Ahmed Ben Bella and Modibo Keita – strove to achieve genuine independence for their countries and for Africa as a whole and exercised a remarkable degree of independence in their dealings with world powers. And Mugabe was the only other leader who fit in this category, in spite of his shortcomings.

According to Ben Bella, the six leaders – Nkrumah, Nyerere, Sekou Toure, Nasser, Modibo Keita and Ben Bella himself – constituted what came to be known as "The Group of Six" within the Organisation of African Unity (OAU). In an interview in Switzerland in 1995 with Jorge G. Castañeda, the author of *Companero: The Life and Death of Che Guevara*, Ben Bella said the six leaders worked together secretly within the OAU on a number of issues including the Congo and African liberation, excluding other African leaders. It is a subject Godfrey Mwakikagile has also addressed in his book *Nyerere and Africa: End of an Era*.[27]

Godfrey Mwakikagile's background as a Tanzanian has played a major role in his assessment of many African leaders because of the central role his country played in the liberation struggle in the countries of Southern Africa, and not just in South Africa – the bastion of white minority rule on the continent.[28]

Zimbabwean President Robert Mugabe was one of the African leaders who had strong ties to Tanzania, Godfrey Mwakikagile's home country, since liberation days. Others with strong ties to Tanzania include Thabo Mbeki, former president of South Africa; Joaquim Chissano, former president of Mozambique; and Sam Nujoma, former president of Namibia.[29]

Tanzania, then known as Tanganyika, was also the first independent African country Nelson Mandela first visited when he secretly left South Africa for the first time in 1962 to seek support from other African countries for the liberation struggle in his home country. And Julius Nyerere was the first leader of an independent African country he met when he went to see him in Dar es Salaam during that time. It was also Nyerere who authorised the government of Tanganyika to give Mandela a travel document that enabled him to go to Addis Ababa, Ethiopia, to attend a conference of African leaders and to go to other African countries. Mandela wrote about that in his book *Long Walk to Freedom*:

> Because I did not have a passport, I carried with me a rudimentary document from Tanganyika that merely said, 'This is Nelson Mandela, a citizen of the Republic of South Africa. He has permission to leave Tanganyika and return here.' I handed this paper to the old Sudanese man behind the immigration counter and he looked up with a smile and said, 'My son, welcome to the Sudan.' He then shook my hand and stamped my document.

Newspaper background

In those days, Dar es Salaam, Tanzania, was the headquarters of all the African liberation movements, under the leadership of President Julius Nyerere, and Godfrey Mwakikagile got the chance to know many of the freedom fighters who were based there when he worked as a young news reporter in the nation's capital.[30]

They included Joaquim Chissano Joaquim Chissano who was the head of the FRELIMO office in Dar es Salaam and who later became the minister of foreign affairs and then president of Mozambique when his country won independence after 500 years of Portuguese colonial rule.[31]

Many other freedom fighters who were based in Dar es Salaam, Tanzania, also went on to become national leaders in their respective countries after the end of white minority rule in Southern Africa. And they all still have strong ties to Tanzania even today.

Tanzania played a big role in supporting the African liberation movements not only by giving sanctuary to the freedom fighters but by providing them with military training and guerrilla bases and by supporting them financially because of Nyerere's leadership. As the legendary British journalist David Martin stated after interviewing Nyerere one day:

> I remember one day sitting in his office questioning that a number of African countries had not paid their subscriptions to the OAU Liberation Committee Special Fund for the Liberation of Africa. He looked at me for some moments, thoughtfully chewing the inside corner of his mouth in his distinctive way. Then, his decision made, he passed across a file swearing me secrecy as to its contents. It contained the amount that Tanzanians, then according to the United Nations the poorest people on earth, would directly and indirectly contribute that year to the liberation movements. I was astounded; the amount ran into millions of US dollars.
>
> It was the practice among national leaders in those days to say that their countries did not have guerrilla bases. Now we know that Tanzania had many such bases providing training for most of the southern African guerrillas, who were then called 'terrorists' and who today are members of governments throughout the region....
>
> Tanzania was also directly attacked from Mozambique by the Portuguese. But, in turn, each of the white minorities in southern Africa fell to black majority political rule and Nyerere saw his vision for the continent finally realized on 27 April 1994 when apartheid formally ended in South Africa with the swearing in of a new black leadership. – (David Martin, "A Candle on Kilimanjaro," in *Southern African Features*, 21 December 2001).

Tanzania was also threatened by the apartheid regime many times. South Africa's defence minister, P.W. Botha – who later became president - publicly stated in 1968 that countries which support "terrorists" – freedom fighters – should receive a "sudden hard knock," in pointed reference to Tanzania, which had the largest number of guerrilla camps, and Zambia which also had a number of such bases. According to *Africa Contemporary Record*:

> By 1968 the potential threat of escalating guerrilla attacks became elevated to a top priority of the South African regime....This threat was taken a stage further on April 24 (1968) by the Commandant-General S.A. Melville, former head of the S.A. Defence Force, who said that South Africa already had sufficient justification and provocation for

retaliation against countries which 'harboured' and encouraged terrorists whose only intention was to penetrate South Africa or South West Africa. He supported the Minister of Defence's view that such countries should receive a 'sudden hard knock.'

On April 25, the Deputy Minister of Police, Mr. S.L. Muller, informed parliament on information about fresh groups of 'terrorists' gathering in Zambia....Accoding to Muller, there were in Zambia '19 training and transit camps for terrorists as well as officers of all the African subversive organisations'....the South African Minister of Defence, Mr. P.W. Botha, warned on April 5 (1968) that countries aiding and inciting terrorism and guerilla warfare against South Africa could eventually provoke South Africa into 'hitting back hard'....

The Rhodesia rebel Minister of Law and Order, Mr. Lardner Burke, extending the state of emergency at the beginning of 1968, said that the number of 'terrorists' waiting in Zambia and Tanzania to cross the Rhodesian border continued to mount. The South African Deputy-Minister of Police, Mr. S.L. Muller, said Tanzania posed 'the greatest potential threat to the Republic.' He claimed there were '40 camps in Tanzania for the training of terrorists and all the offices of subversive organisations'.

A new external service of Radio Tanzania was inaugurated in 1968 to assist in 'propagating the ideological principles of the liberation movements in Tanzania.'

Tanzania's relations with its southern neighbour, Malawi, continued to decline in 1968 for three reasons. First, because of Dr. Banda's growing relations with South Africa. Second, because Malawi accuses Tanzania of supporting its exile Ministers, like Mr. Chipembere, in subversive activities. And third, because of frontiers disputes.

Malawi's territorial claims to districts in Tanzania provoked President Nyerere to retort that Dr. Banda was 'insane'; but, he warned, 'Dr. Banda must not be ignored; the powers behind him are not insane'....

A Tanzanian note in January, 1967, objected to maps which showed the Malawi-Tanzanian boundary as running along the eastern and northern shores of Lake Nyasa. Tanzania contended the boundary passes through the middle of the lake and that the change was made illegally by the British government on the declaration of the Rhodesian Federation.

Dr. Banda counter claimed that the lake had always belonged to Malawi, and that he had every right to change its name to Lake Malawi. The Portuguese Foreign Minister, Mr. Nogueira, supporting Malawi in March, recalled that under a Portuguese-British treaty still in effect, Malawi owned one part of the lake and Portugal the other.

By September, 1968, Dr. Banda had not only laid further claim to four districts in Tanzania, but to four Zambian districts as well. Speaking at the Malawi Congress Party's annual convention on September 17, Banda said that 'the real boundary' between his country and Zambia should be the Luangwa River, thus incorporating the whole of the Zambian eastern province. At the same time he announced he was putting the first of many gunboats on Lake Nyasa to start patrols as an answer to Tanzania's 'claim.'

Dr. Nyerere described these claims as 'expansionist outbursts which do not scare us, and do not deserve my reply.'

On September 27, President Kaunda said his country could not establish diplomatic relations with Malawi until claims to Zambian territory had been renounced....(and) challenged Dr. Banda 'to go ahead and declare war on Zambia'....

Suspicious that Swaziland's independence on September 6 (1968) was more apparent than real, President Nyerere declined to permit Tanzania to be represented at their celebrations....

On May 17, Mr. Vorster (the prime minister), speaking at the National Party's 'twenty years of Nationalist rule festival,' said that slowly but surely an army would be built up in certain Central African States for an eventual 'now or never' attack on South Africa....'These people have put it very clearly that they will abandon their plans only if South Africa is prepared to hand over to the Blacks'....Two days before, on May 15, at a summit meeting of 14 Central and East African leaders in Dar es Salaam, full support was promised to the guerilla movements fighting in Southern Africa. – (Colin Legum and John Drysdale, eds., *Africa Contemporary Record: Annual Survey and Documents 1968 - 1969*, London: Africa Research Limited, 1969, pp. 291, 292, 249, 373 - 374, 220, 180, and 250).

Dr. Banda's territorial claims extended to Mozambique; he even tried to convince Nyerere in the early sixties to share the territory with him. As Nyerere said years later:

In 1961 we became independent. In 1962, early 1962, I resigned as prime minister and then a few weeks later I received Dr. Banda. We had just, FRELIMO had just been established here and we were now in the process of starting the armed struggle.

So Banda comes to me with a big old book, with lots and lots of maps in it, and tells me, 'Mwalimu, what is this, what is Mozambique? There is no such thing as Mozambique.' I said, 'What do you mean there is no such thing as Mozambique?' So he showed me this map and he said: 'That part is Nyasaland. That part is part of Southern

Rhodesia. That part is Swaziland, and this part, which is the northern part, Makonde part, that is *your* part.'

So Banda disposed of Mozambique just like that. I ridiculed the idea, and Banda never liked anybody to ridicule his ideas. So he left and went to Lisbon to talk to Salazar about this wonderful idea. I don't know what Salazar told him. That was '62. - (Julius K. Nyerere, at an international conference, University of Dar es Salaam, Tanzania, 15 December 1997, in Godfrey Mwakikagile, *Nyerere and Africa: End of an Era*, Pretoria, South Africa: New Africa Press, 2010, pp. 556 - 557).

Mozambique won independence in 1975 after almost 500 years of Portuguese colonial rule with its territory intact; so did Angola, in the same year, from the same colonial power. Three countries in southern Africa remained under white minority rule: Rhodesia, Namibia, and South Africa.

In 1976, the American secretary of state, Henry Kissinger, went to Tanzania and met with President Nyerere three times – once in April, twice in September – in an attempt to help find solutions to conflicts in the countries of southern Africa still under white minority rule, especially Rhodesia where the white minority had unilaterally declared independence, excluding the black majority from the government.

Nyerere was chairman of the Frontline States – Tanzania, Zambia, Mozambique, Angola and Botswana – in the struggle against the white minority regimes and was critical to finding solutions to conflicts in the region. As David Martin stated about Nyerere's prominent status and the meetings he had with Kissinger:

Tanganyika became independent on 9 December 1961 and a year later...the country became a republic. For the next 24 years Nyerere was to fill the African and international stage like a colossus.

When he met the astute American Secretary of State Henry Kissinger for the first time in Dar es Salaam in 1976, the two men began a mental verbal fencing match of David and Goliath proportions. One began a quote from Shakespeare - some of whose works Nyerere translated into Swahili setting them in an African context - or a Greek philosopher and the other would end the quotation. Then Nyerere quoted an American author. Kissinger laughed: Nyerere knew Kissinger had written the words.

Neither man trusted the other. Kissinger wanted the negotiations kept secret. Nyerere, understanding the Americans' duplicity, took the opposite view and as Africa correspondent of the London Sunday newspaper, *The Observer*, I was to become the focal point of the Tanzanians' strategic leaks. That year the newspaper led the front page on an unprecedented 13 occasions on Africa. All the leaks, as Kissinger knew, came from Nyerere. One political fox had temporarily outwitted the other.

Apart from his simplicity and piercing intellect, one of Nyerere's most endearing traits was his honesty. – (David Martin, "Mwalimu Julius Kambarage Nyerere: Obituary," Southern African Research and Documentation Centre (SARDC). David Martin was a founder-director of the Southern African Research and Documentation Centre of which Nyerere was a patron. He lived in Tanzania for 10 years from 1964 to 1974 and frequently talked with Nyerere through the decades, a period of 35 years, until Nyerere's last days).

His simplicity belied his intellect and leadership potential demonstrated by his meteoric rise to power. He returned to Tanganyika in October 1952 after earning a master's degree from the University of Edinburgh in Scotland. Nine years later, he led his country to independence becoming the youngest national leader in the world. He was 39.

When he was at Edinburgh, no-one thought he would become a titan not only on the African political landscape but on the world stage years later. He did not stand out among other students as a leader or future politician anymore than he did when he was a student at Makerere University College in Uganda before he went to Scotland for further studies.

One of his fellow students from Tanganyika, Abdallah Said Fundikira who was with him at Makerere and who became a cabinet member in the first independence cabinet, said people did not really notice Nyerere. It was when he spoke that others noticed he had leadership qualities in addition to his sharp intellect. As Fundikira put it:

> If you want to know the truth, one did not particularly notice Nyerere. – (Abdallah Said Fundikira, *Africa News Online*, 8 November 1999).

He had a passionate desire to see his country and Africa as a whole free. Trevor Grundy, who was a critic of Nyerere, stated the following in his review of *Nyerere: The Early Years*, a book written by Thomas Molony, a senior lecturer in African studies at the University of Edinburgh:

> He went on to use his Edinburgh years to great advantage, bewildering – some might say bamboozling – liberal-minded journalists in the 1960s and 1970s with his formidable intellect which was the result of his reading of Jacques Rousseau and John H. Stuart Mill, T. H. Green's *Principles of Political Organization*, Benard Bosanquet's *Philosophical Essay of the State* and Harold Laski, the famous London School of Economics theorist.
> He had a blotting paper brain.
> Hardly a soul at Edinburgh guessed he would turn into Africa's number one brain box in years to come. As the historian George Shepperson put it in a BBC interview: 'We at Edinburgh were very surprised in mid-1950s when Dr Nyerere's name became widespread throughout the world press. We never felt when he was here that he was going to become a leading politician.'
> Statesmen and journalists were amazed at his knowledge....
> With his eager tongue, (and) a formidable intellect...he is presented by Commonwealth groupies as the politician who did the most to mastermind the downfall of Portuguese and British/Afrikaner rule in Africa....The Rhodesian leader Ian Smith several times referred to Nyerere as Africa's 'evil genius'....
> He did so much to help liberate different parts of Africa from European rule. – Trevor Grundy, "Julius Nyerere Reconsidered," 4 May 2015, africaunauthorised.com).

The years he spent at Edinburgh were some of the most rewarding in terms of intellectual preparation for his role as a national leader after he returned to Tanganyika. He had a passionate desire to see his country and Africa as a whole free.

Nyerere's commitment to the liberation struggle and his uncompromising stand on racial equality was also demonstrated in his negotiations with Kissinger. He did not trust the United States and did not make concessions Kissinger wanted him to make. As James Spain, the American ambassador to Tanzania during that time, stated:

> One of the amusing sidelights of Henry Kissinger's second or third visit was this. He stayed in the Kilimanjaro Hotel. When the party was clearing out to go to the airport, I was told that the Secretary of State wanted me. I went upstairs. People were carrying away files and suitcases.
>
> In the middle of a table there was a 'bug' protector that was still making weird electronic sounds. Henry gets both of us hunched over this thing. He said 'Thank you very much. This visit has been useful. Your arrangements were fine, but I want to warn you about one thing: This fellow Nyerere is not our side.'
>
> This was a pretty accurate reflection of the spirit of the times....
>
> If I did anything useful, it was to convince Washington that Nyerere was not a brutal African dictator and a Communist stooge....
> He...loved word play. I never read a book that he hadn't read. He translated Shakespeare into Kiswahili....
>
> He was a hopeless socialist. Still, he was clearly a very sincere and humane man....Most Western development aid to Tanzania came from Scandinavia, particularly the Swedes. They like the intellectual socialist, the benign father of his people who didn't kill or imprison people, while trying to create a new way of life with better prospects....
>
> The fact was that Nyerere certainly wasn't on our side, but he wasn't a tool of the Chinese or the Russians either....
>
> He was a very remarkable man and, I think, a very constructive element in the peaceful solutions to the problems of Southern Africa that eventually emerged. – (James W. S. Spain, interviewed by Charles Stuart Kennedy, 31 October 1995, *The Association for Diplomatic Studies and Training (ADST), Foreign Affairs Oral History Project*, copyright 1998, pp. 36 and 34).

Kissinger's failure to extract concessions from Nyerere prompted American reporters who had accompanied him, as well as other journalists, to conclude that Kissinger's mission was a failure. When Nyerere was asked at a press conference in Dar es Salaam if he considered Kissinger's mission to be a failure, he said in response:

> A mission of clarity is not a mission of failure.

The immediate concern was Rhodesia where guerrilla warfare was most intense during that period. Nyerere played a critical role in helping end white minority rule in that country. Frustrated by Nyerere's intellectual manoeuvres, political skills and determination to remove white minority regimes from power, Rhodesia's prime minister, Ian Smith, called him Africa's "evil genius."

Once Rhodesia was free, Namibia would be next, and finally South Africa. Nyerere was seen as a critical player in all those theatres. Kissinger acknowledged Nyerere's vital role in resolving conflicts in the region, as did others leaders. As Richard N. Viets who served as American ambassador to Tanzania from 1979 to 1981 stated:

> At that time in mid-1979, the so-called front-line states in Southern Africa, I think there were five of them...the organization was chaired by Julius Nyerere, the President of Tanzania, a very remarkable gentleman. Nyerere really towered over the other four heads of state and this organization in many respects was a one-man operation. Because of his long association with the independence movements in East Africa and throughout Southern Africa he was highly respected.
>
> Nyerere is an intellectual of very considerable dimensions, an extraordinarily articulate person. So the leadership of this group was essentially his without any challenge. He was offering almost daily advise to the Zimbabwean leadership on tactics, strategy, etc. in their negotiations with the British and the Americans and the others involved....
>
> I decided I needed to know more about Julius Nyerere than anybody else on the face of the earth....He is a very shrewd man.
>
> He was...a most remarkable figure in contemporary African political history. I always said, and others who knew him well I think shared this view, that if Nyerere had been born in Western Europe or the Far East or even in North America, he would have been an

exceptional figure in public life. He was a superb politician.

He had an acute brain, the memory of an elephant, intellectual horsepower that was second to none.

He was cunning. He could be warm-hearted one moment and cut you off at the legs at the next if it met his political or personal needs.

Nyerere...remains as far as I know the principal translator of Shakespeare from English into Swahili and one of the most gifted orators I have ever heard in English, and a marvelous drafter of the English language. – (Richard N. Viets interviewed by Charles Stuart Kennedy, April 1990, *The Association for Diplomatic Studies and Training, Foreign Affairs (ADST), Oral History Project*, copyright 1998, pp. 56, 58, 59, 61, 67 - 68).

Nyerere was also interviewed in Dar es Salaam in 1976 on an American television programme, ABC's "Issues and Answers" about the escalating conflict in southern Africa. Her made it clear that the United States and other Western powers were supporting the apartheid regime in South Africa and asked a pointed question:

> Why are Western countries arming South Africa? Why are you arming South Africa? Against what military combination? And you expect us to sit just like that.

His pivotal role in the region also prompted an American journalist on ABC's "Issues and Answers" to ask Nyerere:

> Can you use your influence, which is tremendous influence, and ask Castro to withdraw his troops from Angola?

Nyerere responded:

> Even if I had that kind of influence, it would be unnecessary. First, you remove the cause....

He was also asked:

> Will you commit troops (in a war against South Africa)?

Nyerere: Yes, I will commit troops. We would rather hang together than hang separately....

Nyerere blamed the United States for fomenting trouble and fuelling conflict in Angola. When he was asked on the American television programme, "Issues and Answers," who was causing turmoil in the country, he responded:

I believe the CIA. Who is doing it? Who else could be doing it? Why do we keep on hearing these whispers coming from Washington, saying, 'Let us create another Vietnam for the Russians in Angola'?...You are causing *us* trouble.

His commitment to the liberation of Africa was clearly evident to the freedom fighters themselves based in Tanzania and even to other people elsewhere. Many Tanzanian soldiers fought and died in the liberation wars in southern Africa and are honoured at a memorial site in Tanzania; so are those who fought and died in the war with Uganda under Idi Amin.

Nyerere's relentless support for the liberation struggle was also underscored by Professor Piero Gleijeses who stated in his book, *Conflicting Missions: Havana, Washington, and Africa, 1959 - 1976*:

Of all the African leaders who proclaimed their support for the liberation struggle in Africa – Nkrumah, Nasser, Ben Bella, Sekou Toure – he was the most committed. And by the second half of 1964, spurred by events in Zaire and the obvious failure of peaceful attempts to end white rule in southern Africa, this commitment, and his disappointment with Western powers, was increasingly evident.

By the time Che (Guevara) arrived (in Tanzania in 1965), Dar es Salaam had become the Mecca of African liberation movements...Dar es Salaam 'has become a haven for exiles from the rest of Africa,' the CIA lamented in September 1964. 'It is full of frustrated revolutionaries, plotting the overthrow of African governments, both black and white'....

In September 1964, Frelimo, the movement against Portuguese rule in Mozambique, had launched the opening salvo of its guerrilla war from bases in southern Tanzania, its only rear guard.

Following Stanleyville, Nyerere had thrown his full support to the Simbas, and Tanzania had become their main rear guard and the major conduit of Soviet and Chinese weapons for them.

It was also the seat of the Liberation Committee of the OAU. The head offices of Frelimo and a host of other movements struggling against the white regimes in South Africa, Namibia, and Rhodesia were in Dar es Salaam.

The Cuban embassy there was, the CIA reported accurately in March 1965, 'the largest Cuban diplomatic station in sub-Saharan Africa.' The ambassador, Captain Pablo Ribalta, was a close friend of Che Guevara. – (Piero Gleijeses, *Conflicting Missions: Havana, Washington, and Africa, 1959 - 1976*, Chapel Hill, North Carolina, USA: The University of North Carolina Press, 2002, pp. 84 and 85).

About ten years later, Kissinger was in Tanzania trying to find a diplomatic solution to the conflicts in southern Africa, a mission that was somewhat compromised because of American – Western – support for the white minority regimes in the region. As Nyerere stated in his article, "Rhodesia in the Context of Southern Africa" published in *Foreign Affairs* in April 1966:

The deep and intense anger of Africa on the subject of Rhodesia is by now widely realized. It is not, however, so clearly understood. In consequence the mutual suspicion, which already exists between free African states and nations of the West, is in danger of getting very much worse....

Successive Western governments have declared their hostility to apartheid, and their adherence to the principles of racial equality. They have frequently made verbal declarations of their sympathy with the forces in opposition to South African policies. But they have excused their failure to act in support of their words, on the grounds of South Africa's sovereignty. Africa has shown a great deal of scepticism about this argument, believing that it masked a reluctance to intervene on the side of justice when white privilege was involved. Now, in the case of Southern Rhodesia, legality is on the sde of intervention. What is the West going to do? Will it justify or confound African suspicions?

So far the West has demonstrated its intentions by the gradual increase of voluntary economic sanctions; there has been a refusal even to challenge South African and Portuguese support for Smith by making sanctions mandatory upon all members of the United Nations.

And there have been repeated statements by the responsible authority that force will not be used except in case in case of a break-down in law and order - which apparently does not cover the illegal seizure of power! What happens if the economic sanctions fail to bring down the Smith regime is left vague.

The suggestion therefore remains that, despite legality, the domination of a white minority over blacks is acceptable to the West....It is time for...Britain and the United States of America to make clear whether they really believe in the principles they claim to espouse, or whether their policies are governed by considerations of the privileges of their 'kith and kin.' – (Julius K.Nyerere, "Rhodesia in the Context of Southern Africa," *Foreign Affairs*, New York, April 1966; Julius K. Nyerere, *Freedom and Socialism/Uhuru na Ujamaa: A Selection from Writings and Speeches, 1965 - 1967*, Dar es Salaam, Tanzania: Oxford University Press, 1968, pp. 143, 154 - 155, and 156).

The critical role Nyerere played in finding solutions to the conflicts in southern Africa was also demonstrated by the fact that not only did Kissinger meet with him three times but longer than he did with any other African leader during his mission to the continent in 1976. In acknowledging Nyerere's role, Kissinger wrote the following, "Julius Nyerere and Tanzania: The Ambivalent Intellectual," in his book, *Henry Kissinger: Years of Renewal*:

Tanzanian President Julius Nyerere proceeded to arrange an official reception that could not have been more cordial. The motive, however, was altogether different from Kenyatta's. Nyerere...was, at heart, deeply suspicious of American society and American intentions.

In international forums, Tanzania's ministers frequently castigated us. Nyerere would not have described friendship with the United States as a national priority; instead, he tended to think of relations with us a necessary evil....

Brilliant and charming, Nyerere had an influence in Africa out of proportion to the resources of his country, proof that power cannot be measured in physical terms alone....Because Tanzania was involved in the armed struggle that was taking place in Rhodesia, and because of Nyerere's intellectual dominance, Nyerere would be a key to any solution....

Many of Nyerere's American admirers thought he and his

colleagues were the embodiment of American values and liberal traditions. By contrast, his American critics viewed Nyerere as a spokesman for Communist ideology. Neither view was accurate. Nyerere was his own man. His idiosyncratic blend of Western liberal rhetoric, socialist practice, nonaligned righteousness, and African tribalism was driven, above all, by a passionate desire to free his continent from Western categories of thought, of which Marxism happens to be one. His ideas were emphatically his own....

For our first meeting, Nyerere, a slight, wiry man, invited me to his modest private residence. it was a signal honor, and he introduced me to his mother and several members of his family. He was graceful and elegant, his eyes sparkling, his gestures fluid.

With an awesome command of the English language (he had translated *Julius Caesar* into Swahili), Nyerere could be a seductive interlocutor. But he was also capable of steely hostility. I had the opportunity to see both these sides during my three visits to Dar es Salaam....

Nyerere was the key to the frontline states....

The two most impressive leaders I encountered on this trip, Nyerere and Senghor, were at opposite ends of the African sppectrum. In a sense, they represented metaphors for varying approaches to African identity.

Nyerere was a militant who used ideology as a weapon; Senghor was an intellectual who had taught himself the grammar of power.

Nyerere considered himself as a leader of an Africa that should evolve in a unique way, separate from the currents in the rest of the world which Africa would use without permitting them to contaminate its essence. Senghor saw himself as a participant in an international order in which Africa and *négritude* would play a significant, but not isolated, role.

When all is said and done, Nyerere strove for the victory of black Africa while Senghor sought a reconciliation of cultures within the context of self-determination. – (Henry Kissinger, *Henry Kissinger: Years of Renewal*, New York: Touchstone, 1999, pp. 931 - 932, 936, 949 - 951).

In its assessment of Nyerere, the CIA prepared a report, released in May 1965, about his passionate desire to see Africa free and united and how determined he was to achieve his goal:

On the question of African liberation, Nyerere is a fanatic. Beneath a charming personality which disarms many Westerners, he is a man of strong conviction, prepared to pay almost any price to achieve a united Africa ruled by black Africans.

Nyerere's commitment to African liberation was indisputable; so was his ambition to see Africa united which even surpassed his desire to achieve socialism. As he stated in an interview in 1998 not long before he died:

> I have always said that I was African first and socialist second. I would rather see a free and united Africa before a fragmented socialist Africa. – (Julius K. Nyerere, in an interview with Ikaweba Bunting, *New Internationalist*, Oxford, UK, December 1998).

And he stated in his speech in Accra on 6 March 1997 on Ghana's 40th independence anniversary:

> Without unity, there is no future for Africa.

It is also true that Nyerere wanted Africa to be ruled by Africans – just as Europe is ruled by Europeans, America by Americans and so on – and wanted Africans to maintain their identity as Africans. As he stated when spoke about the Portuguese colonies in Africa and their policy of assimilation which was actually never implemented as they claimed it was on the basis of racial equality:

> Portugal pretends that her colonies are really part of Europe, and that she abjures racial discrimination. She claims instead to be in the process of making European Gentlemen out of the African inhabitants of those areas, and talks proudly of the policy of equality for the 'assimilado.' But Africans are not European, could not become European, and do not want to become European. They demand instead the right to be Africans in Africa, and to determine their own cultural, economic, and political future. This right is what Portugal denies. The inhabitants of her colonies can certainly be 'African'; but if they are, then they are subjected to special laws, and special taxation and labour levies; their participation in the functions of their own government is ruled out.
> In South Africa there is no longer even the pretence that citizens of different races are equal before the law, or in social and economic

rights and duties. – (Julius K. Nyerere, "The Honour of Africa," an address to the National Assembly, 14 December 1965, before Tanzania broke off diplomatic relations with Britain the following day, the first country to do so – followed by Ghana under Nkrumah and Egypt under Nasser the day after – because of Britain's refusal and unwillingness to use force to remove the white minority government from power in Rhodesia after it unilaterally declared independence on11 November 1965; in Julius K. Nyerere, *Freedom and Socialism/Uhuru na Ujamaa: A Selection from Writings and Speeches 1965 - 1967*, Dar es Salaam, Tanzania: Oxford University Press, 1968, pp. 123 –124).

Because of the prominent role he played on the political scene in southern Africa, President Nyerere was also invited to Washington by President Jimmy Carter in August 1977 in an attempt to find solutions to the conflicts in the region. He was the first black African leader to be invited by Carter for a state visit.

High on Carter's agenda was Rhodesia, Namibia and the war in Angola and the involvement of Cuban troops in the conflict supporting the MPLA government against South African-backed UNITA forces. As the American ambassador to Tanzania during that time, James Spain, stated in an interview years later:

> Nyerere was the first African chief of state that Carter invited back. I accompanied him. Only twice in my life have I been in substantive sessions in the White House.
> I was with Carter and Nyerere, Vance, Moose and Brzezinski for something like five hours. Then too, five or six days are allotted for the distinguished visitor to see the US. We took our own plane out to Chicago, San Francisco and Los Angeles, and the rural Midwest and South. Nyerere didn't play bridge but his foreign minister (Benjamin Mkapa who later became president of Tanzania and was Nyerere's student at St. Francis College, Pugu, on the outskirts of Dar es Salaam) did....
> Rhodesia and Namibia were high priority issues at the time. Kissinger had devoted three or four days to them in 1976....David Owen, the British Foreign Secretary, joined him for a couple of his meetings with Nyerere....
> Nyerere made no bones that he would give all the support he

could, including arms, to the Namibian and Rhodesian rebels. That was to end 'colonialism.' But he saw the situation within South Africa differently. That was a fight between African and Africans. The Boers, as he always called the Afrikaners, were Africans too, bad Africans, but Africans. As he told an American visitor, 'Unlike the British in Rhodesia, they have no place to go home to'....

We were in the middle of the negotiations for an independent Rhodesia.

The personal chemistry between Carter and Nyerere was great. Toward the end of the discussions Carter shuffled his papers and said, 'Well, I think that is all Mr. President. It has been very useful.'

His National Security Adviser who had been sitting down the table and hadn't said a word coughed pointedly.

'Oh, yes,' said Carter. 'There is the matter of the Cubans in Angola.'

'Yes, indeed Mr. President,' Nyerere responded. 'I thought we were going to agree on everything, but that is something that we can disagree on. Let's talk about it.'

Carter didn't seem very eager. He said, 'We feel that's bad.'

Nyerere gave his standard reply: as soon as the South Africans get out of Angola the Cubans will get out.

'How can you guarantee that?'

'Because the president of Angola has promised me and I will see to it that he lives up to his promise.'

There isn't.

Brzezinski broke in. 'Mr. President, are you aware that the number of Cubans in Angola compared to the total population of Angola is larger than the number of Americans who were in Vietnam at the height of our involvement?'

'Oh, really, how interesting,' replied Nyerere.

Carter started folding up his papers.

'And, Mr. President,' asks Brzezinski, 'Are you aware that the number of Cubans in Angola compared to the total population of Cuba is very much larger than the number of Americans in Vietnam at the height of our involvement compared to the total population of the United States?'

This time Nyerere didn't say a word. He waved his hand with a condescending smile.

Carter grabbed his papers, stood up, and announced 'Well, it looks like we are really finished!' – (James W. Spain, interviewed by Charles Stuart Kennedy, 31 October 1995, *The Association for Diplomatic Studies and Training (ADST), Foreign Affairs Oral History Project*, copyright 1998, p. 41).

On the Rhodesian question, there was hope that the conflict could be resolved diplomatically. But the intransigence of the white minority regime left little room, if any, for a diplomatic solution. As the leader of the white minorities in Rhodesia, Prime Minister Ian Smith, said, there would be no black majority rule in his life time, not even in a thousand years. Africans insisted, there would be, in his lifetime. As he put it:

'No African rule in my lifetime. The white man is master of Rhodesia. He has built it, and he intends to keep it.' – (Ian Smith, in Alan Cowell, "Ian Smith, Defiant Symbol of White Rule in Africa, Is Dead at 88," *The New York Times*, 21 November 2007).

His defiance was even more pronounced in the same year Kissinger went to Africa in his abortive attempt to find a diplomatic solution to the conflict. As the Rhodesian leader bluntly stated in 1976:

'I don't believe in black majority rule ever in Rhodesia – not in a thousand years.'

War seemed to be the only solution. As *The New York Times* stated in its report when President Nyerere visited the United States at the invitation of President Carter:

Other Americans who spoke with Nyerere today (5 August 1977) said that he feared it was too late for a projected new British-American peacekeeping effort in Rhodesia and that the issue between the white minority Government and black nationalist forces would have to be decided by war....
Mr. Nyerere is chairman of a committee of presidents of the so-called 'front-line countries' that lie on or near Rhodesia's borders. The Administration believes he could be the single most influential African leader in getting a fair hearing for the British-American proposals both from the other 'front-line' presidents and from the Patriotic Front, which is waging guerrilla war against Rhodesia's white minority government.
Joshua Nkomo and Robert Mugabe, the leaders of the Patriotic Front coalition, have publicly rejected any further efforts to negotiate

a settlement in Rhodesia, a country of 270,000 whites and more than six million blacks, and have said the issue must be resolved by war. – (Graham Hovey, "Nyerere Is Called Hopeful on Rhodesia," *The New York Times*, 5 August 1977).

Without Nyerere's direct involvement, there was little hope a solution to the conflict could found. President Carter knew that. According to *The Washington Post*:

> Tanzania's President Julius Nyerere, probably black Africa's most widely respected figure, arrives in Washington today (4 August 1977) on his first official trip to the United States since he was President Kennedy's guest 14 years ago. He is the first black African leader invited by President Carter to visit him at the White House.
> Since the Vietnam war, the United States and Tanzania have been on opposite sides of almost every major world issue and Tanzania's U.N. ambassador, Salim Salim, has stood out as one of the Third World's most distinguished critics of American policies. Relations between the two countries first soured in 1964 when Tanzania accused the United States of plotting to overthrow the government and they have never been warm since.
> Improving bilateral relations is unlikely to be the substance of Nyerere's talks with Carter, however.
> Nyerere is chairman of the presidents of the so-called frontline states – Angola, Botswana, Mozambique, Zambia and Tanzania – the independent African countries most directly involved in the southern African drama. This makes him the continent's most influential spokesman on strategies for achieving majority rule in Rhodesia, granting legitimate independence to Namibia (Southwest Africa) and ending apartheid in South Africa.
> Nyerere is personally considered to be above reproach. A wealthy Nairobi-based Greek businesswoman, whose family has been involved in Tanzania for two generations, says, 'Nyerere is the only man in East Africa who cannot be bought.' A practicing Roman Catholic of simple tastes, the 55-year old philosopher-president is said to be the lowest paid head of state in Africa.
> To much of the continent, the United States...is still regarded as one of the leading collaborators in maintaining white supremacy and black exploitation in southern Africa....
> Part of Carter's success in convincing Africans that he is sincere about changing American policy something former Secretary of State Henry Kissinger tried and failed to do, stems from U.N. Ambassador Andrew Young's open identification with the African cause....

Ten months before his 1969 trip to Canada, Nyerere let it be known that he would also like to visit Washington to help improve relations with the United States, but he was told that President Nixon would be too busy.

The following year, when Nyerere came to New York to address the U.N. General Assembly on southern Africa - with a speech that had such an impact on African and black American students that mimeographed copies were passed hand-to-hand throughout American campus communities - no effort was made to see President Nixon.

In 1975, however, Nyerere was invited to deliver the commencement address at Boston University and he asked for a brief meeting with President Ford. He was rebuffed yet by another American President and later declined the Boston invitation. – (Roger Mann, "Nyerere Visit Seen as Symbol of Shift in U.S. Policy on Africa," *The Washington Post*, 4 August 1977).

This deliberate snub of a prominent and highly respected African leader by presidents Nixon and Ford reflected their attitude towards Africa in general as a continent which they saw as a peripheral actor on the global stage and one that could simply be ignored by the United States at will. It is an attitude that was shared by Henry Kissinger who served under both presidents as national security advisor and secretary of state.

It is also a sentiment that was echoed by President Donald Trump decades later when, on 11 January 2018, he described African countries as "shithole countries." As James K. Bishop, a veteran foreign service officer since the Kennedy Administration who also served as deputy director for West Africa at the State Department and as United States ambassador to Nigeria, Liberia and Somalia among other posts, stated about Nixon and Kissinger:

For countries I covered, we had a pretty broad spectrum of US interests at a time when the US administration was not particularly concerned about Africa. In addition to other issues that Nixon and Kissinger had to face – Vietnam, China, the Soviet Union, disarmament – they both had also had very disparaging views of Africa.

Nixon told one of our ambassadors – with whom I was working

when he made his farewell call on the President at the White House – that Africans were a bunch of children and should be treated as such. Those were the ambassador's marching orders.

Kissinger went to Africa once during my period in Washington when I was the Deputy Office Director for West Africa. Bill Schaufele was the Assistant Secretary at the time; he looked over the manifest for Kissinger's plane and realized that he was the only African expert aboard. He asked whether he could bring an assistant along to help him. I was marched up to Kissinger's office and inspected - as a slave might have been inspected 200 years earlier on a block in Annapolis. He looked at me as if I were a piece of rancid meat.

During the inspection, Kissinger went out of the room to take a telephone call from the President. Winston Lord, who remained with Schaufele and I, was kind enough to tell me not to be offended because Kissinger treated all of his staff the same way.

The bottom line was that I didn't go on the plane; Schaufele went by himself. – (James K. Bishop, Jr., interviewed by Charles S. Kennedy, *The Association for Diplomatic Studies and Training (ADST), Foreign Affairs Oral History Project*, 15 November 1995, p. 30).

Kissinger had a bad reputation as a very arrogant person since his student days at Harvard University and probably even before then.

One of his professors at Harvard, William Yandell Elliott who was his supervisor when he was a doctoral candidate, and who later served in both Democratic and Republican administrations as presidential advisor, told him years later:

Henry, you're brilliant. But you're arrogant. In fact you're the most arrogant man I've ever met. Mark my words, your arrogance is going to get you in real trouble one day. – (William Yandell Elliott, in Greg Grandin, *Kissinger's Shadow: The Long Reach of America's Most Controversial Statesman*, New York: Metropolitan Books, p. 39, 2015).

It was when he served as secretary of state under President Gerald Ford that he had to go to a continent he despised so much and whose leaders he equally despised. The presidents he worked for had no more respect for

Africans than he did.

Nixon believed in scientific racism, legitimised by pseudoscience, and expressed extremely racist views. According to *Newsweek*, he described black people in recorded conversations as "Negro bastards" who "live like a bunch of dogs"; "they are not going to make it for 500 years." His predecessor, Lyndon Johnson, routinely called blacks "niggers," civil rights bills "nigger bills."

Blacks were also intellectually "inferior" to whites and members of other races, a belief common among racists.

But when Kissinger went to Tanzania and met with President Nyerere, he met his intellectual equal who was not intimidated by him. And he knew that, despite his arrogance.

It is only when American interests – and the interests of American allies – are at stake that American leaders start to pay attention to African leaders. That was the case with the countries of southern Africa where the white minority rulers, who were allies of the United States, came under increasing pressure from Africans to relinquish power to the indigenous people.

With the war intensifying in Rhodesia, waged by the freedom fighters to end white minority rule in that country, it was clear that Nyerere could no longer be ignored by the United States as a major player on the political scene in southern Africa. It was President Ford who sent Kissinger to Africa to seek a diplomatic solution to the conflict. But Kissinger failed to achieve his goal when he met with Nyerere.

When Carter became president, the new American leader went a step further not only by inviting Nyerere to the White House but by seeking his guidance and support in the quest for an amicable solution to the conflict in Rhodesia and in trying to get Cuban troops out of Angola. He made some progress with Nyerere on the question of Rhodesia but not on the withdrawal of Cuban troops from Angola.

Nyerere's disagreement with the United States on the presence of Cuban troops in Angola sent a clear signal to the Carter administration that Cuban troops were not going to leave Angola, and he would not ask Castro to withdraw his troops, unless South African troops were out of Angola.

President Carter acknowledged Nyerere's role as a major political force in southern Africa and did not want to alienate him by seeking concessions he knew Nyerere would not make. As *The Washington Post* stated about Nyerere's prominence as a leader and as a prime factor and determinant in the calculus of the political events unfolding in southern Africa:

>President Carter asked visiting Tanzanian President Julius K. Nyerere yesterday (4 August 1977) for his crucial support of a new diplomatic attempt to resolve the conflict over majority rule in white-dominated Rhodesia.
>
>The two leaders were said to have agreed there is still 'a possibility' of heading off 'massive bloodshed and civil war' throughout Rhodesia, where black guerrilla spokesmen say the time for diplomacy is gone.
>
>However, 'It cannot be overemphasized,' White House press secretary Jody Powell told reporters after the first Carter-Nyerere meeting, 'that hope for a realization of that [diplomatic] possibility involves an extremely difficult and complex process.'
>
>Nyerere...is a pivotal figure in the Carter administration's African diplomacy in Rhodesia and in South African-ruled Namibia (Southwest Africa).
>
>The United States and Britain are now drafting proposals to try to produce a peaceful transition to majority rule in Rhodesia, where 270,000 whites rule 6 million blacks....
>
>Nyerere...was publicly asked by Carter yesterday for his advice and his counsel and his friendship and his guidance for achieving 'peace with justice' in Africa.
>
>Welcoming Nyerere on the South Lawn of the White House with full military honors, Carter reached back to the memories of the Kennedy administration, when Nyerere last visited the White House, to re-kindle and strengthen the U.S. link with Tanzania.
>
>During the Nixon-Ford years, the relationship was frigid, until 1976 when Secretary of State Henry A. Kissinger suddenly reversed

U.S. policy toward black African nationalism, and launched an aborted attempt at a Rhodesian settlement and 'majority rule' in all Africa.

Carter lauded Nyerere yesterday as 'a senior statesman...a scholar, a philosopher, a great writer,' who 'has forgone material wealth and ease in a sacrificial way for his own people.'

The gray-haired Nyerere, whose mild humble appearance conceals the intellect and political skill to bargain shrewdly with the world's Communist and non-Communist leaders responded warmly to the welcome.

There was no allusion on either side yesterday to Nyerere's long-standing complaint about U.S. policy in Africa, that for years it looked at Africa 'through anti-Communist spectacles,' ignoring Africa's basic needs.

Nyerere...has maintained that Africa's nationalists must 'accept help from wherever they can get it' to achieve their own objectives. To achieve black majority rule in Rhodesia and Namibia and South Africa, the stronghold of white-minority rule, Nyerere has said the United States must join in efforts to assure that South Africa is 'isolated economically, politically and socially,' by the rest of the world.

Nyerere...added to his schedule a meeting with members of the Congressional Black Caucus. – (Murray Marder, "President Asks Nyerere for Support on Rhodesia," *The Washington Post*, 5 August 1977).

At the welcoming ceremony after his arrival in Washington, President Nyerere underscored the importance of the United States as a global power exercising economic and military might - including the enormous influence it had on the white minority regimes in southern Africa - when, responding to President Carter who had just welcomed him, he said in his speech:

We in Tanzania, Mr. President, and in Africa generally, follow American politics with close attention. There is the intrinsic interest of the affairs of the most powerful nation the world has ever known. But more to the point, your politics do affect us. Indeed, we in Tanzania sometimes think that the world should somehow join n the process of electing the American President--[laughter]--for though we realize that the American people do not elect an absolute monarch, the world power structure is such that other peoples in other nations have a vital interest in the person whom the American people choose as their executive head of state. – (The American Presidency Project, University of California, Santa Barbara: Jimmy Carter, XXXIX President of the United States: 1977 – 1981. Visit of President Julius K. Nyerere of Tanzania – Remarks of the President and President Nyerere at the Welcoming Ceremony, 4 August 1977).

After his meetings with President Nyerere, President Carter was asked at a press conference in Washington, D.C.:

Question: "What can you tell us, sir, about the outcome of the visit with President Nyerere?"

Carter: "Well, President Nyerere is a man who has the best insight into African problems of anyone I've ever met. I think he has the trust and confidence of almost all the other nations in Africa and obviously is a natural scholar, student, historian, and political leader.

He and I have reached, I think, almost complete agreement over the goals and purposes of diplomatic efforts relating to Rhodesia and Namibia. And we will try to carry out those purposes, working as closely as we can together, recognizing, of course, that many other nations and leaders will be involved.

But we have, I think, made a great deal of progress in our meetings these last 2 days, and I've developed an increasing respect for him." – (The American Presidency Project, University of California, Santa Barbara: Jimmy Carter, XXXIX President of the United States: 1977 – 1981. Visit of President Nyerere of Tanzania – Remarks to Reporters Following The President's Departure, 5 August 1977).

Pressure exerted on the Rhodesian white minority regime by the freedom fighters and their supporters, who continued to wage war, finally led to a peaceful resolution of the conflict. At a conference at Lancaster House in

London in 1979, an agreement was reached for a transition to majority rule through democratic elections. The elections were held in February 1980. Robert Mugabe won. He became prime minister in April. White minority rule had finally ended in Rhodesia which was later renamed Zimbabwe.

Decades later, President Robert Mugabe launched a book, *Julius Nyerere: Asante Sana, Thank You Mwalimu*, a tribute to Nyerere for the major role played in the liberation of the countries of southern Africa. As he stated, the liberation of all the countries in southern Africa was planned in Dar es Salaam under the leadership of Nyerere. He went on to say:

> When we gained our independence in Mozambique and Angola in 1975, in Zimbabwe in 1980, Namibia in 1990, and a new democratic dispensation, in South Africa in 1994, we said – Asante sana, Thank you, Mwalimu....
>
> Mwalimu Nyerere was honoured this year (2015) by the African Union with the naming of the AU Peace and Security headquarters after him....
>
> The time is now to recognise the role played by Julius Nyerere in the political liberation of Africa, and to enshrine his legacy to reside with the present and future generation of Africans. – (Robert Gabriel Mugabe, foreword to *Julius Nyerere: Asante sana, Thank You, Mwalimu*, Harare, Zimbabwe, 2015).

Remembering those days, Philip Ochieng, who worked at the *Daily News* in Dar es Salaam during that period, stated the following:

> Under Julius Kambarage Nyerere, Dar es Salaam served as the external headquarters of practically every one of the nationalist movements fighting to bring down Europe's racially conceited tyrannies all over our continent - all the way from the borders of Egypt in the north to the Cape of Good Hope in the south, including Kenya (Ochieng's home country).
>
> That was how I first met Robert (Bob) Mugabe, a great nationalist, at that time considered as the most redoubtable of all of Southern Africa's campaigners for indigenous self-rule.

For, in the Tanzanian capital, Robert Mugabe was seen then as the topmost and most cherished among Africa's nationalist leaders fighting to bring down European tyranny all over our vast continent, especially in that Southern African colony, and throughout the world.

Power corrupts

Southern Rhodesia, as Ian Smith and other white supremacists conceitedly insisted on calling it, was what Robert Mugabe would soon lead into independence as Zimbabwe – in triumph and to the accompaniment of *vigelegele* all over the continent and the world, especially in Kambarage's Tanzania, where, in Dar es Salaam, I was then working as a weekend newspaper editor and weekly columnist.

Unfortunately, however – as one of Britain's own top political historians had already noticed – power corrupts and absolute power corrupts absolutely.

If anybody doubted it, the Third World's own history since independence, especially Africa's, has powerfully proved the correctness of that dictum by a noted observer of human behaviour.

Corruption is the name of it in all capitals of Africa and the Third World - including ours - and death is frequently the result of all reactions to anybody intrepid enough to criticise and attempt to put paid to it.

In our own country, a number of true fighters for freedom have paid for it with their own personal lives.

However, although Robert Mugabe was initially adored at home and profoundly respected throughout the continent and, indeed, throughout the world, his regime began to be increasingly personified by economic grabbing, political heavy-handedness, social decay and personal arrogance by every one of that country's top leaders.

Independence

Power drunkenness has been the most spectacular characteristic of all leaders in all the countries the world over in which - encouraged by Europe's own economically dominant classes pursuing their own gluttonous self-interests all over the world – 'independence' was granted precisely under that kind of leadership throughout what Europe now contemptuously calls the Third World.

Quiet evidently, nevertheless, times do change. Of all the nationalists fighting to bring down Britain's colonial high-handedness and arrogance, Robert Mugabe was at one time one of Africa's most cherished darlings.

When I worked in Dar es Salaam, I often met and deeply admired the person whom fellow nationalists in exile called 'Dear Bob.'

Time was indeed when I wholeheartedly recommended 'Bob' as the chief spokesman for our continent and for humanity's downtrodden classes all over the world, including even in that same Western Europe which had, for the nonce, assumed the role of model of what was alleged to be 'democracy.'

Specifically, I would wholeheartedly have recommended Robert Mugabe as the future leader of my Zimbabwean cousins.

When I first met face to face and interviewed what was then our 'dear Bob' in an hotel room in Dar es Salaam at some point in the early 1970s, he proved overwhelmingly charming, courteous, captivating in manner, overpowering in intellect and overwhelmingly knowledgeable of history and the modern human world.

Of all the nationalists seeking to defeat Caucasian racist tyranny and conceit in Africa, especially in Namibia and Southern Rhodesia, Robert Mugabe remained what William Shakespeare - the great bard of England's own intellectual and cultural celebration - would have embraced in poetry and drama as 'the nonpareil.'

Quite evidently, it would have been a terrible and embarrassing mistake. – (Philip Ochieng, "The Mugabe We All Adored in Dar Turned Out an Embarrassment," *Daily Nation*, Nairobi, Kenya, 25 November 2017).

Mugabe looked up to Nyerere when he was in prison in Rhodesia for about 11 years for opposing white minority rule and remained close to him from the time he set foot in Dar es Salaam after he was released from confinement.

When Mugabe assumed power in April 1980, Nyerere told him, "You have inherited the jewel of Africa" and advised him to keep it that way. He did for some time and then something went wrong.

Nyerere's influence could not be underestimated. He was an inspiration to freedom fighters throughout the continent as much as Nkrumah was. As Professor Ali Mazrui stated in his lecture at the University of Ghana in 2002:

The torch of African radicalism, after the coup which overthrew

Nkrumah in 1966, was in fact passed to Nyerere. The great voice of African self-reliance, and the most active African head of government in relation to liberation in Southern Africa from 1967 until the 1980s was in fact Julius Nyerere....

On the question of Nyerere's commitment to liberation...Nyerere was second to none in that commitment. – (Ali A. Mazrui in his lecture, "Nkrumahism and The Triple Heritage: Out of the Shadows," University of Ghana-Legon, 2002).

It is an observation shared by others. As Trevor Grundy stated:

He did so much to help liberate different parts of Africa from European rule while bankrupting Tanzania in the process.

At a meeting of the leaders of the member states of the Southern African Development Community (SADC) in Harare, Zimbabwe, in April 2015 chaired by Robert Mugabe and whose participants included Tanzanian President Jakaya Kikwete, the Zimbabwean leader lamented that Nyerere had not been accorded the respect, recognition and gratitude he deserved for the major and decisive role he played in the liberation of the countries of southern Africa and others elsewhere on the continent. As he stated, among other things:

The reckonings, the consciousness, of our forefathers, those who formed the Frontline States, we don't have them all now. Only one of them still remains alive, KK.

Mwalimu is gone. Neto of Angola is gone. Machel of Mozambique is gone. Sir Seretse Khama of Botswana is gone. They are the ones who formed the Frontline States which grew and transformed into SADCC, with two Cs, which was a coordinating body at that time; and the coordinating body, on the strength of whose reckonings, much more happened.

Greater freedom came. A new political dispensation later came for South Africa. We got our independence. Namibia got its independence. But must not also be forgotten that it was the - because of the earlier stand of these founding fathers of our region that the OAU decided that the liberation of the whole of Africa would be done now through a body called the Liberation Committee to be hosted in Tanzania, Mwalimu's country. And all the freedom movements were harboured there; some of them divided, ZANU, ZAPU, we were two. ANC, PAC. SWAPO, SWANU. We were all there.

And the results, of course, were resounding. Africa became free.

So the arm of southern Africa freed, played a great part in freeing the whole of Africa and rendering each independent.

We have not done done much by way of paying tribute to our forefathers. Yes, something has been done to Kwame Nkrumah at the AU, and recently the hall was named after Mandela.

But we forgot, perhaps because we are a new generation, a new generation of leaders, that the greatest burden of freeing Africa was borne by the one country Tanzania, and that one - I am saying the greatest, not that he was alone, Nyerere, Mwalimu.

No mention has been made, no symbol, to remember his part. And I say, no, we must do something, we will do something. Even if Zimbabwe was - we can't be that ungrateful. No. So I would want to say, help us, help me, my thought that we respect Mwalimu at the AU, somehow. N – ("President Robert Mugabe Pays Tribute to Mwalimu," Harare, Zimbabwe, April 2015).

Kwame Nkrumah's eldest son, Gamal Nkrumah, a journalist with a leading Egyptian newspaper *Al Ahram*, who said Nyerere became a father to him after his own father died, also paid tribute to Nyerere when the Tanzanian leader died in October 1999. Coincidentally, both leaders, Nkrumah and Nyerere, died of cancer. Also, both died at hospitals in Europe; Nkrumah in Romania, Nyerere in Britain. As Gamal stated in his tribute to Nyerere, "The Legacy of a Great African":

Former Tanzanian President Julius Kambarage Nyerere had the gift of incandescence. Undaunted by the multiplicity and complexity of the development problems his people faced, Nyerere's presence at political rallies, remote poverty-stricken villages, academic conferences and international forums where he pleaded the case of the South always lit up the occasion.

He had a way with words, especially in his native Kiswahili. He was the philosopher-king, intellectual, enlightened, the polar opposite of the despotic ruler so common in the Africa of his day. But he was also a man of the people....

Two years ago, at celebrations marking the 40th anniversary of Ghana's independence, I met and spoke to Nyerere for the last time. I would never have guessed that he was ill. As always, he spoke so eloquently and with such intellectual vigour....

He was not only a man of great integrity, but he also had the courage and modesty to admit to past mistakes. I have heard him speak in London, at the Commonwealth Institute, in several forums in the United States and at the United Nations, as well as in many an African setting. To me personally, Nyerere was always the attentive father figure, never missing an opportunity to remind me that my own father's vision for a united Africa was the only way forward.

With his wit, humour, sharp intellect and disarming sincerity, Nyerere was always a winning personality....

He...continued to champion the liberation movements of southern Africa and provide training camps for their freedom fighters on Tanzanian soil....

However we judge him on particular issues, there is no denying Nyerere's enormous contribution to the post-independence African political scene. His greatest achievement is undoubtedly the successful unification of mainland Tanganyika with the Indian Ocean island of Zanzibar....It was to Nyerere's credit that he managed to unite this most ethnically, linguistically and religiously diverse of nation-states and make it one of Africa's most politically stable countries....

Until his death, Nyerere continued to serve as the Leader and chief spokesman of the Geneva-based South Commission. He also remained actively involved in scores of developmental and peacekeeping missions both in Africa and throughout the developing world....

Nyerere bequeathed his country and Africa a great legacy, that of unity, solidarity with the poor and down-trodden worldwide and political secularism, together with a real pride in the continent's languages and cultural heritage.

He could have chosen an academic career in the West, after graduating from Kampala's celebrated Makerere University, then one of Africa's finest institutions of higher learning, and then again when he left Africa to do post-graduate work at Edinburgh in 1949. He translated two of William Shakespeare's plays into Kiswahili, his namesake *Julius Caesar* and *The Merchant of Venice*. But instead, he wisely chose to return to Africa and lead the anti-colonial struggle. In 1960, he even offered to delay Tanganyika's independence plans if the move would facilitate the creation of an East African Federation of Tanganyika, Kenya and Uganda.

That dream failed, and Nyerere officiated instead over the union of Tanganyika and Zanzibar. It is a union that has lasted long, and there are no signs of cracks in it to this day. That this is so is thanks in large measure to Nyerere's own force of character and vision. – (Gamal Nkrumah, "The Legacy of a Great African," *Al Ahram*, Cairo, Egypt, 21 – 27 October 1999).

Not long before he died, Nyerere had also started translating Plato's work, *The Republic*, into Kiswahili.

Probably Nyerere's most enduring legacy in a Pan-African context – besides his success in uniting two countries, Tanganyika and Zanzibar, to form Tanzania, the only union of independent states ever formed on the continent and that still exists to day – is the prominent role he played in helping liberate the countries of southern Africa which were still under white minority rule.

He will always be remembered for that as much as Nktumah will always be remembered for his quest for immediate continental unification and his support of liberation movements in Africa.

Nyerere also will be remembered for his approach to continental unity, formation of regional federations as a practical step towards uniting the continent under one government, after he failed to convince the leaders of Kenya and Uganda to form a federation with Tanganyika and achieve independence on the same day as one political entity.

Both leaders shared a vision for a united Africa under one government unlike most of their colleagues with a few exceptions such as Ahmed Sekou Toure of Guinea, Modibo Keita of Mali, Milton Obote of Uganda, Sorou-Migan Apithy of Dahomey, and Kenneth Kaunda of Zambia. As Nyerere stated in his speech in Accra, Ghana, in March 1997:

"Without unity, there is no future for Africa."

In Nkrumah's case, most African leaders ignored him when he exhorted them to unite their countries under one government, immediately, in Addis Ababa, Ethiopia, where they met in May 1963 and formed the Organisation of African Unity (OAU).

Nkrumah's quest for immediate continental unification was sharply contrasted with Nyerere's gradualist approach which was dictated by pragmatic considerations. As Nyerere stated in an interview with the *New Internationalist* in 1998 not long before he died the following year:

> Kwame Nkrumah and I were committed to the idea of unity. African leaders and heads of state did not take Kwame seriously. However, I did.
>
> I did not believe in these small little nations. Still today I do not believe in them. I tell our people to look at the European Union, at these people who ruled us who are now uniting.
>
> Kwame and I met in 1963 and discussed African unity. We differed on how to achieve a United States of Africa. But we both agreed on a United States of Africa as necessary. Kwame went to Lincoln University, a black college in the US. He perceived things from from the perspective of US history, where 13 colonies that revolted against the British formed a union. That is what he thought the OAU (Organisation of African Unity) should do.
>
> I tried to get East Africa to unite before independence. When we failed in this way, I was wary about Kwame's continental approach. We corresponded profusely on this. Kwame said my idea of 'regionalization' was only balkanization on a larger scale. Later, African historians will have to study our correspondence on this issue of uniting Africa.
>
> Africans who studied in the US like Nkrumah and Azikiwe were more aware of the Diaspora and the global African community than those of us who studied in Britain. They were therefore aware of a wider Pan-Africanism. Theirs was the aggressive Pan-Africanism of W.E.B. Du Bois and Marcus Garvey. The colonialists were against this and frightened of it. – (Julius Nyerere, in an interview with Ikaweba Bunting, "The Heart of Africa: Interview with Julius Nyerere on Anti-Colonialism," in the *New Internationalist*, Oxford, UK, January-February 1999).

He also explained in the same interview what happened when he and Ugandan leader Milton Obote went to see Jomo Kenyatta of Kenya in an attempt to form an East

African federation:

> I respected Jomo immensely. It has probably never happened in history. Two heads of state, Milton Obote and I, went to Jomo and said to him: 'Let's unite our countries and you be our head of state.' He said no. I think he said no because it would have put him out of his element as a Kikuyu Elder. – (Nyerere, *New Internationalist*, ibid.).

In an interview with *The New York Times* in his home village of Butiama near the shores of Lake Victoria in 1996, Nyerere said his biggest failure was that he failed to convince the other leaders in East Africa to form an East African federation; his biggest achievement, he said, was forming a united nation out of more than 120 different ethnic groups:

> I felt that these little countries in Africa were really too small, they would not be viable – the Tanganyikas, the Rwandas, the Burundis, the Kenyas. My ambition in East Africa was really never to build a Tanganyika. I wanted an East African federation.
>
> So what did I do in succeeding? My success is building a nation out of this collection of tribes. – (Julius Nyerere in an interview with James C. McKinley Jr., "Many Failures, and One Big Success," *The New York Times*, and in the *International Herald Tribune*, 2 September 1996, p. 2).

In another interview, Nyerere also explained the differences he had with Kwame Nkrumah in an attempt to unite African countries under one continental government:

> My differences with Kwame were that Kwame thought there was somehow a shortcut, and I was saying there was no shortcut. This is what we have inherited, and we'll have to proceed within the limitations that that inheritance has imposed on us.
>
> Kwame thought that somehow you could say, 'Let there be a United States of Africa' and it would happen. I kept saying, 'Kwame, it's a slow process.'
>
> He had tremendous contempt for a large number of leaders of Africa and I said, 'Fine, but they are there. What are you going to do with them? They don't believe as you do – as you and I do – in the need

for the unity of Africa. BUT WHAT DO YOU DO? THEY ARE THERE, AND WE HAVE TO PROCEED ALONG WITH EVERYBODY!'

And I said to him in so many words that we're not going to have an African Napoleon, who is going to conquer the continent and put it under one flag. It is not possible.

At the OAU conference in 1963, I was actually trying to defend Kwame. I was the last to speak and Kwame had said this charter has not gone far enough because he thought he would leave Addis with a United States of Africa.

I told him that this was absurd; that it can't happen. This is what we have been able to achieve. No builder, after putting down the foundation, complains that the building is not yet finished. You have to go on building and building until you finish; but he was impatient because he saw the stupidity of the others. – (Julius Nyerere, in an interview with Bill Sutherland in Bill Sutherland and Matt Mayer, eds., *Guns and Gandhi in Africa: Pan African Insight on Nonviolence, Armed Struggle, and Liberation in Africa*, Trenton, New Jersey, USA: Africa World Press, 2000; reproduced by Chambi Chachage, "Excerpt from Interview with Bill Sutherland," Centre for Consciencist Studies and Analyses (CENSCA), 5 September 2008. See also Bill Sutherland in William Minter, Gaily Hovey, and Charles Cobb Jr., eds., *No Easy Victories: African Liberation and American Activists over a Half Century, 1950 - 2000*, Trenton, New Jersey, USA: New Africa Press, 2007).

Prime Minister Abubakar Tafawa Balewa of Nigeria was resolutely opposed to a continental government and bluntly stated in his speech at the OAU summit in Accra, Ghana, in October 1965 that Nigeria would never surrender its sovereignty to a higher authority. As Professor Willard Scott Thompson stated in his book, *Ghana's Foreign Policy, 1957 - 1966: Diplomacy Ideology, and the new State*:

Sir Abubakar (Tafawa Balewa) let them go no further. An African government was a dream, he said, 'Or a nightmare.' Nigeria, for its part, would never surrender its sovereignty. 'This request, Mr. Chairman, is indirectly a vote of no confidence in the Oirganisation of African Unity. When we started this Organisation only a year ago, we were working, progressing and now we are trying to impose something.' Union government might come, so might world government, he said. – (Willard Scott Thompson, *Ghana's Foreign Policy, 1957 – 1966: Diplomacy Ideology, and the new State*, Princeton, New Jersey, USA: Princeton University Press,1969, p. 355).

And as Nyerere stated in his speech in Accra on Ghana's 40th independence anniversary where he was an official guest invited by President Jerry Rawlings:

> Prior to independence of Tanganyika, I had been advocating that East African countries should federate and then achieve independence as a single political unit. I had said publicly that I was willing to delay Tanganyika's independence in order to enable all three-mainland countries to achieve their independence together as a single federated state.
>
> I made the suggestion because of my fear, proved correct by later events, that it would be very difficult to unite our countries if we let them achieve independence separately.
>
> Once you multiply national anthems, national flags and passports, seats at the United Nations, and individuals entitled to 21-gun salute, not to speak of a host of ministers, prime ministers, and envoys, you will have a whole army of powerful people with vested interests in keeping Africa balkanised. That was what Nkrumah encountered in 1965.
>
> After the failure to establish the union government at the Accra (OAU) summit of 1965, I heard one head of state express with relief that he was happy to be returning home to his country still head of state. To this day I cannot tell whether he was serious or joking. But he may well have been serious, because Kwame Nkrumah was very serious and the fear of a number of us to lose our precious status was quite palpable.
>
> But I never believed that the 1965 Accra summit would have established a union government for Africa. When I say that we failed, that is not what I, for that clearly was an unrealistic objective for a single summit. What I mean is that we did not even discuss a mechanism for pursuing the objective of a politically united Africa. We had a Liberation Committee already (based in Dar es Salaam, Tanzania). We should have at least had a Unity Committee or undertaken to establish one. We did not. And after Kwame Nkrumah was removed from the African political scene nobody took up the challenge again. – (Julius K. Nyerere, speech on Ghana's 40th independence anniversary, Accra, March 1997).

The coup against Nkrumah was engineered by the CIA and masterminded by the CIA station chief in Accra, Howard T. Bane. After he returned to the United States from Ghana, he was quickly promoted and given a senior position at the CIA and the Distinguished Intelligence Medal, the agency's highest award, for his role in overthrowing Nkrumah.

It was an achievement that was well-received by American officials, President Lyndon B. Johnson among them, and was even celebrated in some quarters including the CIA and the State Department. As Robert P. Smith, who once served as United States ambassador to Ghana and was working at the State Department when Nkrumah was overthrown, stated when he explained how Secretary of State Dean Rusk reacted to the news about Nkrumah's downfall:

> I also remember, the morning of the coup, I got the call about 2 a.m. here at the house and went into the Department and immediately set up a little task force in the Operations Center. Later in the same morning, about 8 or 8.30, Secretary Rusk wandered down the hall and came in and said, 'I've seen the early reports, but I just want to hear it firsthand. What's going on in Ghana?' When I related how Nkrumah had landed in Peking and had been informed by his Chinese hosts of what had happened in Ghana, Dean Rusk broke into an ear-splitting grin. I've never seen him look so happy. – (Robert P. Smith, interviewed by Charles Stuart Kennedy, *The Association for Diplomatic Studies and Training (ADST), Foreign Affairs Oral Project,* 28 February 1989, p. 14).

It was also when Dean Rusk was secretary of state that the State Department recommended arming some groups in Tanzania to destabilise the government in an attempt to overthrow President Nyerere. As John Prados states in his book, *Safe for Democracy: The Secret Wars of the CIA:*

> The Special Group (at the CIA) reportedly considered a State Department proposal to supply arms to certain groups in Tanzania,

where secret-war wizards saw President Julius Nyerere as a problem, in the summer of 1964....Like Nyerere, Washington viewed Ghana's leader Kwame Nkrumah as a troublemaker. – (John Prados, Safe for Democracy: The Secret Wars of the CIA, Chicago, Illinois, USA: Ivan R. Dee, Publisher, 2006, p. 328).

Yet the CIA was wary of supporting covert operations against Nyerere to undermine his government in order to overthrow him because he was not corrupt, did not use his position to enrich himself and his family members, and was extremely popular. His commitment to the well-being of the masses and everybody else was beyond question. The CIA knew a coup against him would not have the support of the people, especially the masses who constituted the vast majority of the population and who sincerely believed he cared about them and was doing his best to improve their lives.

Even his opponents who wanted to overthrow him would not have been able to justify his ouster and convince the people that he did not care about them. They included former foreign affairs minister Oscar Kambona who was the mastermind of the 1969 coup attempt.

The coup was exposed by the Tanzanian intelligence service with the assistance of the South African freedom fighters of the Pan-Africanist Congress (PAC) based in Dar es Salaam. The accused started in March 1968 working on plans to overthrow the government. They were arrested in October 1969, the same month they were going to launch the coup.

Kambona sought the assistance of the guerrilla fighters who were being trained in Tanzania but the PAC leader, Potlako Leballo, notified the Tanzanian authorities about that. He continued to cooperate with the coup plotters while working with the Tanzanian intelligence service monitoring the conspirators. Kambona hoped that the guerrilla fighters would team up with some members of the Tanzanian army to overthrow Nyerere.

One colonel, one captain, and one lieutenant of the Tanzanian army were among the leading conspirators who were arrested, tried and convicted of treason. Others were a former cabinet member; the former secretary-general of the only opposition party in the country, the African National Congress (ANC) which died out in the mid-sixties after being overwhelmed at the polls by the ruling Tanganyika African National Union (TANU); a former editor of the ruling party's newspaper; and one woman who was the leader of the women's movement in the country and who played a major role campaigning for independence with Nyerere.

Two of them, the army captain and the former secretary-general of the opposition ANC, were brothers and cousins of Oscar Kambona.

Leballo's testimony proved critical to the outcome of the trial. He was deeply involved in the coup plot in order to provide evidence against the conspirators later during the trial in the high court of Tanzania. He also mentioned the South African minister of foreign affairs, Hilgard Muller, as one of the people Kambona approached to help overthrow Nyerere. According to Colin Legum in *Africa Contemporary Record, 1970 - 1971*:

> The central prosecution witness was Potlako K. Leballo, a founder of the Pan-African Congress (Pan-Africanist Congress) of South Africa (PAC), which had its exile headquarters in Dar es Salaam.
>
> The state maintained that seven defendants attempted to enlist Leballo in the plot but that he informed government officials and only appeared to go along with the plot in order to assist in capturing the conspirators.
>
> Leballo testified that he frequently met with Kambona in London and that Kambona had shown him a cache of $500,000 and told him that he could 'get more where that came from' by contacting a U.S. Information Service 'friend' in London (*The New York Times*, 19 July 1970, 12).
>
> Leballo further testified that Kambona had an agreement with the South African foreign minister, Hilgard Muller, that South Africa would support the coup. – (Colin Legum and John Drsydale, eds.,

Africa Contemporary Record: Annual Survey and Documents 1970 – 1971, London: Africa Rsearch Limited, 1971, pp. 170 – 71).

The coup attempt is covered extensively in Godfrey Mwakikagile's book, *Nyerere and Africa: End of an Era*, in which the author uses transcripts of the court proceedings during the treason trial to document his work. As he stated in his book:

> In spite of his immense popularity, President Nyerere was not immune from subversion. He became a target of a number of attempts, from within and without, to oust him from power. There were also many attempts to destabilize and weaken his government which his enemies and detractors hoped would eventually lead to his downfall.
>
> He was fiercely independent, a stance that rankled Western powers as he went on to forge links with Eastern-bloc countries including the People's Republic of China and the Soviet Union, but especially with China, while maintaining ties with the West in pursuit of his policy of non-alignment. And his strong support for the African liberation movements was not endorsed by Western powers which wanted to perpetuate white minority rule in Africa for hegemonic control of the continent by the West.
>
> So, Western powers wanted him out. Apartheid South Africa and other white minority regimes on the continent including Rhodesia and the Portuguese colonial governments - hence their mother country Portugal - also wanted him out. They did everything they could, including infiltrating and bombing Tanzania, to destabilize his government. One of the attempts to undermine his government involved the United States in the mid-sixties. As Nyerere himself stated in June 1966:
>
> 'We have twice quarrelled with the US Government, once when we believed it to be involved in a plot against us, and again when two of its officials misbehaved and were asked to leave Tanzania....The disagreements certainly induced an uncooperative coldness between us.'
>
> Dr. Kwame Nkrumah, in his book *Dark Days in Ghana*, also discusses attempts by the CIA and the American government to undermine and overthrow Nyerere. He himself was ousted from power in a coup engineered and masterminded by the CIA in February 1966.
>
> The most dramatic attempt to overthrow Nyerere came to public

attention in October 1969 when the accused conspirators were brought to court in Tanzania's most celebrated treason trial. There was another treason trial in 1983. But it was not as dramatic as the other one mainly because of the people involved, although the plot in 1982 to overthrow the government led to the arrest of 600 soldiers and about 1,000 civilians in January 1983 for their alleged involvement in and support of the coup attempt.

The 1969 treason case involved some of Tanzania's most prominent politicians, including luminaries in the independence movement and two former cabinet members. The leader of the treasonous coterie was Oscar Kambona, Tanzania's former minister of foreign affairs who earlier had also served as minister of home affairs and then as minister of defence. He was also one of the country's three most influential and powerful leaders, together with President Nyerere himself and Vice President Rashidi Kawawa, who spearheaded the independence movement in Tanganyika; Kawawa was vice president of Tanganyika until April 1964 when he became second vice president after Tanganyika united with Zanzibar, and the president of Zanzibar, Abeid Karume, became first vice president under the union constitution.

In July 1967, Kambona left Tanzania and went into self-imposed exile in London, Britain. He continued to exercise some influence on his supporters in Tanzania, disgruntled with Nyerere's socialist policies and one-party rule, but gradually faded into obscurity as a "potent" force on the nation's political scene. His opposition to Nyerere's leadership and socialist policies reached a dramatic point towards the end of January in Arusha just before the adoption of the famous Arusha Declaration which became Tanzania's economic blueprint and political manifesto, covering all aspects of national life across the spectrum including foreign affairs and the liberation of Africa from colonialism and imperialism. Nyerere wrote the Declaration which, even years later just before he died, he said he would not change except for a few words here and there in its Swahili version. As Arthur Wille, a Catholic priest who knew Nyerere well and was close to him since the 1940s, stated:

'When the TANU National Executive Committee met in Arusha January 26 - 29 it turned out to be a stormy session. At this meeting Nyerere proposed that *Ujamaa* become the official policy of the government. Oscar Kambona objected strongly to this policy. Twice during these sessions, the Executive Committee adjourned in order to allow their three leaders, Nyerere, Kambona and Kawawa to go into private session. Each time that they returned to the Executive Committee it was apparent that Kawawa had supported Nyerere to defeat Kambona. The result was that the Arusha Declaration was adopted.'

The Arusha Declaration was adopted on February 5, 1967. It was the most ethical economic and political document ever written by an African leader. As Andrew Nyerere, Mwalimu Julius Nyerere's eldest son with whom I was in regular contact when I worked on the second edition of this book, stated in his comments in August 2003 when he looked at my work in progress:

'The Arusha Declaration forbade leaders to have two salaries. And there is one African businessman who told me that when Nyerere did this, when he restrained his colleagues from becoming rich, that is how we came to prominence; by that, he meant a whole generation of noveau rich people. The man who told me this has since died. He was suffering from a terminal illness. He spoke to me a few months before he died.'

Kambona left Tanzania about five months after the Arusha Declaration was adopted and continued to criticize Nyerere from Britain. And following Tanzania's recognition of Biafra in April 1968, a move that infuriated the Nigerian federal government, Nigerian leaders invited Kambona to Nigeria to lecture. He took this opportunity to denounce Nyerere and pursue his political ambitions. The Nigerian government also immediately broke off diplomatic relations with Tanzania because of her recognition of Biafra as an independent state, the first country to recognize the secessionist region of Eastern Nigeria as a sovereign entity.

Kambona left Tanzania via Kenya where some of his supporters lived and used Kenya's capital Nairobi as one of their operational bases in their conspiracy to overthrow Nyerere. But even in Kenya itself, a neighbouring country whose policies were different from Tanzania's - Kenya was capitalist and pro-Western, Tanzania socialist and non-aligned - there were many people who saw Kambona as a spent force fading into oblivion, although he could not be entirely dismissed as a non-entity. As the *Kenya Weekly News* stated on July 26, 1968, almost exactly one year after Kambona went into voluntary exile in Britain:

'Every lost turning, every sign of human weakness and failing will be exploited by people like Mr. Kambona. While this might be legitimate political opposition at home, it smacks of straw-clutching and opportunism coming from abroad. This is Mr. Kambona's problem; but it is unlikely to dissuade him from seeking to exploit every twist and turn in Tanzania's politics. It is the only way he can remain in business.'

One year and three months later, Kambona was accused of treason. The charges against him and his alleged conspirators were brought before the High Court of Tanzania in Dar es Salaam presided by Chief Justice Philip Telford Georges from Trinidad, who later served in the same capacity in newly independent Zimbabwe under President Robert Mugabe, himself with strong ties to Tanzania before and after he became the leader of his country. The prosecution team was led by Attorney-General Mark Bomani, and later by Senior State Attorney Nathaniel King, also from Trinidad, who almost single-handedly handled the case for the government.

I was a student then, at Tambaza High School in Dar es Salaam, in Form VI, or standard 14, and attended the treason trial with some of my schoolmates; the high court was only within walking distance from our school. I had just reached the age of 20 in October, the same month the treason charges became known to the public in 1969, four months after I was first hired as a reporter by the *Standard*, the country's largest English newspaper, in the nation's capital. But the trial did not start until June 1970. I went to the high court, not as a reporter, but simply as a spectator following the proceedings of the most important case in the history of Tanzania since independence in 1961. It was also the country's first treason trial, but not the last.

Kambona sought help from the CIA to overthrow Nyerere, just as Simon Kapwepwe did in his attempt to oust Zambian President and his childhood friend Kenneth Kaunda. But neither got the help they needed, at least not enough of it to carry out a coup. The immense popularity of both leaders, their high international stature as highly respected statesmen, and their incorruptible nature, made it highly unlikely that their ouster would be accepted domestically or internationally; thus making it very difficult for their would-be successors to win support and recognition. As Andrew Nyerere stated in his written remarks to me on what I said about the CIA in this chapter when he read my manuscript:

'We were discussing it at Msasani (where President Nyerere and his family lived on the outskirts of Dar es Salaam) one day, the supposed CIA infiltration of our government. We were talking about it with my mother, and Mwalimu Nyerere was present. And my mother said, there was much confusion nowadays. Everyday one hears of more government leaders who are on the payroll of the CIA. And I said that surely there is a misunderstanding concerning this, because the CIA argue with those whom they consider to be the enemies of the

United States, and this had nothing to do with us. And I saw that this statement made my mother calm.'

Some observers have emphasized the integrity of the two leaders, as incorruptible individuals, as the prime factor in the refusal or unwillingness of the CIA to support coup attempts against them. As Ben Lawrence, a Nigerian, stated in his article, "Privatization: Nigeria's New Gold Rush":

'The survival of Kenneth Kaunda and Julius Nyerere for so long in power was because of their alliance with the masses. When Oscar Kambona of Tanzania and Kapwepwe of Zambia requested the Central Intelligence Agency's (CIA) help to overthrow their former friends, they were plainly told that those leaders were impregnable because they were incorruptible and had no loot stashed in foreign vaults.'

But none of this was enough to dissuade Kambona from pursuing his goal of trying to overthrow Nyerere. What I wrote about the CIA in this chapter inspired more remarks from Andrew Nyerere who said the following in his comments to me:

'One day Mwalimu Nyerere was speaking in praise of various US presidents, and then he lowered his voice and spoke in a very hushed tone referring to President Ronald Reagan, saying that, now they have elected this murderer, that is Ronald Reagan. Now that the American people have elected this murderer, there is much chaos in the world. But I do not think that Mwalimu Nyerere meant that he feared his life was in danger. I think he was just wondering how he was going to get aid from the United States now that there was a hostile government in power. Or maybe he was half-hoping that Jimmy Carter would be re-elected and that he would be able to make another visit to the White House. Because he had been very pleased with that visit he made to the White House, he put the picture on the wall at Msasani.'

In the treason trial which began in June 1970 before Chief Justice Philip Telford Georges, a Trinidadian, it was alleged that Kambona was the mastermind behind the coup attempt. The coup was to take place in October 1969. The conspirators wanted not only to overthrow the government but also to assassinate President Nyerere. I was in court and remember during the proceedings when Senior State Attorney Nathaniel King, also a Trinidadian, asked one of the accused, John Lifa Chipaka, what he meant when he said they wanted to 'eliminate' the president. Chipaka responded by saying that they wanted to 'eliminate him politically, not physically.' Nathaniel King looked at Chipaka and laughed when Chipaka said that. Chipaka's denial was not convincing and the evidence presented in court demonstrated otherwise. The plan to overthrow the government included a plot to assassinate the president.

The accused were Colonel William Makori Chacha, a senior army officer in the country's army, the Tanzania People's Defence Forces (TPDF), who, not long before the treason trial, was a military attache at the Tanzania embassy in Peking in the People's Republic of China; John Dustan Lifa Chipaka, 38, former secretary-general of the defunct African National Congress (ANC) led by Zuberi Mtemvu in the 1960s. In the 1990s, after he was released from prison, Chipaka was still active in politics and became one of the opposition leaders in Tanzania and once led a party founded by Oscar Kambona after Kambona returned to Tanzania from Britain where he had lived in self-imposed exile for 25 years.

Others who appeared before the court on treason charges were: Michael Kamaliza, 46, a polio victim and former secretary-general of the National Union of Tanganyika Workers (NUTA) who also once served as minister of labour; Bibi Titi Mohammed, 45, a fiery orator, once a junior minister of labour and community development in the sixties and Tanzania's most prominent female politician who was head of the ruling party's women's movement known in Kiswahili as Umoja wa Wanawake wa Tanzania (UWT), translated as Women's Union of Tanzania; Gray Likungu Mataka, 34, a journalist; Captain Elia Dustan Lifa Chipaka, 32, of the Tanzanian army, the Tanzania People's Defence Forces (TPDF), and younger brother of one of the accused, John Dustan Lifa Chipaka; and Lieutenant Alfred Philip Milinga, 27, also of the Tanzania People's Defence Forces, and the youngest among the accused. They all denied all the charges brought against them.

One of the most remarkable things about this trial was the fact that some of the people involved in the coup attempt were once, or were supposed to be, some of the most loyal to the president. Before his departure from Tanzania in 1967, especially before 1966, the minister for foreign affairs, Oscar Kambona, was one of Nyerere's closest colleagues who even helped quell the army mutiny in 1964 when he went directly to speak to the mutinous soldiers and negotiate with them on their salary demands and insistence that the British army officers should be immediately replaced by indigenous ones. Nyerere also attended Kambona's wedding to Flora Moriyo at St. Paul's Cathedral in London in on 19 November 1960 and gave away the bride. Kambona asked Nyerere to be his best man; they were also very close and worked together campaigning for independence.

Oscar Kambona and Flora Moriyo were the first black couple to be married at the cathedral.

Kambona was also one of the founders of TANU, together with Nyerere and others, a party which led Tanganyika to independence. Another veteran politician and founding member of TANU, Bibi Titi Mohammed, also was known to be a close friend and very loyal supporter of Nyerere; so was former labour minister Michael Kamaliza, even if only by virtue of his position as a cabinet member under Nyerere. Colonel Chacha was also said to be a loyal supporter of President Nyerere.

Yet, they turned out to be the most prominent conspirators against him and his government. Ironically, not long before the treason trial, Nyerere himself had publicly stated in 1966 what turned out to be one of the most "prophetic' statements he had ever made during his presidency, unequivocally saying:

'I've been one of the luckiest presidents in Africa. My colleagues are very loyal to me.'

They proved him wrong; not all, but many of them, including those who lied to him throughout his tenure to promote their own interests. And others, of course, plotted to get rid of him right away, as the treason trial tragically demonstrated.

The most ominous sign of things yet to come was the abrupt resignation of Oscar Kambona from his ministerial post and other positions in June 1967. This came only about four months after the adoption of the Arusha Declaration in February, the country's economic and political manifesto he strongly opposed. In July, he left the country. And within two years or so, he was accused of treason and of being the mastermind behind the coup attempt to overthrow and assassinate Nyerere, his erstwhile compatriot.

His attempts to undermine and oust Nyerere from power gained momentum soon after he settled in London where he launched a blistering attack on the president and his government in a concerted effort to win support and turn the people of Tanzania against him, but to avail. Nyerere's popularity was immense, even if his socialist policies and one-party rule weren't among a significant number of people; a disenchantment Kambona tried to capitalize on and use as a lightning rod to galvanize the opposition against Nyerere within the country.

However, there are different opinions on how much, if any, opposition to Nyerere's economic policies were generated or fuelled by the Arusha Declaration. As Andrew Nyerere stated in some of his comments to me on this second edition which he read when I was working on it:

'No one opposed the Arusha Declaration. There was only one problem in that the young students of primary school accepted it more readily than the older students of secondary school. The young were more idealistic.'

Safe in London, Kambona was not arrested for his involvement in the coup plot. But six of his fellow conspirators were arrested in October 1969. They were all arrested in Tanzania, with the exception of Gray Likungu Mataka who once served as news editor of the TANU ruling party's daily newspaper, *The Nationalist*, a fiercely nationalistic and uncompromising publication whose managing editor, Benjamin Mkapa, became president of Tanzania from 1995 - 2005. Mataka was arrested in Nairobi, Kenya, where he had been acting as a conduit between Kambona and the other conspirators in Tanzania. It was one of the ironies of this trial that Mataka was not only once editor of the ruling party's newspaper but of a paper that was fiercely loyal to the president.

I also remember when I was a news reporter of the *Standard* in Dar es Salaam that we had a sort of an adversarial relationship with *The Nationalist* whose reporters, and sometimes even editorials, now and then lambasted us for working for 'an imperialist newspaper.' The *Standard* was then owned by Lonrho, until it was nationalized in 1970 when it became a state-owned newspaper and rechristened *Daily News*. President Nyerere became editor-in-chief of the *Daily News* but only as a ceremonial head. It was the editor of the paper who exercised power over us. Coincidentally, the treason trial started in the same year in which the paper was nationalized.

And in spite of its reputation as an "imperialist" newspaper before it was nationalized, the *Standard* adhered to the highest journalistic standards in covering the treason trial; so did *The Nationalist,* without slanting facts in favour of the government, despite its strong nationalist bias and unswerving loyalty to President Nyerere.

The first accused was Oscar Kambona. There was speculation that the government would seek extradition of the former foreign affairs minister. But nothing was done, and he was tried in absentia. Andrew Nyerere remembers Oscar Kambona well, as much as he does the early days of independence when our country was still called Tanganyika, and had the following to say in his remarks to me when he read this chapter:

'I remember the day when we went to State House. Mr. Kambona took over the house that we were staying in, the one at Sea View, the residence of the Chief Minister. I gazed at him for a long time as the car sped away. He was taking charge of the house which was to be his new home. It is a pity that he turned out to be such a traitor. If Nyerere knew that he would turn out to be such a heinous traitor, he would not have given him all those responsible positions in government. But I went to his funeral. I felt that all these evils of the past should be forgotten.'

When I asked Andrew what he thought about Kambona since the early days of Tanganyika's independence in the sixties, in terms of what type of person he was, he responded by saying:

'He was a good man. But there was misunderstanding, and what happened, happened. For example, he strongly disagreed with Mwalimu Nyerere about Kassim Hanga, the Zanzibar (cabinet) minister who was sent back and killed. And Kambona was right about this. He did not want Hanga sent back to Zanzibar. And Mwalimu Nyerere said that, concerning Hanga, he sent him back, but he did not know that they were going to kill him.'

During the 1970 treason trial involving Kambona, it was alleged by the prosecution team that the conspirators intended to launch a military coup between October 10 and 15, 1969. During that time, President Nyerere and a large number of high ranking government officials including cabinet members, as well as the head of the Tanzania People's Defence Forces (TPDF), Major-General Mrisho Sarakikya, were out of the country. The plotters felt that this was the perfect time for a coup. Some people in Zanzibar were also implicated in the coup plot.

The director of the Criminal Investigation Department (CID), Geoffrey Sawaya, who was also an intelligence officer, told the high court that Oscar Kambona sent large sums of money to the people in Tanzania who were to take part in the coup; and that all the conspirators used aliases.

One key figure in uncovering the plot was a South African freedom fighter living in exile in Tanzania, Potlako Leballo, the leader of the Pan-Africanist Congress (PAC), a black nationalist group which was formed in 1959 by members who left the African National Congress (ANC) over policy differences. The first leader of the PAC was Robert Mangaliso Sobukwe, a professor at Witwatersrand University and compatriot of Nelson Mandela. Mandela remained in the African National Congress and later became president of the organization which spearheaded the struggle against apartheid.

Leballo became head of the PAC after Sobukwe was sent to prison by the apartheid regime. And his testimony in Tanzania's first treason trial proved to be critical.

The coup plotters approached Leballo and enlisted his help in carrying out the coup, possibly with the help of his guerrilla fighters based in Tanzania, and he went along with the plan to gather intelligence for the government. Leballo met with the conspirators on a number of occasions. He had already informed the government and the conspirators were now under surveillance, with all their meetings being monitored by Tanzania's intelligence officers. Leballo became the government's key witness who unlocked all the secrets of the coup plotters. He also testified in court that Kambona had been given a lot of money to finance the coup.

When Tanzania's Attorney-General Mark Bomani asked Tanzania's head of the Criminal Investigation Department (CID) how he knew for sure that Leballo met the conspirators, Sawaya said whenever he knew in advance that there would be a meeting, he would assign his intelligence officers to monitor the proceedings in a clandestine operation the coup plotters never knew about. He also testified before the court that Leballo told him, in advance, about a trip to Nairobi, Kenya, on March 25, 1969; and that Leballo did go on that trip and returned to Dar es Salaam on April 1st.

Leballo told the director of the Criminal Investigation Department the purpose of the trip was to meet with Gray Likungu Mataka, who then lived in Nairobi which was one of the operational bases for the coup plotters, to get confirmation of the coup plot as Mataka had explained to him earlier.

awaya went on to say that he already knew that Leballo and Colonel Chacha had a meeting and that Leballo had been introduced to Prisca (one of the code names used by one of the conspirators) and Bibi Titi Mohammed. Chacha and Leballo met at Twiga Hotel in Dar es Salaam. Leballo also met with Bibi Titi Mohammed at an Islamic Centre at Chang'ombe in Dar es Salaam and discussed how President Nyerere and other senior government officials including some cabinet members would be assassinated.

The director of the Criminal Investigation Department further testified that on March 24, 1969, Leballo went to him and told him about the meeting he (Leballo) had with Chacha at Twiga Hotel. When Attorney-General Mark Bomani asked him how he knew the meeting had taken place, Sawaya said he sent his intelligence officers to Twiga Hotel on a surveillance mission after he was told about the meeting in advance. And they observed the meeting taking place.

On the following day, March 25, Leballo left for Nairobi, the intelligence director said, and was 'escorted' by some intelligence officers who had been assigned by the director to accompany him.

Sawaya went on to tell the court that in April 1969, he went on a trip overseas. He said he met again with Leballo on May 2, 1969, and that Leballo told him that the plan for the coup as explained by Gray Mataka in Nairobi was very well received by Colonel Chacha, Michael Kamaliza and Bibi Titi Mohammed in a jovial mood. He also said Mataka had promised to ask for some money from Kambona to facilitate the operation. The intelligence chief further stated that Leballo produced a letter written to Prisca by Mataka, and that Mataka himself copied the letter in his own handwriting and gave the copy to Leballo:

'**Mark Bomani:** Can you recognize the copy of this letter if you see it?
CID director: Yes, I can.
Bomani: How can you recognise this letter?
CID director: I can recognise it by the name of Chaima.
Leballo: He (the CID director) told me that after I met with Mataka for the first time, the accused changed his name and gave himself the code name of Chaima.
Chief Justice: Was the letter translated?
CID director: Soon after the copy of the letter was made, it was translated so that I could understand what it said.
Bomani: Did you know the letter was delivered?
CID director: I was informed that it was being delivered.'

The CID director went on to say that according to the information he got from Leballo, Chipaka, Titi, Kamaliza, Leballo and Prisca were going to have a meeting to discuss what they would be doing when they were waiting for some money from Kambona.

At that meeting, Kamaliza asked Leballo to go to London and ask Kambona to send more money. Kamaliza also asked Chipaka to write Kambona a letter and send him a 10-shilling note for Kambona to sign it. With Kambona's signature on the 10-shilling note, Kamaliza said the note would be passed around to convince some cabinet members and members of parliament to support Kambona in overthrowing the government.

It was also expected that the note would be used to raise more funds for the coup and get support from TANU leaders and workers and from the leaders and members of the country's labour union, the National Union of Tanganyika Workers (NUTA), to oppose the government; thus encouraging others to overthrow it.

Kamaliza told Leballo there was no doubt that the workers of Tanzania would support the coup because the president had removed him (Kamaliza) from the leadership of NUTA against the wishes of the workers.

Geoffrey Sawaya, the CID director, went on to say that Leballo met Titi (Bibi Titi Mohammed) at her house on June 23, 1969. She told him that she had been to Nairobi where she stayed for four days and made a telephone call to Kambona asking him to send one million shillings for overthrowing the government within two weeks.

Titi gave Leballo 400 shillings and said she had received 2,000 shillings, $1,000 for Colonel Chacha, for incidental expenses. Titi told Leballo she would give him 600 shillings in a few days, and did so on June 26. The money was presented in court as evidence.

On June 28, Colonel Chacha made arrangements to meet with Leballo on June 30 in order to introduce him to Major Herman. Chacha and Lieutenant-Colonel Marwa went to Leballo's residence at 3 a.m. on June 30. Chacha and Leballo went into the bedroom, leaving Marwa in the sitting room. There in the bedroom, Chacha told Leballo that he was ready to overthrow the government if he was paid 20 million shillings, and wanted Leballo to tell Kambona to send the money right away.

On July 3, Chacha and Leballo met again at the army headquarters at Chacha's request. Chacha told Leballo he was disappointed because the money was being delayed. And he wanted Leballo to go to the officers' mess at Lugalo Barracks where Captain Elia Dustan Lifa Chipaka would introduce him to Major Herman.

Leballo went there and found Captain Chipaka waiting for him. Captain Chipaka told Leballo that he did not trust Major Herman as someone who would be involved in overthrowing the government because he was a half-caste from Iringa (in the Southern Highlands of southwestern Tanzania); and that he would give him a list of army officers which would include the name of one officer from Zanzibar. From that list would be chosen a person who would lead the coup.

Afterwards, Captain Chipaka introduced Leballo to Major Herman.

After this meeting, Leballo met with John Chipaka and Michael Kamaliza in the main office of NUTA in Dar es Salaam. They had a discussion and agreed that Leballo should go to London and ask Kambona to send more money.

Around 4.15 p.m. on the same day, Leballo was again asked to go to the same office. He went and found Kamaliza alone in the office. Kamaliza told Leballo that he had sent someone to Kambona to get and bring the money. He also told Leballo that he personally would like Major Herman, and not Colonel Chacha, to lead the coup.

There were conspirators in Zanzibar but, because the former island nation was an autonomous entity with its own legal system even after uniting with Tanganyika to form Tanzania, the authorities in the isles dispensed swift justice against them. So, it was only the ones on the mainland who had to appear before the Tanzania High Court in Dar es Salaam presided over by the Trinidadian jurist Philip Telford Georges.

The head of the Criminal Investigation Department, Geoffrey Sawaya, told the court that the coup did not take place because some of the conspirators were arrested and detained before the scheduled date for the takeover. He said some of them made statements after their arrest admitting most of the allegations about their involvement in the abortive coup attempt. And he produced evidence showing instructions on how strategic locations would be taken over. He also presented to the court lists of prominent people who were to be detained by the coup makers.

There were moonlight trips by dhow between Dar es Salaam and Zanzibar, made by the conspirators and their couriers. Secret meetings were held in expensive hotels in Nairobi, Kenya, in London, and in Dar es Salaam. Nightclubs were another hot spot where the coup plotters met to discuss their nefarious scheme which included a plot to assassinate President Nyerere. There was even a plan, for whatever reason they deemed appropriate, to bomb the University of Dar es Salaam; probably to cause panic while they executed the coup, or simply to wreak havoc and cause mayhem.

One of the most damaging pieces of evidence against the coup plotters presented in court was the 'wedding guest list' found at the residence of Captain Elia Dustan Lifa Chipaka.

All 37 'guests' named on the list were army officers. Captain Chipaka told the court that the names were part of a list of the names of guests he was going to invite to his wedding. But, as Chief Justice Philip Telford Georges said at the end of the trial, the list contained comments which an average person would consider to be totally irrelevant to preparation for a wedding. For example, against the name of one colonel was this comment:

'Dissatisfied, but his stand is not known.'

Other evidence included letters from Oscar Kambona written to the conspirators.

What the coup plotters did not know was that Potlako Leballo, the South African political exile and president of the Pan-Africanist Congress (PAC) was already working for the Tanzania intelligence service but gained their confidence. The outlandish claim by the that Leballo had manufactured the whole thing and was really a spy for the South African apartheid regime was dismissed as nonsense by the court.

In delivering the verdicts, the chief justice denied pleas for clemency made by the defence lawyers and made it clear that overthrowing governments was not an acceptable way to change leadership, emphasizing that the young African nations needed peace and stability to consolidate their independence and serve their people.

The trial lasted 127 days, the longest in the country's history. Chief Justice Philip Telfer Georges did not sentence the conspirators to death as he could have under the law, but nonetheless gave them stiff sentences as follows:

– Bibi Titi Mohammed: life imprisonment for treason.
– Gray Likungu Mataka: life imprisonment for treason.
– Elia Dustan Lifa Chipaka: life imprisonment for treason.
– John Lifa Chipaka: life imprisonment for treason.
– Michael Kamaliza: ten years' imprisonment for misprision of treason.
– William Makori Chacha: ten years' imprisonment for misprision of treason.

Alfred Philip Milinga was acquitted of all charges, but after spending 16 months in detention under the Preventive Detention Act during the investigation and trial of the treason case. The act was passed by parliament to allow the government to detain people if they posed a threat to national security but was criticized by the chief justice during the treason trial for detaining people for too long before they were brought to court.

The ringleader and mastermind of the treasonous coterie, former foreign affairs minister Oscar Kambona, was tried in absentia. Only three years earlier, President Nyerere had said of his cabinet colleague and close political aide:

'Oscar is extremely loyal - to the party, to me, and to the people.'

President Nyerere could be extremely tough when you encroach on his authority. Yet he also had a reputation for being very tolerant, kind, and forgiving. And he lived up to both. About seven years after the treason trial, Bibi Titi Mohammed received a presidential pardon in 1977 and walked out of prison in Dodoma, central Tanzania. She had written the president asking for forgiveness, but had no hope that she would get it.

On 5 February 1978, Otini Kambona, former education and information minister under Nyerere in the first independence cabinet, and Mattiya Kambona, the younger brothers of Oscar Kambona, were released from detention together with 22 other detainees and 7,000 petty criminals. They were all pardoned by President Nyerere. They were freed on the first anniversary of the founding of the ruling Chama Cha Mapinduzi (CMM), formed from a merger of the mainland TANU and its sister counterpart in Zanzibar, the Afro-Shirazi Party (ASP). February 5, 1978, was also the eleventh anniversary of the Arusha Declaration.

Otini and Mattiya Kambona were detained for more than 10 years. They were arrested and detained in December 1967 for supporting their brother's political activities and using a Kiswahili newspaper Otini Kambona published to help further his political ambitions, even if by making oblique references to his brother's agenda.

But more often than not, the newspaper *Ulimwengu* (The World) was explicit in its condemnation of the government. It published articles written by Oscar Kambona highly critical of the government. After the two brothers were arrested, the paper also immediately ceased publication.

Also released in 1972, like Bibi Titi Mohammed, was Eli Anangisye, former secretary-general of the TANU Youth League, who had been detained for his involvement in another plot to overthrow the government by trying to enlist the help of some army officers to carry out the coup. He was the alleged mastermind of the plot.

Why Nyerere freed all these people, despite their attempts to undermine his government, remained a mystery. And he gave no reason for setting them free, in spite of the overwhelming evidence implicating them in the plots. He was not ruthless but took a firm stand against his enemies. And he could have let them rot in prison, instead of pardoning them. Yet, he set them free, demonstrating one of his qualities as a compassionate man.

Kambona, of course, was never arrested. No extradition proceedings took place and he remained in Britain until he willingly returned to Tanzania in April 1992 after the country adopted the multiparty system which enabled him to form a political party and challenge the ruling Chama Cha Mapinduzi (Revolutionary Party) which had been in power since independence, first as TANU. Ironically, multiparty democracy was introduced with the full support of former President Nyerere when he started questioning the functional utility of the one-party state of which he was the architect and which was officially adopted in 1965. But it had become corrupt, he said, and needed to be replaced. Yet his position on the multi-party system was not fully understood. As Andrew Nyerere stated in his written comments on my work in August 2003 when I was writing this expanded edition:

'Mwalimu Nyerere was chairman of the party. And he said, we have been discussing this multi-party democracy at the CCM meeting in Dodoma (Tanzania's new capital). We notice that in many countries there is much talk about the multi-party form of government. After discussing this, we have decided that there is no reason why this country should not follow this kind of multi-party democracy. So we invite everyone to discuss this.

In connection with this, I would like to make a comment about the notes which Mwalimu had been making for a speech which he was going to make, but which he never made, because death overtook him.

He wrote that he hoped he had made a good decision when he spoke in favour of multi-party democracy. This is good, in so far as Mwalimu hoped that all the decisions he had made during his life were good decisions.

But the mere fact that he wrote this meant that he did not see any necessity for a multi-party state, even as he did not see any necessity for a single party state. The only thing that mattered was that the government should serve the people well.'

Twelve years after the treason trial, Oscar Kambona gave an interview in April 1982 in which he explained why he was highly critical of Nyerere, and by implication tried to justify his attempt to overthrow the government, although nothing he said could justify that. As he stated in the interview with *Drum*:

'Nyerere and I go back a long way - we founded TANU. Nyerere was the chairman and I was the secretary-general.

Problems between us began in 1964 during the army mutiny. Nyerere and Kawawa hid themselves in a grass hut while I was left to face the music (Kambona was then minister of defence).

I negotiated with the army and managed to settle the uprising. When Nyerere returned, the army wanted to mutiny again - that was when we asked for military assistance from the British.

After the mutiny, some friends told him that he was losing his grip on the country and I think he believed them.

When Nyerere visited China, he was very impressed with the glorification of Mao Tse-Tung. I think the seeds of a single, all-powerful individual, an autocrat, were sown in him on this trip. And when he came back, he wanted a one-party state.

I sat on the commission that looked at the question of a one-party state and produced a minority report in which I wanted to know what mechanism we had of changing government peacefully.

Nyerere persuaded me not to present my report and said that I should go along with the majority report which was in favour of a one-party state and that at the end of five years, we would review the situation and if we found any weaknesses we could put them right. I agreed, but I refused to sign as a member of the committee.

I think that *Ujamaa* was badly implemented and that is why it has been a failure. The government should have had pilot schemes which were successful so that people could go to see them.

The farmers in Tanzania are very conservative. They want to know what they get from their labour. If a man has a farm and earns 200 British pounds from it, and is then asked to go into an *Ujamaa* village and gets 20 pounds for the same work, he begins to ask: 'How is *Ujamaa* good for me?'

The system in Tanzania is such that Nyerere will continue to remain in power. The president chooses all the candidates for elections. Whichever way you vote, you still vote for his man.

In the presidential elections, there are only two boxes - one for Nyerere and the other against him. When you go into the polling booth, there is a soldier standing there. He tells you, 'If you want Nyerere, vote there, and if you are an enemy of the people, then vote in the 'no' box.'

Nyerere has been in power for 21 years now. And nowadays he is always saying that he is going to resign. Then the parliamentarians stamp their feet and shout that he is their leader and Nyerere says: 'Well, what can I do? A captain cannot abandon his ship and let it sink.'

But why is it that during all this time he hasn't been able to find anyone who can rule the country besides himself?

I feel very sorry for the person who will take over because the country is bankrupt. If I took over I would change the economic policies and do away with detention for longer than ten days.'

But even after multiparty politics was introduced, Kambona was still not able to get significant support among the people after he returned to Tanzania in April 1992 from 25 years of exile in Britain. Whatever lure and lustre he had before, especially among his admirers, was now gone; having faded after so many years of absence from his country, and tarnished by his treasonous acts of trying to undermine and overthrow an immensely popular president who was also the founding father of the nation. Many people simply saw him as a traitor, and his party, the Tanzania Democratic Alliance (TADEA), never won the support he hoped it would be able to get across the country....

Kambona faded into obscurity and died discredited in his own country he helped lead to independence; yet whose government, of which he once was a prominent member, he tried to overthrow, thus tarnishing his image forever.

Yet, he remained and died a patriot to some people. On his grave, he may have wanted a fitting epitaph written along these lines:

Here lies Oscar Salathiel Kambona, a leader of the independence movement, and once a prominent cabinet member who tried to change the government by unconstitutional means, and who died a traitor to some, but a patriot to others.'

He was both, at different times, in Tanzania's 'turbulent' history. – (Godfrey Mwakikagile, *Nyerere and Africa: End of an Era*, New Africa Press, 2010, pp. 361 – 375, and 380).

Kambona also attempted to overthrow Nyerere at the wrong time. The Tanzanian leader, who was the father of the nation and was affectionately called Mwalimu, meaning "teacher" because he was once a teacher, was at the peak of his popularity, only a few years after independence. The country had a robust economy and there was no widespread discontent over living conditions. All those factors militated against any attempt to depose him.

He was not infallible. But his integrity was unimpeachable even with all the mistakes he made as a mere mortal with frailties. And the CIA knew that. A coup against him could have resulted in chaos and even retaliation against the coup makers probably in a form of a counter-coup and civil protests and disobedience even if muted. It would have been unpopular.

Resistance to the coup from some segments of the security forces would have made things worse because of Nyerere's popularity across the nation especially among the workers and peasants Even when he made mistakes, they believed he did so with the best of intentions because he had their best interests at heart. It would have been very hard to justify a coup against him.

Also, it would have been hard to justify his ouster even in a geopolitical context where he was an anchor of stability because of his genuine commitment to non-alignment in the ideological rivalry between the East and the West during the Cold War and because of the enormous influence he had on other leaders in the region.

His popularity and commitment to the well-being of

his people was even acknowledged by American diplomats accredited to Tanganyika, later Tanzania, even when they disagreed with on a number of issues including his socialist policies. They still acknowledged that he was a man of high moral integrity, highly principled and selfless. As US Deputy Ambassador Robert Hennemeyer who was in Tanganyika, later Tanzania, from 1961 - 1964, stated:

> (He was) a great leader of his people. I don't believe for a moment that he meant anything but to do the best he could for the wellbeing of his people....He was so revered as the great father. – (Robert Hennemeyer, in Godfrey Mwakikagile, *Why Tanganyika united with Zanzibar to form Tanzania*, New Africa Press, 2014, pp. 56, 113).

But that did not stop the CIA from conducting its espionage activities in Tanzania. It is part of the agency's mandate to have agents in every country. The CIA even recruits foreign students in the United States to work for the agency. For example, there was a report in *The Detroit News* in 1975 stating that the agency was busy on college campuses recruiting foreign students. It named the University of Michigan and Michigan State University as some of the fertile grounds for recruitment by the CIA. The report stated:

> The emphasis is on the emerging nations of Africa.

Even the University of Dar es Salaam in Tanzania was infiltrated by the CIA. One American lecturer, Dr. Stephen Andrew Lucas who taught sociology at the university for seven years in the 1960s, was a CIA agent. He also worked as a CIA agent in Madagascar, Angola and Mozambique. Some students at the university were suspicious of some faculty members from western countries including the United States whom they accused of being spies.

It was a suspicion that could have been misconstrued as a form of xenophobia. But it was subsequently justified, although a blanket condemnation of all Westerners as infiltrators or saboteurs could not be justified and was even criticised by President Nyerere who described the students as "petty nationalists." As Professor Ronald Aminzade states in his book, *Race, Nation, and Citizenship in Postcolonial Africa: The Case of Tanzania*:

> The exclusion of foreigners from university-level education proved more contentious. Marxist-Leninist students at the university, who organized the United African Students Revolutionary Federation (USARF) in 1967 following the Arusha Declaration, regarded the presence of expatriate faculty from Western capitalist countries as imperialist infiltration.
> Angered by the presence of U.S. professors in the law school, they occupied the Faculty of Law in March 1969 and demanded the East Africanization of the faculty, the appointment of a Tanzanian to dean of the Faculty of Law, and the hiring of teaching staff from socialist countries.
> Radical students claims that some foreign faculty members at the university might be spying on left-wing activists were supported by subsequent revelations, years later, that a visiting U.S. lecturer in sociology, Stephen Lucas, was, in fact, a CIA agent.
> When the students confronted President Nyerere, who was also Chancellor of the university, with their demand to remove expatriate faculty from the campus, he responded by asking them where Che Guevara was born (Argentina), where he fought (Cuba), and where he died (Bolivia). He chastised the students for being 'petty nationalists' rather than 'internationalists.'
> There were few highly educated Tanzanians to replace the foreign faculty, and the university was necessary for training high-ranking government officials and of, course, future faculty. in this way, foreign faculty remained a vital resource for the socialist project.
> Interestingly, government officials were not averse to appealing to antiforeign sentiments to justify their actions in confrontations with Marxist-Leninist students and faculty at the university. They claimed that the Marxist-Leninist rhetoric of radical students was an unwelcome foreign influence in a country trying to build its own distinctive national brand of socialism.
> In November 1970, the government banned the USARF and shut down its Marxist-Leninist magazine *Cheche*, which means 'the spark' in Swahili and was a reference to the Leninist journal of the Russian Bolsheviks. In government administrators' view, the organization

violated the principle of self-reliance because it was borrowing a foreign ideology and because it gave the false impression that Tanzania was building a 'Russian socialism.'

Student editors Karim Hirji and Naijuka Kasihwaki responded by arguing:

If people think we are building 'Russian Socialism' because of the name *Cheche*, then will they not also think we are building 'American Socialism' since our nationalized institutions get advice from American management consultancy agencies?' – (Ronald Aminzade, *Race, Nation, and Citizenship in Postcolonial Africa: The Case of Tanzania*, New York: Cambridge University Press, 2013, pp. 187 - 188).

But the students were right on target in the case of Dr. Stephen Lucas when they said there were some faculty members who were spying for governments hostile to Tanzania even if they did specifically identify him as as an agent or conclusively say he was one but may have suspected that. It was years later, after he left the University of Dar es Salaam, that he was identified as a CIA agent. KGB agents in Tanzania probably knew he was one when he was teaching at the university as much as they probably did when he was in Congo-Leopoldville and elsewhere.

Some of the information has come from former CIA agents who have turned against the agency for different reasons and have exposed their colleagues working in different parts of the world.

Before going to Tanzania, Stephen Andrew Lucas was an agent in Congo-Leopoldville and worked under Larry Devlin, the CIA station chief in that country when Patrice Lumumba was arrested and assassinated; so was Frank Carlucci, a senior CIA agent under diplomatic cover, who even befriended Lumumba and was involved in his assassination.

Lumumba's arrest was orchestrated by the CIA, probably by Carlucci himself. Joseph Mobutu who was the head of the army was already on the CIA payroll when he served as Lumumba's secretary before Lumumba promoted him. He ousted Lumumba, in collaboration with the CIA, and sent him to Katanga to be executed. In fact, when Mobutu was president of Zaire (formerly Congo-Leopoldville), the largest CIA station in Africa was in the capital Kinshasa, before then known as Leopoldville.

There were CIA agents in Elisabethville, the capital of Katanga Province, where Lumumba was sent to his arch-enemy, Moise Tshombe, to be assassinated. And there was probably more than one CIA agent on the scene when Lumumba and his colleagues, Joseph Okito and Maurice Mpolo, were shot to death on the outskirts of Elisabethville on 17 January 1961. They were brutally beaten on their flight from Leopoldvile to Elisabethville, and even when they landed at the airport, before they met their fate. Okito, who once served as vice president of the senate, was shot first; he was also the oldest of the three.

Even President Nkrumah blamed Frank Carlucci for being directly responsible for Lumumba's death, as Carlucci himself said then and years later, although he consistently denied any involvement in the assassination of the Congolese leader:

> I arrived (in Congo) 15 days before independence. We had a Consul General who was leaving and an ambassador had been designated, Clare Timberlake. The situation was one of considerable confusion....
> I set about to get to know the political figures....I persuaded the DCM (deputy chief of mission), Rob McIlvaine, a marvelous man, to allow me to rent a Volkswagen so I had my own car and didn't go around in an embassy chauffeured car. I then got myself some press credentials because the press moved around more freely than anybody else could. Lumumba tended to hold a press conference a day and I figured it was important to get into those. Then I got myself a pass to the Parliament which was in formation. And basically spent all day outside the embassy. Just floating in from time to time....
> We developed a relationship (with Mobutu)....Larry Devlin and I went to see him shortly after he took over....
> There wasn't a lot to be obtained in Leopoldville. Most of the action had taken place in Katanga and we had to depend on our consul

in Elisabethville to report on what had transpired there. Our best assessment was that he (Lumumba) had been killed after he arrived in Katanga...., probably in the presence of (Godefroid) Munongo....

When this happened, as I recall, I was in Stanleyville. This was shortly after they had arrested all the Europeans in Stanleyville and thrown them out. Timberlake asked me if I'd go up there, back and forth, and act as consul for Stanleyville. They announced on Stanleyville radio that Lumumba had been murdered and that I was the man who had done it. They claimed I was a paratroop captain or colonel, I guess. I had made it up to the rank of colonel. They were going to see that justice was done.

And as I recall, Kwame Nkrumah sent a cable to Dag Hammarskjold about me killing Lumumba and a few other things like that. So we had to worry a little bit about survival. I had to find my way out of Stanleville. I did that by hitchhiking. In fact, I hitchhiked in a UN plane to Bukavu and then to Elisabethville and then back to Leopoldville.

I went back up to Stanleyville a couple of weeks later and they arrested me....They put me under house arrest. They declared me *persona non grata*....It was a breakaway government in Stanleyville, headed by Antoine Gizenga. Kabila was a member of that government. I didn't know him well.

We had Gizenga, Gbenye, Weregemere, and a number of other Lumumba supporters in Stanleyville. They had broken away when - I guess after Lovanium - I can't recall the exact sequence, certainly when Mobutu had taken over. They declared their own government. I had been going back and forth, meeting with them, when they declared me *persona non grata*.

About then, I wanted to introduce my successor, Tom Cassilly, (who later himself got arrested), so I said I'd go up one more time. I flew up and at the airport, they arrested me. – (Ambassador Frank Charles Carlucci III interviewed by Charles Stuart Kennedy, 1 April 1997, *The Association for Diplomatic Studies and Training (ADST), Oral History Project*, copyright 2000, pp. 7, 8, 20 - 21).

Three years after Lumumba's assassination, Carlucci was sent to Zanzibar where he became head of the American consulate. He was there during the revolution in January 1964.

Three months after the revolution, Zanzibar united with Tanganyika to form Tanzania. Carlucci was later expelled from the country. As he himself stated in an interview in 1997:

> I arrived in 1964...in early '64 and...I was expelled in January 1965. – (Ibid., p. 28).

When he was in Zanzibar, he befriended the leader of the new revolutionary government, Abeid Karume, who did not know English and spoke to him in Swahili:

> One of the reasons that I think I got kicked out was that I managed to develop a good relationship with Karume. Karume spoke very little English....I was the only senior diplomat on the island who could converse with him in Swahili and he loved that. So we had a very good relationship....
> One of my neighbors, a minister named Jumbe, who later became vice president, had a tendency to drink a bit and one night he came over to my house. No sooner did he come in than the police arrived and essentially told him to get out. We were pretty much isolated. We were socially ostracized. Virtually every Sunday there would be a demonstration against me. I would get my tear gas [mask] and my beer and I'd go to the embassy and watch the demonstrators....
> (It was) anti-American. It got serious when the Belgians sent paratroopers into Stanleyville....
> The only people at ceremonies I could talk to were the Brit, the Israeli, and the Soviet. I'd have to listen to all the diatribes. In one of the more humorous incidents, I decided to visit the neighboring island of Pemba, which was being run by a Commissar, named Ali Sultan Issa, a man who was trained in Beijing. He was so indoctrinated that he insisted we even share the same bed. 'This is the way we do it in the People's democracy.'
> He took me around the island with people chanting and singing since it was in the 'workers' paradise.' Then he had a rally and meeting and I could see during the rally, this was in the early stages of my stay, that he would point at me and the crowd would applaud and yell and scream. So I asked someone what he was saying and he told me he was saying, 'There's the enemy. Why don't you applaud or don't you think we ought to throw the Americans out?'
> Right then and there, I decided that learning Swahili was essential....
> There was one other African that I could talk to. He was the Chairman of the Afro-Shirazi Party, Thabit Kombo, who was probably in his 70s or 80s at the time, and was such a revered figure in Zanzibar

that he could talk to me without fear of retaliation. He and the President were essentially the only two that I could talk to. – (Ibid., pp. 29, 31, 34, 35).

Carlucci also was the first American diplomat to establish informal ties with the African National Congress (ANC) and the Pan Africanist Congress (PAC) of South Africa.

The CIA had already infiltrated both organisations and other groups in South Africa including the South African Communist Party (SACP). Donald Rickard, a CIA agent working under diplomatic cover in South Africa and who was responsible for Nelson Mandela's arrest when Mandela returned from Tanganyika in 1962 after secretly leaving his home country to seek support for the ANC in the struggle against apartheid, had informers in the upper echelons of the ANC.

They provided him with information on Mandela's return to South Africa and he tipped off the authorities who arrested Mandela on 5 August 1962 when he was driving a car from Durban to Johannesburg disguised as a chauffeur.

But it was Carlucci who openly, even if surreptitiously, interacted with some members and leaders of the ANC and the PAC when it was not official policy of the United States to do so. As he stated in an interview:

I became personally interested in the evolution of apartheid and while I was a commercial officer in essentially an economic and consulate-post in Johannesburg (1957 - 1959), I undertook on my own initiative to go to a number of ANC [African National Congress] meetings.

They were allowed to meet. There was surveillance on me when I went to the meetings. And after I had gone to a certain number of them, the South African Government complained to our ambassador, Ambassador Byroade, at the time about my activities. So although I wasn't doing anything illegal, they thought it was suspect activity....

I got a sense of what their politics were, how militant they were. Frankly, I felt they were less militant than they'd been described. I got to know some of the splinter groups. I was the first person, for example, to talk to Robert Sobukwe, who founded the Pan Africanist Congress. He later died.

But I got acquainted with the movement, which, interestingly, nobody in Pretoria had been able to do. Our embassy was constrained from attending the meetings. The meetings were in Johannesburg. So I established a relationship, a personal relationship, with some of the political officers in Pretoria and reported to them.

I wrote a number of political – what in those days were airgrams you may recall – political airgrams on these meetings on the ANC. They were well-received in Washington and I think were basically responsible for my subsequent assignment to the Congo as a political officer. – (Ibid., pp. 5, 6).

Carlucci was adept at forging ties with national leaders, very quickly, wherever he was assigned and was linked to dramatic events which took place when he was there or soon after he left. Whenever he left a station where he was assigned, trouble followed. He said his colleagues even joked about that.

Donald Petterson who was a consular officer in Zanzibar from 1963 to 1965 and once served as United States ambassador to Tanzania (1986 – 1989) had the following to say about Carlucci and some of the experiences he himself had in Zanzibar during and after the revolution:

A phone call from the rebels finally came. It was from Aboud Jumbe, one of the ministers in the new government, who said he wanted to come over and take Picard to the revolutionary headquarters. In due course he arrived in an open Land Rover with armed people in it. Jumbe himself was heavily armed. Fritz (Frederick "Fritz" Picard, the consul) and I, along with Jim Ruchti and the executive officer, got into the Land Rover and were driven to Raha Leo, the site of the radio station and the African community center.

Raha Leo was now the command headquarters of the revolution. There was electricity in the air when we neared Raha Leo. Hundreds of Africans who were in a very fierce mood ringed the place, many or most armed with everything from sticks to old swords; an occasional rifle was seen. As we approached the headquarters, better-armed revolutionaries came into sight. They carried police rifles, and a few had automatic weapons. We saw Arab prisoners, some of them bloodied, some lying near the entrance to the revolutionary headquarters, all looking despondent. The crowd was so excited because they knew at that moment, or soon thereafter, Ali Muhsin, whom they hated, would be brought in....

The air was so tense as they began to swarm toward the Land Rover that Aboud Jumbe yelled at them in Swahili - he had a bullhorn - to get back or he would open fire. They obliged, and a way was cleared for us. We got out of the Land Rover and waited for somebody to come out of revolutionary headquarters.

After a while, a figure emerged, a man dressed in a semi-military uniform. He had on dark shorts and a dark blue shirt, a peaked cap, knee socks in the British style. He approached us, went up to the executive officer, pulled out a revolver out of his holster, stuck it right at the exec, either in his ribs as I remember it, or in his face as Jim Ruchti remembered it, and said, 'How do you do? I am John Okello.'

With that, he put his revolver back in the holster and said there was going to be some target practice behind revolutionary headquarters. Would we like to join in? Well, figuring that the targets might well be some of the captured Arabs, we declined.

He escorted us into Raha Leo. We went up the stairs into a meeting room, where after another wait we were ushered into the room. Sitting there behind a table with Okello were Abaid Karume, leader of the Afro-Shirazi Party and now president of the new government, Babu, Hanga, and several others....Karume had come back to Zanzibar...from Dar es Salaam...by boat early that morning with Babu and Hanga.

The British high commissioner had met with them just before we did, and as he left we entered. The discussion began. Fritz, first of all, told Okello - who had put his revolver on the table with the barrel pointing at Fritz - that we would not negotiate at gunpoint. Okello made no reply, but picked up and reholstered his weapon. He didn't say much during the ensuing discussion, in which Fritz made the request for an evacuation (of Americans from Zanzibar).

Babu replied angrily, so did Hanga; Karume was uncomfortable. They were angry that the Americans had brought in this warship. And it seemed to us, as we thought about it a bit later, that they didn't know whether the *Manley* might open fire. in any case, they really didn't care for the evacuation. They didn't want to see it happen, but they agreed to it, fearing there might be consequences otherwise.

Finally, Karume indicated that he would not oppose the request. Then he turned to Okello and said, 'It's your decision.'

Okello sort of shrugged and said, 'All right.'

This made it clear to us there that Okello was indeed of great importance. I say this because later on there were those who belittled Okello's role in the revolution. In fact, the official history of the revolution barely mentions him. But he was the force that pulled it off. Weeks later, others with more political sagacity took control....

My Swahili...was very useful. I formed a friendship with Karume as a result, because I was the only American who spoke Swahili and my Swahili was getting better and better all of the time. We carried out our conversations in Swahili. I was very deferential to him; Fritz was not. Fritz, unfortunately, was a bit patronizing with Karume, and that came back to haunt him, as I'll explain.

On the morning of January 16, four days after the revolution... (there) were American, British and Canadian newspapermen - reporters for *Time, Newsweek, The New York Herald Tribune*, a Canadian paper and a British paper - and an Indian photographer for *Life* magazine....They had sailed from in the dhow from the mainland (Tanganyika), arriving in Zanzibar the previous night.

They started asking me questions. Foolishly I answered. At that point a rifle was pointed right in my face, and I was told to 'Shut up!' So I stopped talking, [laughter] the better part of valor! Some authorities from the revolutionary government joined these armed people at the dockside. They said that the men in the boat were spies and we were going to be taken to revolutionary headquarters. Off we went. I tried to explain to the rebels who I was. They couldn't care less, nor did they accept that these were just newspaper people....

I formed a relationship with Karume, and also with Babu, who was a very charming guy, a militant left-winger, to say the least, and very shrewd, very intelligent. Karume was a stolid man, not nearly as bright as Babu, but a man of very real native intelligence. I don't mean to use that term in a derogatory sense at all. He was a very able man in many ways, but impressionable and unsophisticated. As time would go by the results of that would be harmful to Zanzibar....

Frank (Carlucci) was well-regarded by Joe Palmer, the Assistant Secretary of State for African Affairs and by Charlie Whitehouse, and by everybody else. It had been decided that Frank would be the new chargé d'affaires in Zanzibar. He came with a letter from President Johnson that indicated recognition (of the new revolutionary government that had replaced the sultan) would be coming soon.

Frank and Leonhart (the American ambassador to Tanganyika) tried to convince Karume that with recognition just around the corner, it would be much better if he didn't throw me off the island.

By the way, the whole Revolutionary Council, which included all the wild men along with some of the more able and moderate Zanzibari Africans who were in the cabinet, were at this meeting. The discussion went on for a couple of hours, but in the end Karume and the Council rejected the American proposal. Karume, when he said goodbye, said, 'If you come back, if recognition takes place, and you come back, Mr. Carlucci, we'll have a parade in your honor.'

So with that, Frank and Ambassador Leonhart returned to Dar es Salaam.

I went back to the embassy to finish burning the classified materials. I had just started when there was a pounding on the front door. Ali Mahfoudh, the head of the newly created special police force, demanded to come into the embassy. When I refused him entry, he said he would have to take me in custody. He drove me to State House, the seat of the government. An official there told Mahfoudh to take me back to the embassy and not to interfere with me.

After I did some burning, I went home for a quick lunch. When I returned, the officer in charge of the soldiers who had surrounded the building said I could not reenter it. When I argued with him, he told me a government official wanted to see me and he drove me to a government office. I was taken to the office of Abdul Aziz Twala, one of the more militant members of the cabinet. Unbeknownst to me, an argument had preceded my arrival. some of the people there wanted to kill me.

At least that's what a man named Mohammed Ali Foum, who was there at the time and later became a diplomat in Tanzanian diplomatic service, told me years afterward. We met at the United Nations one day, and he told me this. I don't know if it's true but he swore it was. he said that after some argument, it was decided that killing me would cause too many problems.

At any rate, when I got there, Twala simply me to return to the embassy, then go home and get ready to leave later that day....

Frank had been in the Congo, where he acquired a reputation as an exceptionally able Foreign Service officer. He was the embassy's trouble shooter in the Congo....

He was an excellent reporter. He got out, beat the bushes, met the people. He was charming. He got people to trust him. He dealt with people who were essentially hostile to us at that time, befriended them, and got a lot out of it. He knew what was going on in Zanzibar before he'd been there very long....

He had extraordinary intelligence, coupled with very good common sense, and outgoing nature. He knew how to get along with Africans. He was sensitive to their culture. He had no false pretensions. He was an excellent writer, had superior analytical skills....Somebody who's willing to get out of the office, travel around the country, to do whatever is necessary to get information, to establish rapport with people so they will talk to you. You collect intelligence from people whom you meet and process it through whatever abilities you have. You learn to sift out good information from bad....

Frank set out to meet and establish a relationship with as many people as possible in the government and other areas....(He) worked long, hard hours and gave a great deal of thought to his work....He had all the qualities that would later propel him to high offices in the U.S. government, including secretary of defense. – (Ambassador Donald Petterson interviewed by Charles Stuart Kennedy, 13 December 1996, *The Association for Diplomatic Studies and Training (ADST), Foreign Affairs Oral History Project*, copyright 2002, pp. 37 – 38, 40, 41, 42, 43, 44, 46, 47).

It is those qualities which also helped him pave the way for Lumumba's elimination although he strenuously denied that, in spite of the fact that he served with distinction – in the field, outdoors – as a foreign service officer in Congo during that period and, at the very least, collected invaluable information for the CIA because of the close ties he had with the Congolese leaders including Lumumba's enemies.

He later served as deputy director of the CIA under President Jimmy Carter and as secretary of defence and national security advisor under President Ronald Reagan, among other high-level positions in the federal government through the years.

Stephen Lucas, who like Carlucci learned Swahili in his role as a CIA agent in Congo-Leopoldville and Tanzania, was awarded the Defense Intelligence Director's Award, the Retirement Medallion and Certificate of Distinction from the Central Intelligence Agency after he retired. He went to teach at Louisiana State University where he became head of international programmes. He also founded a Swahili programme at the school and taught Swahili among other subjects including contemporary Africa, intelligence, globalisation and regionalisation as well as others in the area of international studies.

He is still remembered for the role he played as a CIA

agent in Africa, working for an agency that has in some ways determined the course of events in many African countries, thus partly determining the destiny of the continent.

Many leaders who led their countries to independence, including Jomo Kenyatta who was revered as one of the fathers of the African independence movement, were on the CIA payroll; so was Kenyatta's heir apparent Tom Mboya.

They were the founding fathers, yet sellouts, bought by the CIA.

Even Emperor Haile Selassie, a revered figure and symbol of African independence and resistance to foreign rule – best exemplified by his dignified resistance to the Italian invasion of Ethiopia – who played a major role in the establishment of the Organisation of African Unity (OAU) in Addis Ababa, Ethiopia, in May 1963 and presided over its formation, was on the CIA payroll.

Those who came after them – not all but most of them – were no better than their predecessors. And that is still the case today.

The CIA operates with impunity in many countries across the continent often in collaboration with the leaders of those countries; so do intelligence services of other powers, as they always have since the sixties when most African countries emerged from colonial rule; only to be ruled again as neo-colonies, controlled and manipulated by their former colonial masters and other powers including the United States, the most powerful country in the world.

But there were exceptions such as Kwame Nkrumah, Julius Nyerere, Ahmed Sekou Toure, Patrice Lumumba, Modibo Keita, Gamal Abdel Nasser, Ahmed Ben Bella, Milton Obote, Kenneth Kaunda, Muammar Gaddafi and Marien Ngouabi; and later, Robert Mugabe, Samora Machel, Agostinho Neto, Jerry Rawlings, Murtala Mohammed, and Thomas Sankara. They did not succumb to CIA temptations. They were not, and could not, be bought by the CIA and other foreign agencies.

One of the best examples of CIA interference in African affairs to the detriment of Africa's wellbeing was the military coup against President Nkrumah in the sixties.

The coup would not have been carried out when it was, and would not have succeeded, without CIA involvement. The agency had already infiltrated the government and the military as well as security services including the police in preparation for the coup.

The subject has been addressed by Godfrey Mwakikagile in his book, *Western Involvement in Nkrumah's Downfall*. Other researchers and analysts have also written about it.

Even President Felix Houphouet Boigny of the Ivory Coast who was Nkrumah's political and ideological rival acknowledged that the military coup against Nkrumah was externally engineered. As he stated in an interview with *Jeune Afrique*, 4 February 1981:

> Destabilisation is not a new thing. Did you know why Idi Amin made his coup in 1971? It was not he who did it, but the British. He did not even know what he wanted himself.
>
> It was the same in Ghana when the military overthrew Nkrumah. They [the coup makers] came to see me. I asked them. They replied: 'All is not well anymore.' 'Is that all?' [I asked them]. I also asked them what they were going to do; they did not know. People outside knew it for them.

An indefatigable champion of African unity and independence, Nkrumah was a great inspiration to freedom fighters across the continent. President Nyerere strongly condemned the coup against Nkrumah. As he stated at a press conference in Dar es Salaam soon after Nkrumah was overthrown on 24 February 1966:

> What is happening in Africa? What are the coups about? The last few months have seen changes of governments in many African countries. The latest has been in Ghana. What is behind all this? Are

these 'revolutions' intended to remove humiliation and oppresion from Africa?

Let us take the latest in Ghana. The enemies of Africa are now jubilant. There is jubilation in Salisbury and Johannesburg. Even a fool could begin to wonder whether these 'revolutions' would help Africa.

What was Kwame trying to do? He stood for the liberation of Africa. There is not a single leader in Africa more committed to this than Kwame. Whom did he anger with his commitment to freedom? Certainly not Africa. He was committed to true independence. He was not merely against ordinary colonialism; he was against neocolonialism - against a colonial power going out through the political door and controlling the country through the e conomic door. – (Julius K. Nyerere, quoted by Kwame Nkrumah, *Dark Days in Ghana*, New York: Monthly Review Press, 1968, p. 137; Opoku Agyeman, *Nkrumah's Ghana and East Africa: Pan-Africanism and Interstate Relations*, Madison, New Jersey, USA: Fairleigh Dickinson University Press, 1992, p. 152).

Nyerere offered Nkrumah asylum. Sekou Toure, Nasser and Modibo Keita also offered Nkrumah asylum. They were ideological compatriots. Nkrumah finally decided to go to Guinea.

A bitter foe of neocolonialism like Nkrumah, Nyerere also maintained until the end of his life that economic inequalities in the international system existed because underdeveloped or developing countries were being treated unfairly; they were at the mercy of the industrialised nations. The poor are poor, and are getting poorer, because they are being exploited by the rich and powerful. Their natural resources do not benefit them but instead benefit powerful nations.

Even racial inequalities and injustices in the countries of southern Africa which were under white minority rule continued to exist because rich and powerful nations – almost all of therm white – supported and sustained white minority regimes for political, economic and racist reasons. leaders of Western countries disagreed with him. But he continued to maintain his position. As *The Washington Post* reported when he was about to step down as president of Tanzania:

After 23 years in office, Africa's senior statesman and one of the Third World's most eloquent spokesmen is planning to step down. Tanzanian President Julius Nyerere, 63, says he will retire from office next year, become one of the few rulers in the short history of independent black to relinquish his post voluntarily.

He does not intend to depart quietly. Last month (November 1984) Nyerere accepted the chairmanship of the Organization of African Unity with a blistering attack on U.S. policy toward white-ruled South Africa, and he later urged African nations to withhold payments on their debts to force western governments and financial institutions to negotiate reforms in the international economic order.

The statements were vintage Nyerere, a leader who has forged a reputation as Africa's most vocal critic of the economic inequality between the First World and the Third.

He is also a man of irrepressible intellect and consummate charm who manages to impress even those western diplomats who find his foreign policies unpalatable and his socialist domestic policies unworkable.

'He is a humane, decent person with an extraordinary mind and considerable charm,' said a senior western diplomat here (in Dar es Salaam), 'but he clings to notions that are wrong'....

Nyerere's Tanzania has been...Africa's leader in the struggle for social equity...(and) Nyerere has been sub-Saharan Africa's leading socialist visionary....

anzania boasts black Africa's highest adult literacy rate -- 70 percent -- thanks to his unswerving commitment to public education. Average life expectancy has increased by 10 years during the last generation through improvements in health care and clean water supplies....

He is famous for the learned treatises he has written on underdevelopment and for periodic bursts of self-criticism....

By stressing national institutions and a nationwide public school system, by eschewing favoritism in dealing with Tanzania's 100-plus tribes, and by imposing Swahili as a national language, Nyerere has helped construct one of Africa's rarest entities: a true nation.

By stressing socialist equality, he has given his country a sense of mission, and by invading neighboring Uganda and overthrowing dictator Idi Amin in 1979, he has given Tanzania an epochal moment of moral triumph that may be enshrined in African history as the defeat of Hitler is cherished in Europe.

'For all its problems, this a remarkably stable country, with dignified, intelligent people, a high degree of religious and ethnic tolerance and many of the attributes of nationhood,' said a Western diplomat here.

Nyerere has blamed most of Tanzania's economic woes on outside forces beyond his control. Alternate years of droughts and crippling floods, the 1977 collapse of the East African Community, forcing the country into expensive capital investments for railways and power lines, and the $500 million price tag for the war against Amin are all cited as major contributors to Tanzania's plight.

Most of all, Nyerere see inequities in a world trade system in which exportable commodities of poor nations such as Tanzania have steadily lost value during the past decade while oil, and vital imports from the industrial West, have increased sharply.

In 1972, Tanzania spent 5 percent of its foreign exchange earnings on imported oil. Last year (1983) it spent nearly 60 percent, even though it has cut oil consumption by nearly one-third.

'It is as if we had been robbed,' Nyerere has said. 'To buy a seven-ton truck in 1981, we had to produce and sell abroad about four times as much cotton, or three times as much cashew, or three times as much coffee, or 10 times as much tobacco as we had to produce and sell in 1976.'

He has also said,' It it true internationally that the rich are rich because the poor are poor. The inevitable oversimplification of that statement does not invalidate it.'

Nyerere's supporters dismiss the idea that his socialist policies have contributed to Tanzania's problems, pointing out that capitalist countries such as Kenya and the Ivory Coast are also suffering from extreme economic shocks.

'Other countries don't have our policies and they are suffering too,' said a top presidential aide....

Nyerere's relations with the United States, which improved dramatically during the Carter administration, have deteriorated under President Reagan. Nyerere has been harshly critical of U.S. support for South Africa and has accused the Reagan administration of encouraging South African aggression against its black-ruled neighbors.

Some of his top aides say that they believe that the United States is encouraging the International Monetary Fund (IMF) to coerce Tanzania into politically risky austerity measures and that the Americans are quietly gloating over the failure of Nyerere's socialist experiment.

American officials have insisted that such views are mistaken....

'Julius has been in charge for too long, but people love him...,' said a senior diplomat. – (Glenn Frankel, "Nyerere Resignation to End 23-

Year Era in East Africa," *The Washington Post*, 9 December 1984).

He stepped down from the presidency in November 1985 when white minority rule was coming to an end in southern Africa. Only apartheid South Africa, and Namibia which was ruled by South Africa, remained under white minority governments.

He was one of the greatest leaders Africa has ever produced. As Ugandan President Yoweri Museveni said when assessing Nyerere' role in the liberation of Africa:

> He was the greatest black man that ever lived. There are other black men such as Nelson Mandela and Kwame Nkrumah, but Nyerere was the greatest. – (Yoweri Museveni, *New Vision*, Kampala, Uganda, 4 April 2012).

They all will be remembered for the role they played in liberating Africa from colonial rule and racial oppression. However, unity on a continental scale has remained elusive as much as it was in the sixties when most African countries won independence. But as Nyerere warned in his Accra speech, "Without unity, there is no future for Africa."

And in what amounted to a farewell speech to Africa not long before he died, Nyerere said the following at a conference at the University of Dar es Salaam - the speech was informal and conversational in style, sprinkled with personal anecdotes, and was given before a diverse audience of politicians, academicians, students and diplomats:

> You wanted me to reflect. I told you I had very little time to reflect. I am not an engineer (reference to the vice-chancellor of the University of Dar es Salaam who identified himself as an engineer in his introductory remarks) and therefore what I am going to say might sound messy, unstructured and possibly irrelevant to what you intend to do; but I thought that if by reflecting, you wanted me to go back and relive the political life that I have lived for the last 30, 40 years,

that I cannot do.

And in any case, in spite of the fact that it's useful to go back in history, what you are talking about is what might be of use to Africa in the 21st century. History's important, obviously, but I think we should concentrate and see what might be of use to our continent in the coming century.

What I want to do is share with you some thoughts on two issues concerning Africa. One, an obvious one; when I speak, you will realise how obvious it is. Another one, less obvious, and I'll spend a little more time on the less obvious one, because I think this will put Africa in what is going to be Africa's context in the 21st century. And the new leadership of Africa will have to concern itself with the situation in which it finds itself in the world tomorrow - in the world of the 21st century. And the Africa I'm going to be talking about, is Africa south of the Sahara, sub-Saharan Africa. I'll explain later the reason why I chose to concentrate on Africa south of the Sahara. It is because of the point I want to emphasise.

It appears today that in the world tomorrow, there are going to be three centres of power: some, political power; some, economic power, but three centres of real power in the world. One centre is the United States of America and Canada; what you call North America. That is going to be a huge economic power, and probably for a long time the only military power, but a huge economic power. The other one is going to be Western Europe, another huge economic power. I think Europe is choosing deliberately not to be a military power. I think they deliberately want to leave that to the United States. The other one is Japan. Japan is in a different category but it is better to say Japan, because the power of Japan is quite clear, the economic power of Japan is obvious.

The three powers are going to affect the countries near them. I was speaking in South Africa recently and I referred to Mexico. A former president of Mexico, I think it must have been after the revolution in 1935, no, after the revolution; a former president of Mexico is reported to have complained about his country or lamented about his country. 'Poor Mexico,' said the president, 'so far from God yet so near the United States.' He was complaining about the disadvantages of being a neighbour of a giant.

Today, Mexico has decided not simply to suffer the disadvantages of being so close to the United States. And the United States itself has realised the importance of trying to accommodate Mexico. In the past there were huge attempts by the United States to prevent people from moving from Mexico *into* the United States; people seeking work, seeking jobs. So you had police, a border very well policed in order to prevent Mexicans who *seek*, who *look* for jobs, to *move* into the

United States. The United States discovered that it was not working. It *can't* work.

There is a kind of economic osmosis where whatever you do, if you are rich, you are attractive to the poor. They will come, they'll even *risk* their own lives in order to come. So the United States tried very hard to prevent Mexicans going into the United States; they've given up, and the result was NAFTA. It is in the interest of the United States to try and create jobs in Mexico because, if you don't, the Mexicans will simply come, to the United States; so they're doing that.

Europe, Western Europe, is very wealthy. It has two Mexicos. One is Eastern Europe. If you want to prevent those Eastern Europeans to come to Western Europe, you jolly will have to create jobs in *Eastern* Europe, and Western Europe is actually *doing* that. They are *doing* that. They'll help Eastern Europe to develop. The whole of Western Europe will be doing it, the Germans are doing it. The Germans basically started first of all with the East Germans but they are spending lots of money also helping the other countries of Eastern Europe to develop, including unfortunately, or *fortunately* for them, including Russia. Because they realise, Europeans realise including the Germans, if you don't help *Russia* to develop, one of these days you are going to be in trouble. So it is in the interest of Western Europe, to help Eastern Europe including Russia. They are pouring a lot of money in that part of the world, in that part of Europe, to try and help it to develop.

I said Western Europe has two Mexicos. I have mentioned one. I'll jump the other. I jump Europe's second Mexico. I'll go to Asia. I'll go to Japan. Japan - a wealthy island, *very* wealthy indeed, but an *island*. I don't think they're very keen on the unemployed of Asia to go to Japan. They'd rather help them where they are, and Japan is spending a lot of money in Asia, to help create jobs *in* Asia, prevent those Asians dreaming about going to Japan to look for jobs. In any case, Japan is too small, they can't find wealth there.

But apart from what Japan is doing, of course Asia *is* Asia; Asia has *China!* Asia has *India*, and the small countries of Asia are not very small. The population of Indonesia is twice the population of Nigeria, your biggest. So Asia is virtually in a category, of the Third World countries, of the Southern countries; Asia is almost in a category of its own. It is developing as a power, and Europe knows it, and the United States knows it. And in spite of the *huge* Atlantic, now they are talking about the Atlantic *Rim*. That is in recognition of the importance of Asia.

I go back to Europe. Europe has a second Mexico. And Europe's second Mexico is North Africa. North Africa is to Europe what

Mexico is to the United States. North Africans who have no jobs will not go to Nigeria; they'll be thinking of Europe or the Middle East, because of the imperatives of geography and history and religion and language. North Africa is part of Europe and the Middle East.

Nasser was a great leader and a great *African* leader. I got on extremely well with him. Once he sent me a minister, and I had a long discussion with his minister at the State House here, and in the course of the discussion, the minister says to me, 'Mr. President, this is my first visit to Africa.' North Africa, because of the pull of the Mediterranean, and I say, history and culture, and religion, North Africa is pulled towards the North. When North Africans look for jobs, they go to Western Europe and southern Western Europe, or they go to the Middle East. And Europe has a specific policy for North Africa, specific policy for North Africa. It's not only about development; it's also about security. Because of you don't do something about North Africa, they'll come.

Africa, south of the Sahara, is different; *totally* different. If you have no jobs here in Tanzania, where do you go? The Japanese have no fear that you people will flock to Japan. The North Americans have no fear that you people will flock to North America. Not even from West Africa. The Atlantic, the Atlantic as an ocean, like the Mediterranean, it has its own logic. But links North America and Western Europe, not North America and West Africa.

Africa south of the Sahara is isolated. That is the first point I want to make. South of the Sahara is totally isolated in terms of that configuration of developing power in the world in the 21st century - on its own. There is no centre of power in whose self-interest it's important to develop Africa, *no* centre. Not North America, not Japan, not Western Europe. There's no self-interest to bother about Africa south of the Sahara. Africa south of the Sahara is on its own. *Na sijambo baya.* Those of you who don't know Kiswahili, I just whispered, 'Not necessarily bad.'

That's the first thing I wanted to say about Africa south of the Sahara. African leadership, the coming African leadership, will have to bear that in mind. You are on your own, Mr. Vice President. You mentioned, you know, in the past, there was some Cold War competition in Africa and some Africans may have exploited it. I never did. I never succeeded in exploiting the Cold War in Africa. We suffered, we suffered through the Cold War. Look at Africa south of the Sahara. I'll be talking about it later. Southern Africa, I mean, look at southern Africa; devastated because of the combination of the Cold War and apartheid. Devastated part of Africa. It could have been *very* different. But the Cold War is gone, thank God. But thank God the Cold War is gone, the chances of the Mobutus also is gone.

So that's the first thing I wanted to say about Africa south of the Sahara. Africa south of the Sahara in those terms is isolated. That is the point I said was not obvious and I had to explain it in terms in which I have tried to explain it. The other one, the second point I want to raise is completely obvious. Africa has 53 nation-states, most of them in Africa south of the Sahara. If numbers were power, Africa would be the most powerful continent on earth. It is the weakest; so it's obvious numbers are not power.

So the second point about Africa, and again I am talking about Africa south of the Sahara; it is fragmented, fragmented. From the very beginning of independence 40 years ago, we were against that idea, that the continent is so fragmented. We called it the Balkanisation of Africa. Today, I think the Balkans are talking about the Africanisation of Europe. Africa's states are too many, too small, some make no logic, whether political logic or ethnic logic or anything. They are non-viable. It is not a confession.

The OAU was founded in 1963. In 1964 we went to Cairo to hold, in a sense, our first summit after the inaugural summit. I was responsible for moving that resolution that Africa must accept the borders, which we inherited from colonialism; accept them as they are. That resolution was passed by the organisation (OAU) with two reservations: one from Morocco, another from Somalia. Let me say why I moved that resolution.

In 1960, just before this country became independent, I think I was then chief minister; I received a delegation of Masai elders from Kenya, led by an American missionary. And they came to persuade me to let the Masai invoke something called the Anglo-Masai Agreement so that that section of the Masai in Kenya should become part of Tanganyika; so that when Tanganyika becomes independent, it includes part of Masai, from Kenya. I suspected the American missionary was responsible for that idea. I don't remember that I was particularly polite to him. Kenyatta was then in detention, and here somebody comes to me, that we should break up Kenya and make part of Kenya part of Tanganyika. But why shouldn't Kenyatta demand that the Masai part of Tanganyika should become Masai of Kenya? It's the same logic. That was in 1960.

In 1961 we became independent. In 1962, early 1962, I resigned as prime minister and then a few weeks later I received Dr. Banda. *Mungu amuweke mahali pema* (May God rest his soul in peace). I received Dr. Banda. We had just, FRELIMO had just been established here and we were now in the process of starting the armed struggle.

So Banda comes to me with a big old book, with lots and lots of maps in it, and tells me, 'Mwalimu, what is this, what is Mozambique? There is no such thing as Mozambique.' I said, 'What do you mean there is no such thing as Mozambique?' So he showed me this map, and he said: 'That part is part of Nyasaland (it was still Nyasaland, not Malawi, at that time). That part is part of Southern Rhodesia, That part is Swaziland, and this part, which is the northern part, Makonde part, that is *your* part.'

So Banda disposed of Mozambique just like that. I ridiculed the idea, and Banda never liked anybody to ridicule his ideas. So he left and went to Lisbon to talk to Salazar about this wonderful idea. I don't know what Salazar told him. That was '62.

In '63 we go to Addis Ababa for the inauguration of the OAU, and Ethiopia and Somalia are at war over the Ogaden. We had to send a special delegation to bring the president of Somalia to attend that inaugural summit, because the two countries were at *war*. Why? Because Somalia wanted the Ogaden, a *whole* province of Ethiopia, saying, 'That is part of Somalia.' And Ethiopia was quietly, the Emperor quietly saying to us that 'the whole of Somalia is part of Ethiopia.'

So those three, the delegation of the Masai, led by the American missionary; Banda's old book of maps; and the Ogaden, caused me to move that resolution, in Cairo 1964. And I say, the resolution was accepted, two countries with reservations, and one was Somalia because Somalia wanted the Ogaden; Somalia wanted northern Kenya; Somalia wanted Djibouti.

Throw away all our ideas about socialism. Throw them away, give them to the Americans, give them to the Japanese, give them, so that they can, I don't know, they can do whatever they like with them. *Embrace* capitalism, fine! But you *have* to be self-reliant. You here in Tanzania don't dream that if you privatise every blessed thing, including the prison, then foreign investors will come rushing. No! No! Your are dreaming! *Hawaji*! They won't come! (*hawaji*!). You just try it.

There is more to privatise in Eastern Europe than here. Norman Manley, the Prime Minister of Jamaica, in those days the vogue was nationalisation, not privatisation. In those days the vogue was *nationalisation*. So Norman Manley was asked as Jamaica was moving towards independence: 'Mr. Prime Minister, are you going to nationalise the economy?' His answer was: 'You can't nationalise *nothing*.'

You people here are busy privatising not *nothing*, we did *build* something, we built *something* to privatise. But quite frankly, for the appetite of Europe, and the appetite of North America, this is privatising nothing. The people with a really good appetite will go to Eastern Europe, they'll go to Russia, they'll not come rushing to Tanzania! Your blessed National Bank of Commerce, it's a branch of some major bank somewhere, and in Tanzania you say, 'It's so big we must divide it into pieces,' which is *nonsense*.

Africa south of the Sahara is isolated. Therefore, to develop, it will have to depend upon its own resources basically. Internal resources, nationally; and Africa will have to depend upon Africa. The leadership of the future will have to devise, try to carry out policies of *maximum* national self-reliance and *maximum* collective self-reliance. They have no other choice. *Hamna*! (You don't have it!) And this, this need to organise collective self-reliance is what moves me to the second part.

The small countries in Africa must move towards either unity or co-operation, unity of Africa. The leadership of the future, of the 21st century, should have less respect, less respect for this thing called 'national sovereignty.' I'm not saying take up arms and destroy the state, no! This idea that we must *preserve* the Tanganyika, then *preserve* the Kenya as they *are*, is nonsensical!

The nation-states we in Africa, have inherited from Europe. They are the builders of the nation-states par excellence. For centuries they fought wars! The history of Europe, the history of the *building* of Europe is a history of war. And sometimes their wars when they get hotter although they're European wars, they call them *world wars*. And we all get involved. We fight even in Tanganyika here, we *fought* here, one world war.

These Europeans, powerful, where little Belgium is more powerful than the whole of Africa south of the Sahara put together; these *powerful* European states are moving towards unity, and you people are talking about the atavism of the tribe, this is nonsense! I am telling *you* people. How can anybody think of the tribe as the unity of the future? *Hakuna!* (There's nothing!).

Europe now, you can take it almost as God-given, Europe is not going to fight with Europe anymore. The Europeans are not going to take up arms against Europeans. They are moving towards unity - even the little, the little countries of the Balkans which are breaking up, Yugoslavia breaking up, but they are breaking up at the same time the building up is taking place. They break up and say we want to come into the *bigger* unity.

So there's a *building* movement, there's a *building* of Europe. These countries which have old, old sovereignties, countries of hundreds of years old; they are forgetting this, they are *moving* towards unity. And you people, you think Tanzania is sacred? What is Tanzania!

You *have* to move towards unity. If these powerful countries see that they have no future in the nation-states - *ninyi mnafikiri mna future katika nini*? (what future do you think you have?). So, if we

158

can't *move*, if our leadership, our future leadership cannot move us to bigger nation-states, which I *hope* they are going to try; we tried and failed. I tried and failed. One of my biggest failures was actually that. I tried in East Africa and failed.

But don't give up because we, the first leadership, failed, no! *Unajaribu tena*! (You try again!). We failed, but the idea is a good idea. That these countries should come together. Don't leave Rwanda and Burundi on their own. *Hawawezi kusurvive* (They cannot survive). They can't. They're locked up into a form of prejudice. If we can't move towards bigger nation-states, at least let's move towards greater co-operation. This is beginning to happen. And the new leadership in Africa should encourage it.

I want to say only one or two things about what is happening in southern Africa. Please accept the logic of coming together. South Africa, small; South Africa is very small. Their per capita income now is, I think $2,000 a year or something around that. Compared with Tanzanians, of course, it is very big, but it's poor. If South Africa begins to tackle the problems of the legacy of apartheid, they have no money!

But compared with the rest of us, they are rich. And so, in southern Africa, there, there is also a kind of osmosis, also an economic osmosis. South Africa's neighbours send their job seekers *into* South Africa. And South Africa will simply have to accept the logic of that, that they are big, they are attractive. They attract the unemployed from Mozambique, and from Lesotho and from the rest. They have to accept that fact of life. It's a problem, but they have to accept it.

South Africa, and I am talking about post-apartheid South Africa. Post-apartheid South Africa has the most developed and the most dynamic private sector on the continent. It is white, so what? So forget it is white. It is South African, dynamic, highly developed. If the investors of South Africa begin a new form of trekking, you *have* to accept it.

It will be ridiculous, absolutely ridiculous, for Africans to go out seeking investment from North America, from Japan, from Europe, from Russia, and then, when these investors come from South Africa to invest in your own country, you say, 'a! a! These fellows now want to take over our economy' - this is nonsense. You can't have it both ways. You want foreign investors or you don't want foreign investors. Now, the most available foreign investors for you are those from South Africa.

And let me tell you, when Europe think in terms of investing, they *might* go to South Africa. When North America think in terms of investing, they *might* go to South Africa. Even Asia, if they want to invest, the first country they may think of in Africa *may* be South Africa. So, if *your* South Africa is going to be *your* engine of development, accept the reality, accept the reality. Don't accept this sovereignty, South Africa will reduce your sovereignty. What sovereignty do you have?

Many of these debt-ridden countries in Africa now have no sovereignty, they've lost it. *Imekwenda* (It's gone). *Iko mikononi mwa IMF na World Bank* (It's in the hands of the IMF and the World Bank). *Unafikiri kuna sovereignty gani*? (What kind of sovereignty do you think there is?)

So, southern Africa has an opportunity, southern Africa, the SADC group, *because* of South Africa.

Because South Africa now is no longer a destabiliser of the region, but a partner in development, southern Africa has a tremendous opportunity. But you need leadership, because if you get proper leadership there, within the next 10, 15 years, that region is going to be the ASEAN (Association of South-East Asian Nations) of Africa. And it is possible. But forget the protection of your sovereignties. I believe the South Africans will be sensitive enough to know that if they are not careful, there is going to be this resentment of big brother, but that big brother, frankly, is not very big.

West Africa. Another bloc is developing there, but that depends very much upon Nigeria my brother (looking at the Nigerian High Commissioner - Ambassador), very much so. Without Nigeria, the future of West Africa is a problem. West Africa is more balkanised than Eastern Africa. More balkanised, tiny little states.

The leadership will have to come from Nigeria. It came from Nigeria in Liberia; it has come from Nigeria in the case of Sierra Leone; it will have to come from Nigeria in galvanising ECOWAS.

But the military in Nigeria must allow the Nigerians to exercise that vitality in freedom. And it is my hope that they will do it.

I told you I was going to ramble and it was going to be messy, but thank you very much. – (Julius K. Nyerere in Godfrey Mwakikagile, *Nyerere and Africa: End of an Era*, New Africa Press, 2010, pp. 553 - 560. Source: Mwalimu Nyerere Memorial Site: Written Speeches, South Centre, Geneva, Switzerland, 2001. This is an abridged version of Nyerere's speech at an international conference at the University of Dar es Salaam, Tanzania, December 15, 1997. The transcription of the non-written speech came from Mrs. Magombe of the Nyerere Foundation, Dar es Salaam. Translation of Swahili words, phrases and sentences in Nyerere's speech into English in the preceding text, done by the author, Godfrey Mwakikagile).

Professor Haroub Othman of the University of Dar es Salaam said that was Nyerere at his best; it was one of his best speeches if not the best, he said.

It was a fitting farewell to Africa. Nyerere died almost two years later after warning his fellow Africans as an elder statesman in that speech: "Africa south of the Sahara is on its own."

And as Nkrumah stated years earlier in the sixties: "Africa Must Unite." That was also the title of his book published to coincide with the first meeting of the 32 African heads of state and government who met in Addis Ababa, Ethiopia, from 22 – 25 May 1963 and formed the Organisation of African Unity (OAU) on the last day of the conference.

The countries which were the founding members of the OAU were Algeria, Burundi, Cameroun, Central African republic, Chad, Congo-Brazzaville, Congo-Leopoldville, Dahomey, Ethiopia, Gabon, Ghana, Guinea, Ivory Coast, Liberia, Libya, Madagascar, Mali, Mauritania, Morocco, Niger, Nigeria, Rwanda, Senegal, Sierra Leone, Somalia, Sudan, Tanganyika, Togo, Tunisia, Uganda, United Arab Republic, and Upper Volta.

The rest joined in the following years after they became independent.

Although African leaders failed to unite their countries under one government in the sixties, as urged by Nkrumah, they were at least united in their goal to liberate the countries which were still under white minority rule and eventually succeeded in doing so.

In his seminal work, *Nyerere and Africa: End of an Era,* Godfrey Mwakikagile has written extensively about the liberation struggle, and the liberation movements, in Southern Africa in what is probably one of the best accounts of that critical phase in the history of Africa. He has also, in the same book, written an excellent analysis of the Congo Crisis during the turbulent sixties.

Godfrey Mwakikagile has also written a book about

the struggle against apartheid and the end of white minority rule in South Africa and on the prospects and challenges the country faces in the post-apartheid era. The work is entitled, *South Africa in Contemporary Times.*

The years he spent on the editorial staff at the *Standard* and the *Daily News* were critical to his future career as a writer. Those were his formative years, and had he not become a news reporter, his life, and his career as an author, might have taken a different turn. As he states in *Nyerere and Africa: End of an Era*, he was first hired by renowned British journalist David Martin who was the deputy managing and news editor of the Tanganyika *Standard*. The managing editor was Brendon Grimshaw, also British who, in the seventies, bought Moyenne Island in the Seychelles and became its only permanent inhabitant. Brendon Grimshaw also played a major role in recruiting Godfrey Mwakikagile as a member of the editorial staff at the *Standard*.[32]

It was a turning point in Godfrey Mwakikagile's life.

That was in June 1969 when he was a student at Tambaza High School in Dar es Salaam. He was 19 years old and probably the youngest reporter on the editorial staff at the *Standard* during that time.

The *Standard* which was renamed *Daily News* in 1972 was the largest English newspaper in Tanzania and one of the largest and most influential in East Africa. And it served Godfrey Mwakikagile well, not only in terms of providing him with an opportunity to sharpen his writing skills but also – after it became the *Daily News* – in helping him to go to school in the United States where he became an author many years after he graduated from college.

David Martin, when he worked at the Tanganyika *Standard* and at the *Daily News*, and thereafter, was the most prominent foreign journalist in Eastern and Southern Africa in the sixties and seventies. And he wrote extensively about the liberation struggle in the region for the London *Observer* and for BBC.

He went to the combat zone with FRELIMO guerrilla fighters in Mozambique and also covered the Angolan civil war for BBC and for CBC (Canadian Broadcasting Corporation).

He knew and worked closely with all the leaders of the liberation movements including Robert Mugabe, Dr. Eduardo Mondlane, president of FRELIMO, who was assassinated in Dar es Salaam, Tanzania, in February 1969; and Mondlane's successor Samora Machel who died in a "mysterious" plane crash in 1986 when he was president of Mozambique.

The plane crashed on the South African side of the border with Mozambique and the apartheid regime was suspected of having caused the "accident." He was succeeded by Mozambique's foreign affairs minister, Joaquim Chissano, as president.

David Martin was also very close to many Tanzanian leaders including President Julius Nyerere, and President Benjamin Mkapa who was also his close friend for many years since the sixties when they worked together in the media.

He also interviewed President Kenneth Kaunda of Zambia during the liberation struggle when many freedom fighters were based in that country and used it as an operational base as they did Tanzania.

He wrote more than 20 books. He died at his home in Harare, Zimbabwe, in August 2007, where he went to live after Zimbabwe won independence in April 1980.

President Mugabe delivered an official condolence message and David Martin was accorded a state-assisted funeral in recognition of his works exposing apartheid South Africa's destabalisation campaign in neighbouring countries, racial brutalities and injustices under white minority regimes throughout Southern Africa and for his outstanding role as a champion of racial equality.

The report of his death which included President

Robert Mugabe's long message of condolence on behalf of the government and the ruling party ZANU-PF was published in the Zimbabwean government-owned newspaper, *The Herald*, 22 August 2007, headlined, "President Mourns David Martin."[33]

Another report on David Martin's contributions as a journalist when he reported extensively on the liberation struggle in Southern Africa, and on his support for regional integration of the countries in that part of the continent after the end of white minority rule, was published in the same paper on August 24, headlined, "Martin – Man of Many Talents."[34]

He was buried in Harare, the capital of Zimbabwe. Mozambican President Armando Guebuza and former Tanzanian President Benjamin Mkapa were some of the African leaders who sent condolence messages.

Zimbabwean government leaders including cabinet members, Tanzanian officials, war veterans who fought for Zimbabwe's independence during the liberation struggle in the sixties and seventies, and diplomats, attended the funeral, according to *The Herald*, Harare, Zimbabwe, 25 August 2007, in a report headlined, "Martin Laid to Rest."[35]

David Martin often said he credited his education to the 10 years he spent working as a journalist in Tanzania and was inspired by President Nyerere and by the liberation leaders and movements based there. He interviewed many of those leaders many times during the liberation struggle and thereafter.

In his book *Nyerere and Africa: End of an Era*, Godfrey Mwakikagile has written about David Martin and the role he played as a journalist during the liberation struggle in Southern Africa. But David Martin was also instrumental in opening the door for Godfrey Mwakikagile into the world of journalism, writing everyday, after which both became successful writers.[36]

Godfrey Mwakikagile himself has stated in his books

– *Nyerere and Africa: End of an Era, Africa after Independence: Realities of Nationhood, The Modern African State: Quest for Transformation,Military Coups in West Africa Since The Sixties* and in *Africa is in A Mess: What Went Wrong and What Should Be Done* – that his background as a news reporter which included meeting deadlines when writing news articles prepared him for the rigorous task of writing books.[37]

Criticism of post-colonial Africa

Godfrey Mwakikagile lived and grew up under the leadership of Tanzanian President Julius Nyerere, a legendary figure, liberation icon and staunch Pan-Africanist and one of the most influential and most respected leaders Africa has ever produced, whose socialist policies he has also defended in his writings because of the egalitarian ideals they instilled in the people of Tanzania enabling them to build a peaceful, cohesive nation in which they saw themselves as one people and equal in terms of rights and dignity as fellow human beings in spite of the poverty they endured under ujamaa, Nyerere's African version of socialism.

Yet, in spite of his admiration for liberation icons, he also is highly critical of African leaders from the same generation who led their countries to independence, contending that most of them did not care about the well-being of their people; a position he forcefully articulates in his writings.[38]

He gives them a lot of credit for leading the struggle for independence and contends that they were very successful in mobilising the masses and the elite and in fuelling nationalist sentiments to end colonial rule. But he also bluntly states that they were, in most cases, a tragic failure in terms of nation building and national development during the post-colonial era.

They fostered divided loyalties along ethnic and regional lines, practised tribalism, and pursued wrong policies. They embraced and adopted imported -isms especially Marxism and other alien ideologies while ignoring indigenous knowledge, institutions and systems of thought – which are relevant to African conditions, local circumstances and historical experience – in the quest for development.

They formulated unrealistic development plans and programmes, launched unnecessary capital-intensive projects just for demonstration effect, and underutilised human capital including abundant labour for labour-intensive projects.

They mismanaged the economy, squandered resources, stole from the people, raided national coffers, bankrupted the treasury, enriched themselves, institutionalised corruption, instituted the highly centralised state as an oppressive apparatus for mass regimentation although it also served as an effective instrument of mobilisation of resources and manpower that was unfortunately misused or wasted in most cases.

And they tortured, imprisoned and killed their critics and opponents, muzzled the opposition and stifled dissent instead of encouraging cross-fertilisation of ideas across the spectrum which could have led to formulation of better policies critical to nation building and economic development, as he clearly states in his books, *Economic Development in Africa, Africa After Independence: Realities of Nationhood, The Modern African State: Quest for Transformation,* and *Africa is in A Mess: What Went Wrong and What Should Be Done.*

It is an assessment, and a disillusionment with African leadership, that is shared by his fellow Africans. As Wole Soyinka stated when he saw Nigerian leaders assume power in October 1960 after the end of colonial rule, with pomp and ceremony, he became apprehensive about the future and knew, from then onwards, the enemy was now within, not without. The enemy was the new African leaders who went against everything they had fought for, totally ignoring the wellbeing of their people. Assumption of power was only a means to enrich themselves and trample on the rights of their fellow countrymen.

Godfrey Mwakikagile belongs to a generation that preceded independence and was partly brought up under colonial rule. He even wrote a book, *Life in Tanganyika in The Fifties*, about those years.

Independence meant a lot to him as much as it did to his fellow Africans. He even attended the independence celebrations when Tanganyika attained sovereign status under the leadership of Julius Nyerere.

He witnessed the flags changing at midnight when the Union Jack was lowered and the flag of the newly independent nation of Tanganyika went up. As he states in his autobiographical writings, he vividly remembers attending the independence celebrations with his uncle Johan Chonde Mwambapa, popularly known as Chonde, in the town of Tukuyu. His uncle took him on a bicycle to Tukuyu, four miles north of their home area, to witness the historic occasion. The celebrations were held on a football (soccer) field. He was 12 years old.

Early in his life when he was a teenager, he developed strong Pan-Africanist views under the influence of Julius Nyerere and other Pan-Africanist leaders such as Kwame Nkrumah and Ahmed Sekou Toure. He still holds those views today, crystallised into an ideology for a new African liberation and forcefully articulated in his writings.

He writes as an African more than anything else, not just as a Tanzanian. As Professor Guy Martin states in his book *African Political Thought* about Godfrey Mwakikagile and other Pan-Africanist theorists and thinkers, their individual national identities are secondary to their primary identity as Africans and even irrelevant when they articulate their position from a Pan-African perspective:

> Note that all these scholars are dedicated Pan-Africanists and many would shun the reference to their nationality, preferring to be simply called 'Africans'.... Some of the most prominent Africanist-populist scholars include... Godfrey Mwakikagile....
>
> Chapter 4 is a survey of Pan-Africanism as a political and cultural ideal and movement eventually leading to African unity.... The chapter first shows how the Pan-Africanist leaders' dream for immediate political and economic integration in the form of a 'United States of Africa' was deferred in favor of a gradualist-functionalist approach....
>
> The chapter then analyzes the reasons for the failure of the Pan-Africanist leaders' dream of unity... and surveys past and current proposals for a revision of the map of Africa and a reconfiguration of the African states put forward by various authors such as Cheikh Anta Diop, Marc-Louis Ropivia, Makau wa Mutua, Arthur Gakwandi, Joseph Ki-Zerbo, Daniel Osabu-Kle, Godfrey Mwakikagile, Pelle Danabo, and Mueni wa Muiu....
>
> Chapter eight reviews the ideas and values for a new, free, and self-reliant Africa put forth by African academics who have the best interest of the people at heart and thus advocate a popular type of democracy and development. However, unlike the populist-socialist scholars, these African-populist scholars refuse to operate within the parameters of Western ideologies – whether of the socialist, Marxist-Leninist, or liberal-democratic persuasion – and call on Africans to get rid of their economic, technological, and cultural dependency syndrome.
>
> These scholars are also convinced that the solutions to African problems lie within Africans themselves. Thus they refuse to remain passive victims of a perceived or preordained fate and call on all Africans to become the initiators and agents of their own development.... For the reasons stated previously, the chapter will focus exclusively on the last four scholars mentioned: namely, Osabu-Kle, Ake, Mwakikagile, and Muiu. – Guy Martin, *African Political Thought*, New York: Palgrave Macmillan, 2012, pp. 8, 6).

One of Godfrey Mwakikagile's critics has described him as "a shrewd intellectual in defence of liberation icons" and accuses him of not being intellectually honest about leaders such as Nyerere, Nkrumah and Sekou Toure for not criticising them harshly for their failures because he admires them so much as staunch Pan-Africanists.[39]

In a way, some people may see him as a complex character not always easy to understand, although he articulates his position clearly and forcefully.

Some of the confusion among his readers about his position on African leaders of the independence generation has to do with his own background since he was an integral part of that generation in the sense that he witnessed the end of colonial rule and the emergence of the newly independent African states although he was not old enough to have participated in the independence struggle himself.[40]

He admires the leaders who led their countries to independence, yet he is highly critical of them in most cases for their failures during the post-colonial period. He became disillusioned with the leadership on the continent through the years, filled with broken promises, and not long after the countries won independence. He admires many aspects of Nyerere's socialist policies in Tanzania, yet concedes the policies were also a failure in many cases. And he strongly favours fundamental change in African countries, yet he is nostalgic about the past.[41]

His advocacy for fundamental change is articulated in many of his writings including *The Modern African State: Quest for Transformation*, which was published in 2001 and which is also one of his most well-known books.

In his review of the book, Ronald Taylor-Lewis [born of a Sierra Leonean father], editor of *Mano Vision* magazine, London, described it as "a masterpiece of fact and analysis."[42]

The book has also been reviewed in other publications. Tana Worku Anglana reviewed Godfrey Mwakikagile's *Modern African State: Quest for Transformation* in *Articolo* and described it as "unbiased literature."[43]

Other people have also cited the book in their different analyses of the African condition. They include Dr. Elavie Ndura, a professor at George Mason University in Virginia, USA, who used Godfrey Mwakikagile's book,

The Modern African State: Quest for Transformation, among other works, in supporting her central thesis in her study, "Transcending The Majority Rights and Minority Protection Dichotomy Through Multicultural Reflective Citizenship in The African Great Lakes Region," in *Intercultural Education*, Vol. 17, No. 2, published by Routledge, Taylor & Francis Group, in May 2006.

Professor Elavie Ndura, a Hutu from Burundi where her family experienced genocide, taught for many years at a number of schools in the United States, including the University of Nevada-Reno and George Mason University. Ethnic conflicts in Rwanda and Burundi between the Hutu and the Tutsi is one of the subjects Godfrey Mwakikagile has addressed extensively in his books, *The Modern African State: Quest for Transformation, Identity Politics and Ethnic Conflicts in Rwanda and Burundi: A Comparative Study, Burundi: The Hutu and the Tutsi: Cauldron of Conflict and Quest for Dynamic Compromise, Peace and Stability in Rwanda and Burundi: The Road Not Taken*, and *Civil Wars in Rwanda and Burundi: Conflict Resolution in Africa.*

In many of his writings, Godfrey Mwakikagile focuses on internal factors – including corruption, tribalism and tyranny by African leaders – as the main cause of Africa's predicament, but not to the total exclusion of external forces.

And the position he articulates in his writings on many issues is cited by other people to support their arguments in their works.

One of the works in which Godfrey Mwakikagile is cited and quoted is a compiled study by Professor Robert H. Bates of Harvard University, *When Things Fell Apart: State Failure in Late-Century Africa: Cambridge Studies in Comparative Politics*, published by Cambridge University Press in February 2008.

Godfrey Mwakikagile is also quoted by Professors Robert Elgie and Sophie Moestrup in their book, *Semi-*

Presidentialism Outside Europe: A Comparative Study – Routledge Research in Comparative Politics, Routledge, 2007; Mueni wa Muiu and Guy Martin in *A New Paradigm of the African State: Fundi wa Afrika*, Palgrave Macmillan, 2009; Minabere Ibelema, *The African Press, Civic Cynicism, and Democracy - The PalgraveMacmillan Series in International Political Communication*, Palgrave Macmillan, 2007; James Crawford and Vaughan Lowe in *British Yearbook of International Law 2005: Volume 76*, Oxford University Press, 2007, and in other works.

Others who have cited Godfrey Mwakikagile and his works include Professor Robert I. Rotberg, director at Harvard University's John F. Kennedy School of Government and president emeritus of the World Peace Foundation. He used Godfrey Mwakikagle's book *Ethnic Politics in Kenya and Nigeria*, among other works, to document his study, *Crafting The New Nigeria: Confronting The Challenges*, a book that was published in 2004.

Other researchers and scholars who have cited and quoted Godfrey Mwakikagile in their works include Gabi Hesselbein, Frederick Golooba-Mutebi, and James Putzel,James in their study, "Economic and Political Foundations of State-making in Africa: Understanding State Reconstruction", Crisis States Research Centre, London School of Economics and Political Science, London, UK, 2006; E.M. Poff, "Liberal Democracy and Multiethnic States: A Case Study of Ethnic Politics in Kenya," Ohio University, 2008; PJ McGowan, "Coups and Conflict in West Africa, 1955 - 2004: Part II, Empirical Findings," Armed Forces and Society, Sage Publications, 2006; Christopher Richard Kilford, in his doctoral dissertation, "The Other Cold War," Queens University, Canada, 2009.

Others are Martin P. Mathews, in his book, *Nigeria: Current Issues and Historical Background*, Nova Science Publishers, New York, 2002; Michael Kweku Addison,

"Preventing Military Intervention in West Africa: A Case Study of Ghana," Naval Postgraduate School, Monterey, California, USA, 2002; Isidore Okpewho and N Nzegwu, in their book, *The New African Diaspora*, Indiana University Press, 2009; C.M. Brown, S. Reader and G. Lober, "US National Security Interests in Africa and The Future Global War on Terrorism (GWOT)," Naval Postgraduate School, Monterey, California, USA, 2005.

Nigerian scholar Adaobi Chiamaka Iheduru of Wright State University also used Godfrey Mwakikagile's books, *Relations between Africans and African Americans: Misconceptions, Myths and Realities*, and *Africans and African Americans: Complex Relations, Prospects and Challenges*, to complement her research for her doctorate in psychology. Her dissertation was "Examining the Social Distance between Africans and African Americans: The Role of Internalized Racism."

Another Nigerian scholar, Rotimi T. Suberu, a political science lecturer at the University of Ibadan, Nigeria, used Godfrey Mwakikagile's book *Ethnic Politics in Kenya and Nigeria*, among different works by other scholars, in his analysis, "Federalism and Ethnic Conflict in Nigeria," published in the *African Studies Review 46, No. 2*, September 2003, pp. 93–98.

Godfrey Mwakikagile's book *Ethnic Politics in Kenya and Nigeria* was also used by Dickson Onwuka Uduma, a Nigerian, who earned a master's degree in development and international relations from Aalborg University in Denmark. He wrote a thesis on Nigerian federalism and how it attempts to accommodate ethnicity and nationalism, at the same time, entitled, "Ethnic Identity Politics: Nigeria as a Case Study," and drew on the work of Godfrey Mwakikagile and other scholars.

Jimmy Ssentongo, a Ugandan, used Godfrey Mwakikagile's book, *Ethnicity and National Identity in Uganda*, among other works by other scholars, to write his doctoral dissertation, "Ethnicity and Socio-Economic

Exclusion in Uganda: Perceptions, Indicators and Spaces for Pluralism with Specific Reference to Cosmopolitan Kampala," which he completed at the University of Humanistic Studies, Utrecht, Netherlands.

Professor Michael Vickers, University of Oxford, in his book *Ethnicity and Sub-Nationalism in Nigeria: Movement for a Mid-West State* (Oxford, UK: WorldView Publishing, 2001), also cited Godfrey Mwakikagile, among other scholars, to document and support the central thesis of his book.

Gerald Anietie Ignatius Akata, a Nigerian, used Godfrey Mwakikagile's book, *Military Coups in West Africa Since the Sixties*, together with the works of other scholars, to complete his PhD dissertation in education, "Leadership in the Niger Delta Region of Nigeria: A Study of the Perceptions of Its Impact on the Acquired Leadership Skills of Expatriate Nigerian Postgraduates," at East Tennessee State University.

Another scholar, Paul K. Bjerk, an American, used some of Godfrey Mwakikagile's works, including *Nyerere and Africa: End of an Era*, in his research for his doctoral dissertation at the University of Wisconsin-Madison. His dissertation was "Julius Nyerere and the Establishment of Sovereignty in Tanganyika." Professor Bjerk also taught at Tumaini University in Tanzania for three years before he went to teach at Texas Tech University.

Katrina Demulling of Boston University also relied on Godfrey Mwakikagile's work, *Nyerere and Africa: End of an Era*, together with the works of other scholars, to write her doctoral thesis, "We are One: The Emergence and Development of National Consciousness in Tanzania." As she stated:

> The primary works included in this discussion are: Godfrey Mwakikagile's *Nyerere and Africa: End of an Era*, William Smith's *We Must run While Others Walk: A Portrait of Africa's Julius Nyerere*, A.B. Assensoh's *African Political Leadership: Jomo Kenyatta, Kwame*

Nkrumah, and Julius Nyerere, Juma Aley's *Twenty One Years of Leadership Contrasts and Similarities*, and John Charles Hatch's *Two African Statesmen: Kaunda of Zambia and Nyerere of Tanzania*. A number of other articles and books will also be referenced. – (Katrina Demulling, "We are One: The Emergence and Development of National Consciousness in Tanzania," Boston University Theses and Dissertations, 2015, p. 212).

Prince Kwasi Bediako Frimpong, a Ghanaian, also used Godfrey Mwakikagile's book, *Nyerere and Africa: End of an Era*, to complement his research for his thesis, "Nrumahism and Neo-Nkrumahism," to earn an M.A. degree from the University of Louisville, Kentucky, USA.

Professor Ronald Aminzade of the University of Minnesota also used Godfrey Mwakikagile's books, *Nyerere and Africa: End of an Era*, and *The Union of Tanganyika and Zanzibar: Product of The Cold War?*, among other works by other scholars, in his research for his book, *Race, Nation and Citizenship in Post-Colonial Africa: The Case of Tanzania*, Cambridge University Press, New York, 2013. As he states in his book concerning the union of Tanganyika and Zanzibar which Godfrey Mwakikagile has addressed extensively and which is also one of the subjects he has tackled in his work *Race, Nation and Citizenship in Post-Colonial Africa: The Case of Tanzania*:

> There is considerable disagreement among scholars about why Tanganyika chose to unite with the residents of a relatively small island off its coast. One compelling account highlights the role of foreign powers, especially the United States, which was worried about communists in Zanzibar's government and feared a 'Cuba off the coast of Africa' would spread revolution throughout the African continent. The Union did take place at the height of the Cold War, amid rumors of a Cuban presence on Zanzibar....
>
> An alternative account of the creation of the Union was that it was a victory for African unity and pan-African solidarity. This view is forcefully argued by Godfrey Mwakikagile, who contends that the Union was an African initiative and an expression of Nyerere's pan-African commitment rather than a product of Cold War

pressures....When Nyerere urged the Tanganyikan Parliament to approve the Union, he emphasized it was a first step toward a united Africa. It demonstrated that 'a single Government in Africa is not an impossible dream, but something which can be realized....If two countries can unite, then three can; if three can, then thirty can' (Nyerere, "The Union of Tanganyika and Zanzibar," *Freedom and Unity*, p 292).

In justifying the Union as part of an effort to promote Pan-Africanism, Nyerere emphasized the commonalities between the mainland and the islands, including a common language and historical and cultural ties.... Nyerere further portrayed the Union as a product of 'the overall desire for African unity,' arguing that 'those who welcome unity on our continent must welcome this small move toward it.' 'It is an insult to Africa,' he said, 'to read cold war politics into every move toward African unity' (ibid)....

Support for the merger with the mainland from Abdulrahman Babu and Kassim Hanga, the two Marxist-Leninists who generated the most concern on the part of Western governments, suggests that the union was also not simply the product of a Western anticommunist conspiracy engineered by the United States and Great Britain. (Ronald Aminzade, *Race, Nation and Citizenship in Post-Colonial Africa: The Case of Tanzania*, pp. 99 – 100, 101, 102).

Godfrey Mwakikagile's book, *The Union of Tanganyika and Zanzibar: Product of the Cold War?* cited by Professor Ronald Aminzade, is a strong rebuttal to the argument that Cold War politics provided probably the only context in which the merger of the two East African countries took – and could have taken – place as if union of African countries is impossible unless it is externally engineered.

The union of Tanganyika and Zanzibar and the Zanzibar revolution are subjects Godfrey Mwakikagile has also addressed in detail in two of his other books:*Why Tanganyika united with Zanzibar to form Tanzania* and *Africa in The Sixties*.

Mwakikagile's books have been used by other scholars in their research in different academic disciplines.

German scholar Christa Deiwiks of ETH Zurich, a university in Zurich, Switzerland, where she also earned a master's degree in comparative and international studies, used Godfrey Mwakikagile's book, *Ethnic Politics in Kenya and Nigeria*, a comparative study, in her research for her doctoral degree which she obtained from the same university. Her dissertation was "Ethnofederalism – A Slippery Slope Towards Secessionist Conflict?"

Godfrey Mwakikagile is also cited in the work of Dr. Stephen Macharia Magu, *Political Economy, Social Development and Conflict in Africa*.

Richard L. Whitehead used Godfrey Mwakikagile's book, *Tanzania under Mwalimu Nyerere: Reflections on an African Statesman*, together with the works of other scholars, to write a dissertation for his PhD at Temple University, USA. His dissertation was "Single-Party Rule in a Multiparty Age: Tanzania in Comparative Perspective."

Other people, not just academicians and students, have cited Godfrey Mwakikagile's works in different analyses across the ideological spectrum. They include Tom Hayden, a prominent American radical of the sixties who wrote the *Port Huron Statement* – he was a strong opponent of the Vietnam War and and a leading supporter of the civil rights movement and was a social activist for decades. He used Godfrey Mwakikagile's works including *Congo in The Sixties*, among others by different scholars and political analysts, when he wrote his book, *Listen, Yankee!: Why Cuba Matters*.

Others who also have cited Godfrey Mwakikagile in their studies in different analytical contexts include Rajend Methrie, "South Africa: The Rocky Road to National Building," in a book, Andrew Simpson,*Language and National Identity in Africa*, Oxford University Press, 2008; Valéria Cristina Salles, "Social Representations Informing Discourse of Young Leaders: A Case Study of Tanzania," University of Cape Town, 2005; L.B. Inniss, "A Domestic Right of Return? Race, Rights, and Residency in New Orleans in the Aftermath of Katrina," in the *Boston*

College Third World Law Journal, Boston, Massachusetts, USA, 2007.

Others scholars who have used Mwakikagile's works include Eric M. Edi, in his book, *Globalization and Politics in the Economic Community of West African States (Carolina Academic Press Studies on Globalization and Society)*, Carolina Academic Press, 2007; James John Chikago, in his book, *Crossing Cultural Frontiers: Analysis and Solutions to Poverty Reduction*, 2003; James Kwesi Anquandah, Naana Jane Opoku-Agyemang, and Michel R. Doortmont, in their book, *The Transatlantic Slave Trade: Landmarks, Legacies, Expectations*, Sub-Saharan Publishers, Accra, Ghana, 2007; Luciana Ricciutelli, Angela Rose Miles, Margaret McFadden in their book, *Feminist Politics, Activism and Vision: Local and Global Challenges*, Zed Books, London, 2005; Emmanuel Ike Udogu, in his book, *African Renaissance in the Millennium: The Political, Social, and Economic Discourses on the Way Forward*, Lexington Books, New York, 2007; and others.

Godfrey Mwakikagile's books have been used by many other scholars in different analytical contexts in a number of countries in the Third World and in industrialised nations.

And his diagnosis of – and prescription for – Africa's ailments has also been cited by scholars and other people for its relevance in other parts of the Third World. As Dr. Hengene Payani, a political scientist at the University of Papua New Guinea in Port Moresby, Papua New Guinea, stated in his review of Godfrey Mwakikagile's book *Africa is in A Mess* on amazon.com:

> The book is excellent, honest and thought-provoking and is relevant even in the context of Papua New Guinea, a country which has been ruined by greedy politicians.

He also contacted Godfrey Mwakikagile to

congratulate him for his work.

Although he has written mostly about Africa, and as a political scientist or as a political analyst, his works cover a wide range of scholarship including American studies.

One of Godfrey Mwakikagile's books, *Black Conservatives in The United States*, was cited by Christopher Alan Bracey, a professor of law and African-American Studies at Washington University in St. Louis, Missouri, USA, in support of his research when he also wrote a book about black conservatives entitled *Saviors or Sellouts: The Promise and Peril of Black Conservatism, from Booker T. Washington to Condoleezza Rice*, published in February 2008.

Dr. Michael L. Ondaatje, a lecturer at The University of New Castle, Australia, also used Godfrey Mwakikagile's book on black conservatives, among other works by other scholars, for his doctoral dissertation on the rise of black conservative intellectuals in the United States. He earned his PhD from the University of Western Australia and wrote a book, *Black Conservative Intellectuals in Modern America* (University of Pennsylvania Press 2009) in which he cited Godfrey Mwakikagile's work to complement his research. The book is based on his doctoral dissertation.

But there are limitations to the role played by people like Godfrey Mwakikagile in their quest for fundamental change in African countries. Their contribution is limited in one fundamental respect: They are not actively involved with the masses at the grassroots level precisely because of what they are. They belong to an elite class, and the concepts they expound as well as the solutions they propose are discussed mainly by fellow elites but rarely implemented.

This should not be misconstrued as unwarranted criticism of Godfrey Mwakikagile's writings or the role he plays in the quest for fundamental change in Africa. It is mere acknowledgement of the limitations he faces in his attempt to accomplish this task in conjunction with his brethren across the continent.

Still, there is no question that in many cases, only a few members of the African elite have played and continue to play the role of intellectual activists like Dr. Walter Rodney who wrote his best-selling book, *How Europe Underdeveloped Africa*, in the early 1970s when he was teaching at the University of Dar es Salaam in Tanzania; coincidentally during the same period when Godfrey Mwakikagile was a member of the editorial staff at the *Daily News* in Tanzania's capital Dar es Salaam.

In fact, it was one of his colleagues at the *Daily News*, renowned Kenyan journalist and socio-political analyst Philip Ochieng, who edited Walter Rodney's book, *How Europe Underdeveloped Africa*.

The book was published by Tanzania Publishing House (TPH), Dar es Salaam, in 1973. Ochieng also wrote a feature article, "How Africa Developed Europe," in the *Daily News* in 1972, about Rodney's book, not long before the book was first published by Bogle-L'Ouverture Publications, London, that year.

In an interview with one of Kenya's leading newspapers, the *Daily Nation*, Nairobi, on 6 July 2013, where he worked as an editor and columnist, Philip Ochieng, who coincidentally was also a close friend of Barack Obama Sr., the father of US President Barack Obama, stated that it was he who edited Rodney's book when he was working at the *Daily News* in Dar es Salaam in 1972. As he stated:

> Walter Rodney was my friend and I even edited his seminal work *How Europe Underdeveloped Africa*. Dar es Salaam was the world headquarters of intellectual debate those days.

One of the revolutionary thinkers who was drawn to Tanzania was Che Guevara who, a few years earlier, stayed in Dar es Salaam for many months from October

1965 to the end of February 1966 after his attempts to help Lumumba's followers fight Western-backed forces in the former Belgian Congo failed. He also wrote his famous book, *The African Dream: The Diaries of the Revolutionary War in the Congo*, when he was staying in Dar es Salaam during those months.

It was also in the same year Che Guevara left Tanzania that Walter Rodney, who strongly admired Che, first arrived in Dar es Salaam to teach at the University of Dar es Salaam. He taught there from 1966 to 1967. He then left Dar es Salaam and went to teach at his alma mater, the University of the West Indies, Mona campus, Kingston, Jamaica.

In October 1968, the Jamaican government banned Rodney from teaching at the university. He was declared *persona non grata* and returned to Tanzania to teach at the University of Dar es Salaam from 1969 to 1974 before going back to Guyana, his home country, in the same year. He was actively involved in intellectual debates in Dar es Salaam, and at Makerere University, Kampala, Uganda, where he famously debated renowned Kenyan academic, Professor Ali Mazrui, whose ideological orientation sharply differed from Rodney's. Mazrui was teaching at Makerere during that period. He was the head of the political science department and dean of the faculty of arts and social sciences.

Walter Rodney also founded and led a discussion group at the University of Dar es Salaam whose members included Yoweri Museveni who was a student at the university during that period and who later became president of Uganda. Museveni was also one of Rodney's students.

Before returning to Tanzania from Jamaica in 1969, Walter Rodney was actively involved with the masses when he taught at the University of the West Indies in Kingston. He was expelled from Jamaica because of his political and intellectual activism and went to teach at the

University of Dar es Salaam in a country where his views and his role as an activist intellectual found acceptance under the leadership of President Julius Nyerere who was a superb intellectual himself and who was acknowledged as one even by some of his critics such as Professor Ali Mazrui.

In his book, *On Heroes and Uhuru-Worship: Essays on Independent Africa*, and in some of his other writings, Professor Mazrui described Nyerere as "the most original thinker" among all the leaders in Anglophone Africa, and Senegalese President Leopold Sedar Senghor in Francophone Africa.

Mazrui also described Nyerere as the most intellectual of the East African presidents, an attribute which enabled Walter Rodney to thrive in Tanzania as an intellectual activist. As he stated in his lecture at the University of Nairobi, "Towards Re-Africanizing African Universities: Who Killed Intellectualism in Post-Colonial Africa?," in September 2003:

> The most intellectual of East Africa's Heads of State at the time was Julius K. Nyerere of Tanzania – a true philosopher, president and original thinker.

And in an interview with *The Gambia Echo* in February 2008, Professor Mazrui also stated:

> The fact that Nkrumah had a greater positive impact on me than has any other leader does not necessarily mean that I admire Nkrumah the most. Intellectually, I admired Julius K. Nyerere of Tanzania higher than most politicians anywhere in the world. Nyerere and I also met more often over the years from 1967 to 1997 approximately. I am also a great fan of Nelson Mandela. By ethical standards Mandela is greater than Nyerere; but by intellectual standards Nyerere is greater than Mandela.

Years before then, Professor Mazrui also stated the following:

Julius Nyerere is the most enterprising of African political philosophers. He has philosophized extensively in both English and Kiswahili.

He has tried to tear down the language barriers between ancestral cultural philosophy and the new ideological tendency of the post-colonial era.

Nyerere is superbly eloquent in both English and Kiswahili. He has allowed the two languages to enrich each other as their ideas have passed through his intellect.

His concept of *ujamaa* as a basis of African socialism was itself a brilliant cross-cultural transition. *Ujamaa* traditionally implied *ethnic* solidarity. But Nyerere transformed it from a dangerous principle of ethnic nepotism into more than a mere equivalent of the European word 'socialism.'

In practice his socialist policies did not work – as much for global reasons as for domestic. But in intellectual terms Nyerere is a more original thinker than Kwame Nkrumah – and linguistically much more innovative.

Nkrumah tried to update Lenin – from Lenin's *Imperialism: The Highest Stage of Capitalism* to Nkrumah's *Neo-Colonialism: The Last Stage of Imperialism*. Nyerere translated Shakespeare into Kiswahili instead – both *Julius Caesar* and *The Merchant of Venice*.

Nkrumah's exercise in Leninism was a less impressive cross-cultural achievement than Nyerere's translation of Shakespeare into an African language.

Yet both these African thinkers will remain among the towering figures of the twentieth century in politics and thought. – (Ali A. Mazrui in Ali. A. Mazrui, ed., *General History of Africa VIII: Africa Since 1935*, Berkeley, California, USA: University of California Press, 1993, p. 674; Ali A. Mazrui, *African Thought in Comparative Perspective*, Newcastle upon Tyne: Cambridge Scholars Publishing, 2014, p. 22).

Jonathan Power, a British conservative who described Nyerere as "independent Africa's greatest leader" but who was critical of his socialist policies and one-party rule, stated the following in his article, "Lament for Independent Africa's Greatest Leader":

Tanzania in East Africa has long been one of the 25 poorest countries in the world. But there was a time when it was described, in terms of its political influence, as one of the top 25. It puched far abovoe its weight. That formidable achievement was the work of one man (Julius Nyerere), now lying close to death in a London hospital....

His extraordinary intelligence, verbal and literary originality...and apparent commitment to non-violence made him not just an icon in his own country but of a large part of the activist sixties' generation in the white world who, not all persuaded of the heroic virtues of Fidel Castro and Che Guevara, desperately looked for a more sympathetic role model.

Measured against most of his peers, Jomo Kenyatta of Kenya, Kwame Nkrumah of Ghana, Ahmed Sekou Toure of Guinea, he towered above them. On the intellectual plane only the rather remote president of Senegal, the great poet and author of Negritude, Leopold Senghor, came close to him.

Not only was Nyerere financially open, modest and honest, he was uncorrupted by fame and position. He remained, throughout his life, self-effacing and unpretentious. Above all, he inspired his own people to resist the tugs of tribalism and pull together as one people. To this day Tanzania remains one of the very few African countries that has not experienced serious tribal division....

He was to become the eminence grise of the southern African liberation movements in Angola, Zimbabwe, Namibia and South Africa extending a wide open embrace to their operations. For this his country paid a heavy price, both in material terms but also because of Nyerere's role as interlocutur with the West demanded enormous amounts of time and energy. – (Jonathan Power, "Lament for Independent Africa's Greatest Leader," TFF Jonathan Power Columns, London, 6 October 1999).

Professor Ali Mazrui also paid glowing tribute to Nyerere when Nyerere died in October 1999. As he stated in his article "Nyerere and I":

He was one of the giants of the 20th century.... He did bestride this narrow world like an African colossus....

'The two top Swahili-speaking intellectuals of the second half of the 20th century are Julius Nyerere and Ali Mazrui.' That is how I was introduced to an Africanist audience in 1986 when I was on a lecture-tour of the United States to promote my television series: *The Africans: A Triple Heritage* (BBC-PBS). I regarded the tribute as one of the best compliments I had ever been paid. In reality, Mwalimu Nyerere was much more eloquent as a Swahili orator than I although Kiswahili is my mother tongue and not his.

In the month of Nyerere's death (14 October 1999), the comparison between the Mwalimu and I took a sadder form. A number of organisations in South Africa had united to celebrate Africa's Human Rights Day on October 22. Long before he was admitted to hospital, they had invited him to be their high-profile banquet speaker.

When Nyerere was incapacitated with illness, and seemed to be terminally ill, the South Africans turned to Ali Mazrui as his replacement. I was again flattered to have been regarded as Nyerere's replacement. However, the notice was too short, and I was not able to accept the South African invitation....

Let me also refer to Walter Rodney. He was a Guyanese scholar who taught at the University of Dar es Salaam and became one of the most eloquent voices of the left on the campus in Tanzania. When Walter Rodney returned to Guyana, he was assassinated.

Chedi Jagan, on being elected president of Guyana, created a special chair in honour of Walter Rodney. Eventually I was offered the chair and became its first incumbent. My inaugural lecture was on the following topic: 'Comparative Leadership: Walter Rodney, Julius K. Nyerere and Martin Luther King Jr.'

After delivering the lecture, I subsequently met Nyerere one evening in Pennsylvania, USA. I gave him my Walter Rodney lecture. He read it overnight and commented on it the next morning at breakfast. He promised to send me a proper critique of my Rodney lecture on his return to Dar es Salaam. He never lived long enough to send me the critique....

Julius Nyerere was my Mwalimu too. It was a privilege to learn so much from so great a man. – (Ali A. Mazrui, "Nyerere and I," Africa Resource Center, October 1999; *Daily Nation*, Nairobi Kenya, 26 December 1999).

Professor Walter Rodney himself was a great admirer of Nyerere as a leader and as an intellectual even before he went to Tanzania to teach at the University of Dar es Salaam.

After Rodney left Tanzania in 1974 and returned to Guyana, he continued to be actively involved with the workers at the grassroots level until he was assassinated in June 1980 by a government agent when Guyana was under the leadership of Prime Minister Forbes Burnham.

Most African intellectuals don't do that. They don't work with the masses at the grassroots level. And that severely limits their role as agents of dynamic and fundamental change in Africa.[44]

African writers like Godfrey Mwakikagile and other intellectuals are also severely compromised in their mission because most African leaders don't want to change. Therefore they don't listen to them—in many cases the entire state apparatus needs to be dismantled to bring about meaningful change.[45]

But, in spite of the limitations and the obstacles they face, many African writers and other intellectuals still play a very important role in articulating a clear vision for the future of Africa. And Godfrey Mwakikagile's writings definitely fit this category because of his analysis of the African condition and the solutions he proposes, although he is not a political activist like other African writers such as Ngũgĩ wa Thiong'o in neighbouring Kenya or Wole Soyinka in Nigeria.

But even they had to flee their homelands, at different times, for their own safety, in spite of the courage they had to contend with the political establishment in their home countries, and sought sanctuary overseas although that has not been the case with Godfrey Mwakikagile and many other Africans who once lived, have lived or continue to live in other countries or outside Africa for different reasons.

Writers like Godfrey Mwakikagile and other members of the African elite have a major role to play in the development of Africa.[46]

They do have an impact on constructive dialogue involving national issues. But it is not the kind of impact that reverberates across the spectrum all the way down to the grassroots level precisely because they are not an integral part of the masses, and also because they are not actively involved with the masses to transform society.

So, while they generate ideas, they have not been able to effectively transmit those ideas to the masses without whose involvement fundamental change in Africa is impossible, except at the top, recycling the elite. And while they identify with the masses in terms of suffering and as fellow Africans, many of them - not all but many of them - have not and still don't make enough sacrifices in their quest for social and political transformation of African countries. And Godfrey Mwakikagile is fully aware of these shortcomings, and apparent contradictions, in the role played by the African elite. He's one himself.

Yet, he has not explicitly stated so in his writings concerning this problem of African intellectuals; a dilemma similar to the one faced by the black intelligentsia in the United States and which was addressed by Harold Cruse, an internationally renowned black American professor who taught at the University of Michigan for many years, in his monumental study, *The Crisis of The Negro Intellectual*. The book was first published in 1967 at the peak of the civil rights movement, five years before Godfrey Mwakikagile went to the United States for the first time as a student.

But that does not really explain why Godfrey Mwakikagile has not fully addressed the subject, the dilemma African intellectuals face in their quest for fundamental change, especially in his books – *The Modern African State: Quest for Transformation, Africa is in A Mess: What Went Wrong and What Should Done*, and *Africa After Independence: Realities of Nationhood* – which are almost exclusively devoted to such transformation in Africa in the post-colonial era.

African leaders have failed Africa. But African intellectuals themselves have not done enough to help transform Africa into a better society.

Still, Godfrey Mwakikagile belongs to a group of African writers and the African elite who believe that the primary responsibility of transforming Africa lies in the hands of the Africans themselves, and not foreigners, and that acknowledgement of mistakes by African leaders is one of the first steps towards bringing about much-needed change in African countries; a position he forcefully articulates in his writings.

Political Science Professor Claude E. Welch of the State University of New York-Buffalo, in his review of one of Godfrey Mwakikagile's books – *Military Coups in West Africa Since The Sixties* – published in the *African Studies Review* (Vol. 45, No. 3, December 2002, p.114) – described the author as merciless in his condemnation of African tyrants.

The same book was also cited by James C. Owens of the University of Virginia in his article, "Government Failure in Sub-Saharan Africa: The International Community's Response," in the *Virginia Journal of International Law*, 2002. He used Godfrey Mwakikagile's book, *Military Coups in West Africa Since The Sixties*, among other works, to document the failure of leadership in many African countries in the post-colonial era.

And that is valid criticism of African leadership in post-colonial Africa by Godfrey Mwakikagile and others. Corrupt and despotic rulers don't deserve mercy. They don't deserve sympathy. They are not entitled to it. They have destroyed Africa.

Vision for an African Federal Government

Mwakikagile advocates for a closer union within Africa in the form of an African confederation or African federal government starting with economic integration, leading to an African common market, and eventually, resulting in a political union. Concretely, he proposed the following plan for a Union of African states:

> If the future of Africa lies in federation, that federation could even be a giant federation of numerous autonomous units which have replaced the modern African state in order to build, on a continental or sub-continental scale, a common market, establish a common currency, a common defense and maybe even pursue a common

foreign policy under some kind of central authority - including collective leadership on rotational basis - which Africans think is best for them.

Mwakikagile identifies the type of government best suited for the African situation as a *democracy by consensus,* which, in his view, would allow all social, ethnic and regional factions to freely express themselves. Such a democracy should take the form of a government of national unity, inclusive of both the winners and the losers in the electoral process, and would entail a multiparty system approved by national referendum; it should also be based on extreme decentralization down to the lowest grassroots level to enable the masses, not just the leaders and the elite, to participate in formulating policies and making decisions which affect their lives. That is the only way it can be a people's government and federation that belongs to the masses and ordinary citizens instead of being a government and federation of only the elite and professional politicians. Let the people decide. He has elaborated on that in his other books, *Africa at the End of the Twentieth Century: What Lies Ahead* and *Restructuring The African State and Quest for Regional Integration: New Approaches.*

He also believes that in this democratic system the tenure of the president must be limited to one term (preferably five to six years), and the tenure of the members of the national legislatures to two three-year terms.

Controversy

In what is probably his most controversial book, *Africa is in A Mess: What Went Wrong and What Should Be Done*, Godfrey Mwakikagile strongly criticises most of the leaders of post-colonial Africa for tyranny and corruption, and for practising tribalism, a common theme in the works of many African writers and other people including well-known ones and many African scholars in and outside Africa. But his book stands out as one of the most blunt ever written about Africa's rotten leadership.

Unfortunately, because of its vitriolic condemnation of most African leaders during the post-colonial era, the book has been cited by some people, who obviously have not read it well if at all, as a clarion call for the re-colonisation of Africa (because things are so bad, colonial rule was better) although the author says exactly the opposite in his work.[47]

One of the people he has quoted in his book articulating a similar position is Moeletsi Mbeki, the younger brother of former South African President Thabo Mbeki and head of the South African Institute of International Affairs, who said in September 2004 that Africans were better off under colonial rule than they are today under African leadership in the post-colonial period.

Mbeki also said African leaders and bureaucrats were busy stealing money and keeping it in foreign countries while colonial rulers built and maintained the infrastructure and ran their African colonies efficiently. He was quoted by BBC in a report entitled "Africa 'Better Colonial Times" published on 22 September 2004:

> The average African is worse off now than during the colonial era, the brother of South Africa's President Thabo Mbeki has said. Moeletsi Mbeki accused African elites of stealing money and keeping it abroad, while colonial rulers planted crops and built roads and cities. 'This is one of the depressing features of Africa, he said....
> 'The average African is poorer than during the age of colonialism. In the 1960s African elites/rulers, instead of focusing on development, took surplus for their own enormous entourages of civil servants without ploughing anything back into the country,' he said.
> In July, a United Nations report said that Africa was the only continent where poverty had increased in the past 20 years.
> Moeletsi Mbeki was addressing a meeting of the South African Institute of International Affairs, which he heads." (Africa 'Better in Colonial Times,' BBC, 22 September 2004).

Yet in spite of all that, Godfrey Mwakikagile unequivocally states in his book, *Africa is in A Mess*, that he does not support any attempt or scheme, by anybody, to recolonise Africa, but also bluntly states that African countries have lost their sovereignty to donor nations and multilateral institutions such as the World Bank and the International Monetary Fund (IMF) dominated by Western powers including those who once colonised Africa and are therefore virtual colonies already.

He also contends that African countries have really never been free in spite of the instruments of sovereignty they are supposed to have. He also warns about the dangers of the Second Scramble for Africa by the industrialised nations which are busy exploiting Africa's resources for their own benefit and contends that globalisation is in many ways a new form of imperialism.

Yet he has wrongly been portrayed, along with some prominent African and European scholars including Professor Ali Mazrui, Christoph Blocher, Mahmood Mamdani, Peter Niggli, and R. W. Johnson as someone who advocates the recolonisation of Africa.[48]

Godfrey Mwakikagile states exactly the opposite in his book *Africa is in A Mess*.

The premier of Western Cape province in South Africa, Helen Zille of the Democratic Alliance (DA), the main opposition party in the country, also cited Godfrey Mwakikagile in her speech in parliament on 28 March 2017 in defence of what she wrote about colonialism in her Tweets. She also cited Nelson Mandela, Professor Ali Mazrui, Nigerian author Chinua Achebe and former prime minister of India, Manmohan Singh, saying they articulated the same position she did on the impact of colonialism on the colonised.

The tweets caused a political firestorm in South Africa where her critics contended that she defended colonial rule – she clearly did not – and called for her resignation as premier of Western Cape, although she also had a lot of support across racial lines for what she said; probably more support than criticism as was demonstrated by the comments on social media including South African newspapers and Al Jazeera. Her Tweets were also covered by BBC. Her speech was also posted on Tanzania's leading social media outlet, Jamiiforums.

Helen Zille was a leading political activist during the apartheid era and campaigned against racial oppression and discrimination, incurring the wrath of the white minority regime. She was the first news reporter to report that South African leading political activist, Steve Biko, had been killed in police custody. According to a report by BBC, "Helen Zille of South Africa's Democratic Alliance - A Profile," 25 April 2014:

> Long before pursuing a career in politics, Ms Zille was a journalist with the now-defunct liberal *Rand Daily Mail* newspaper. Her greatest scoop as a political reporter came in 1977 when she uncovered how Black Consciousness activist Steve Biko - Ms Ramphele's partner - had been tortured to death while in police custody.

And as she stated in her speech in the Western Cape parliament, which was reprinted in some South African newspapers including the *Daily Maverick* under the title "From the Inside: A debate of national importance" and on *Times Live*, "Why I raised the subject of colonialism on Twitter":

> There is no question that colonialism was driven by greed and oppressive intent. The question for countries today is whether they are able, like Singapore, to leverage aspects of the legacy of an oppressive past to their advantage....
> In online conversations I wanted to raise this question in a South African context. As we all now know, this caused a volcanic political eruption. In the process many untruths and fabrications were disseminated including false allegations that I defended, justified or praised colonialism or apartheid; failure to distinguish between an evil system and the question of what can be re-purposed from its legacy;

outright fabrications that I have been charged 'over racism'; no such charge exists.

If anyone genuinely (i.e., without animus or a private agenda) thought I was actually defending, justifying or praising colonialism, I apologised unreservedly and stressed that this was not so. Many prominent people have repeatedly made the same point as I, including Nelson Mandela, Chinua Achebe, Ali Mazrui, Godfrey Mwakikagile and even a current matric history text book.

So why the mass hysteria when I made exactly the same point?...

I am glad we are having this debate today because South Africa needs it. Debate requires rational argument. I have no intention of settling scores, only setting out facts.

This debate is about a series of tweets relating to lessons learnt from my recent visit to Singapore and Japan.

None of them defended, justified or praised colonialism or apartheid. I can factually say that few in this house have put as much on the line to fight apartheid as I did.

Of course, colonialism had a diabolical impact worldwide, including South Africa. That was the very premise of my tweets. Anyone who read them without a personal or political agenda would have understood that. If you say the consequences of something were not ONLY negative, you are saying most WERE negative.

But if there was anyone who genuinely thought I was praising, defending or justifying colonialism, I apologised unreservedly and stressed that this was not so. I do so again.

In South Africa, colonialism and apartheid subjugated and oppressed a majority, and benefitted a minority, on the basis of race. This is indeed indefensible, and I have never supported, justified, praised or promoted it, as my life story attests.

My visit to Japan and Singapore, one a coloniser, the other colonised, was eye-opening. It seemed to me that the colonised has overtaken the coloniser on the world stage, and I thought it worthwhile asking why.

Let's start with another question. If I were to state that a worldwide legacy of colonialism was causing on average 3,287 human deaths daily, people would justifiably be outraged if anyone suggested the benefits might outweigh the cost. I am talking about the motorcar. Today in South Africa, this colonial left-over is not only a means of transport but the ultimate status symbol.

Of course, you may argue that the intention of the motorcar was not conquest. It was convenience; People wanted cars.

Fair point.

So let me look at another example: if I said that zealots with a mission using colonialism's methods of conflict and conquest had killed countless millions of people to impose their ideas on others, you would be appalled if anyone suggested the consequences were not only negative.

Of course, I am talking about most of the world's dominant religions, Speaker.

To be consistent on the principle, if people believe the price was too high to acknowledge any advantage, then they mustn't drive a car, or visit most houses of religious worship.

According to modern definitions, there are only 10 countries in the world that have never been colonised. And Africans have not only been the victims of conquest and genocide. They have also been its perpetrators.

Some countries that were brutally colonised in living memory have been spectacularly successful; many that have been free for decades, have not; the same can be said about the handful of countries that have never been colonised. Whether or not a country was colonised is not a predictor of success in the 21st century. In Singapore, they have discussed for decades what factors lead to their economic transformation. I wanted my series of tweets to initiate that debate here.

Many much more famous people have already expressed themselves on the subject and reached the same conclusions I did.

I have written before about how our own former President Nelson Mandela repeatedly discussed this issue. Today I quote from a speech he gave at Magdalene College, Cambridge, on 2 May 2001:

'Britain,' he said, 'was the main colonial power in our history, with all of the attendant problems and consequences of such a relationship.

Much of our traditional systems and institutions still carry the scars of the distortions inflicted by colonial rule. At the same time, so much of what we have to build on in the competitive modern world is also the result of what we could gain from that interaction and engagement with Britain.

Our indigenous understanding of the rule of law, viz that not kings or chiefs but the institutions of law and democracy are supreme, was strengthened and enhanced by our reference to the British understanding of that concept.

If there were one single positive aspect that I had to identify from the history of colonial contact between our two countries, it would be that of the educational benefits our country derived from it.'

Time does not permit me to quote so many others. Nigerian Nobel laureate Chinua Achebe's later work, Ali Mazrui, Godfrey Mwakikagile, Manmohan Singh. I could go on and on.

But more than that, Speaker: we continue to teach exactly the same lesson to our own schoolchildren every day.

I have brought to this house today, Speaker, a history textbook, written in the 21st century, and used in our schools from 2004 to the present. Its lead author is prominent academic historian, Dr Maanda Mulaudzi. For 13 years, Speaker, many thousands of born-free South Africans have studied from this book, maybe even some honourable members here today.

It devotes a significant section to the devastating effects of colonialism in Africa and South Africa. And rightly so.

And then, it asks an interesting question:
'Did colonisation have any positive effects?'
And I quote:

'Although most historians emphasise the negative effects that colonisation had on Africa, some also show that it did have some positive effects. For example, the colonisation of East Africa at last put an end to the slave trade there, which had continued to exist long after it had come to an end in West Africa.

Colonisation also brought with it Western education, medicine and technology as well as language, cultural, and sporting links that have enabled Africa to interact with the rest of the world.

Part of the legacy of colonisation has been the development of Africa into a network of modern, independent states.' (*In Search of History*, sixth impression 2005, page 182).

Why have we tolerated this textbook in our schools for so long? Will we demand that Dr Mulaudzi be fired?

Of course not. So why the political tsunami over what I said?

In his speech on the Motion for Ghana's Independence to the Gold Coast Legislative Assembly on 10 July 1953, Kwame Nkrumah stated:

The strands of history have brought our two countries together. We have provided much material benefit to the British people, and they in turn have taught us many good things. We want to continue to learn from them the best they can give us and we hope that they will find in us qualities worthy of emulation. – (Kwame Nkrumah, in George Padmore, *Pan-Africanism or Communism? The Coming Struggle for Africa*, London: Dennis Dobson, 1956, p. 412).

Yet he was not accused of defending colonialism when he said the British had taught Africans many good things and Africans would continue to learn from them after the end of colonial rule. That is because he did not defend colonialism when he said that. It was a historical fact.

Nkrumah was an uncompromising foe of colonialism who also had fierce pride in his African heritage and identity. He once said: "I am not African because I was born in Africa but because Africa was born in me."

He would be the last person to be accused of being an apologist for colonial rule because of what he said in his speech to the Gold Coast Legislative Assembly about four years before he led his country to independence as the new nation of Ghana.

He blazed the trail for the African independence movement when he led his country to become the first in sub-Saharan Africa to emerge from colonial rule and is sometimes acknowledged as the father of African independence.

Yet that did not stop him from assessing the impact of colonial rule in its proper historical context even if some people thought he was glorifying the colonial rulers when he said the British had taught Africans many good things.

An article about Helen Zille in Wikipedia provides the following details about her and her critics:

In March 2017, after a trip to Singapore and Japan..., Zille commented on Twitter that the legacy of colonialism was not all bad because it had left a legacy of infrastructure and institutions, which South Africa could build upon....

Following accusations that she was defending colonialism, Zille noted that her views had been misconstrued....

Among those who disagreed with her were other DA (Democratic Alliance) members, such as Mbali Ntuli, who stated that colonialism was 'only' negative, and who herself faces a disciplinary hearing in 2017 for 'liking' in December 2016 a Facebook comment that characterised Zille as racist; Phumzile van Damme, who stated that there was not 'a single aspect of [colonialism] that can be said to be positive or beneficial to Africans'; and party leader Mmusi Maimane, who stated 'Colonialism, like Apartheid, was a system of oppression and subjugation. It can never be justified', but also said in the aftermath that Zille was not a racist and that she had 'consistently fought oppression.'

DA MP Ghaleb Cachalia defended Zille as well-intentioned. He agreed with her that colonialism was not solely negative, and noted that many prominent intellectuals, including Chinua Achebe, Ali Mazrui, Godfrey Mwakikagile and Manmohan Singh, have expressed similar sentiments.

Kwame Nkrumah, who led the Gold Coast, renamed Ghana, to become the first country in sub-Saharan Africa to win independence, expressed similar sentiments in his speech on the Motion for Ghana's Independence to the Gold Coast Legislative Assembly on 10 July 1953....

Nkrumah was an anti-colonialist of immense stature and was never accused of being an apologist for colonial rule. He was never subjected to vitriolic condemnation the way Helen Zille was when she articulated the same position he did; nor was Nelson Mandela who expressed the same view. Chinua Achebe and other African scholars, Ali Mazrui and Godfrey Mwakikagile, expressed similar views without incurring the wrath of other Africans the way Helen Zille did.

Moeletsi Mbeki, the younger brother of former South African President Thabo Mbeki and head of the South African Institute of International Affairs, made similar remarks without causing a political firestorm when he said life for Africans was better during colonial times in terms of how governments discharged their responsibilities, according to a BBC report,'Africa 'better in colonial times", 22 September 2004....Yet his remarks did not draw public condemnation as an endorsement of colonial rule the way Zille's comments did.

The ANC and Economic Freedom Fighters (EFF) both demanded that Zille be removed from her position as Western Cape Premier.

As a result of her online comments, Zille was referred to the DA's federal legal commission for a disciplinary hearing on charges of bringing the party into disrepute and damaging the party. Following this news, Zille further defended herself by noting that Nelson Mandela had held the same opinion about colonialism. - (Helen Zille, Wikipedia, 17 September 2017).

Godfrey Mwakikagile has articulated the same position – Nkrumah, Helen Zille, Mandela, Ali Mazrui, Chinua Achebe and others have on the legacy of colonialism – in his book, *Africa is in A Mess* and in his other works including *Africa After Independence: Realities of*

Nationhood.

In fact, the title of his book *Africa is in A Mess*, although not the sub-title, comes from President Julius Nyerere who said exactly the same words in 1985: "Africa is in a mess."

Godfrey Mwakikagile explicitly states that in his book, saying he got the title from Nyerere's statement and felt it was appropriate for his work, although the tone and content might be disturbing to some people. He is brutally frank about the continent's deplorable condition.

But the book echoes the sentiments of tens of millions of Africans across the continent who live in misery and those who are frustrated by lack of fundamental change in African leadership notorious for corruption and other vices including tribalism and tyranny as Godfrey Mwakikagile bluntly states in his work.

His fellow Africans who have reviewed the book amazon.com and elsewhere in different publications and on the Internet strongly support the author and share his concerns about Africa's plight and the misguided leadership the continent has had to endure for decades since independence.[49]

One African reviewer, Khadija Mona Kabba, a member of Sierra Leonean President Ahmed Tejan Kabba's family, also contacted the author to congratulate him for writing such an honest book, as she stated in her review of the book on amazon.com. And she provided an additional perspective, as an insider, that shed more light on Africa's predicament in her review of Godfrey Mwakikagile's book, *Africa is in A Mess*, and said she was going to work with him on a joint project about Africa.

And in the same book, *Africa is in A Mess*, Godfrey Mwakikagile is also highly critical of Western powers for ruthlessly exploiting Africa even today in collusion with many African leaders.

His harsh criticism of bad leadership on the African continent prompted Ghanaian columnist and political analyst Francis Kwarteng to put him in the same category with George Ayittey, a Ghanaian professor of economics at The American University, Washington, D.C., and author of *Africa Betrayed* and *Africa in Chaos*, among other books. As he stated in his article, "Great Lessons From Dr. Yaw Nyarko's Work," GhanaWeb, 8 January 2014:

> Prof. Ayittey's intellectual assault on Africa is, probably, no different from Godfrey Mwakikagile's.

Yet there is a clear distinction between the two African scholars, reinforced by Godfrey Mwakikagile's ideological orientation and strong Pan-Africanist views which separate him from Professor George Ayittey who does not share the philosophical conceptions, in a Pan-African context, of prominent Pan-Africanist leaders such as Nkrumah and Nyerere the way Mwakikagile does.

Academic reviews

Godfrey Mwakikagile's books have also been reviewed in a number of academic publications, including the highly prestigious academic journal, *African Studies Review*, by leading scholars in their fields.

They include *Military Coups in West Africa Since The Sixties* which was reviewed in that journal by Professor Claude E. Welch of the Department of Political Science at the State University of New York, Buffalo; and *Ethnic Politics in Kenya and Nigeria* reviewed by Nigerian Professor Khadijat K. Rashid of Gallaudet University, Washington, D.C.[50]

His other books have also been reviewed in the *African Studies Review* and in the *Journal of Contemporary African Studies*. They include *Nyerere and Africa: End of an Era* and *The Modern African State: Quest for Transformation* which were reviewed in the *African Studies Review*; and *Nyerere and Africa: End of an Era* which was also reviewed in the *Journal of Contemporary African Studies*.

Another one of his books, *Western Involvement in Nkrumah's Downfall*, was reviewed by Professor E. Ofori Bekoe in *Africa Today*, Vol. 62, no. 4, Summer 2016, an academic journal published by Indiana University Press.

See also an analysis of Godfrey Mwakikagile's book, *Ethnic Politics in Kenya and Nigeria*, in A. Simpson and B. Akintunde Oyetade, "Nigeria: Ethno-linguistic Competition in the Giant of Africa," published in *Language and National Identity in Africa*, Oxford University Press, 2007, pp. 172–198; and Godfrey Mwakikagile's *Military Coups in West Africa Since The Sixties* in P.J. McGowan, "Coups and Conflict in West Africa, 1955 - 2004: Part II, Empirical Findings," in *Armed Forces & Society*, Sage Publications, in 2006.

For more reviews of his books, see also *Expo Times*, Sierra Leone; *The Mirror*, Zimbabwe, and other publications including those featured on the Internet.[51]

He has also written about race relations in the United States and relations between continental Africans and people of African descent in the diaspora. His titles in these areas include *Black Conservatives in The United States*; *Relations Between Africans and African Americans*; and *Relations Between Africans, African Americans and Afro-Caribbeans*.

Professor Kwame Essien of Gettysburg College, later Lehigh University, a Ghanaian, reviewed Godfrey Mwakikagile's book, *Relations Between Africans and African Americans: Misconceptions, Myths and Realities*, in *Souls: A Critical Journal of Black Politics, Culture, and Society, Volume 13, Issue 2, 2011*, an academic journal of Columbia University, New York, and described it as an "insightful and voluminous" work covering a wide range of subjects from a historical and contemporary perspective, addressing some of the most controversial issues in relations between the two. It is also one of the most important books on the subject of relations between Africans and African Americans.

The book has also been discussed on different forums on the Internet. It was also the subject of a radio talk show in the United States when it was first published. The talk show was on WCLM, Richmond, Virginia, and the book was discussed three different times in April and May 2006. It was the station's Book Club Choice and generated a lot of interest.

The show was broadcast nationwide and could be heard on the Internet worldwide. Listeners were invited to call in and participate in the discussion. The main guests who discussed the book were Professor Adisa A. Alkebulan, an African American, of San Diego State University, and Professor Albion Mends, a Ghanaian, of Central Missouri State University, also known as the University of Central Missouri. The host of the show said she received hundreds of emails from different parts of the United States and other countries on the subject of relations between Africans and African Americans when the book was being discussed.

Godfrey Mwakikagile's books are found in public and university libraries around the world and have been adopted for class use at many colleges and universities in the United States and other countries. Most college and university libraries in the United States have his books.

Selected publications

Titles by Godfrey Mwakikagile

- *Economic Development in Africa*, 1999
- *Africa and The West*, 2000
- *The Modern African State: Quest for Transformation*, 2001
- *Military Coups in West Africa Since The Sixties*, 2001

- *Ethnic Politics in Kenya and Nigeria*, 2001
- *Nyerere and Africa: End of an Era*, 2002
- *Africa is in A Mess: What Went Wrong and What Should Be Done*, 2004
- *Tanzania under Mwalimu Nyerere: Reflections on an African Statesman*, 2004
- *Black Conservatives: Are They Right or Wrong?*, 2004
- *Nyerere and Africa: End of an Era: Expanded Edition with Photos*, 2005
- *Relations Between Africans and African Americans: Misconceptions, Myths and Realities*, 2005
- *Life in Tanganyika in The Fifties: My Reflections and Narratives from The White Settler Community and Others*, 2006
- *African Countries: An Introduction*, 2006
- *Africa After Independence: Realities of Nationhood*, 2006
- *Life under Nyerere*, 2006
- *Black Conservatives in The United States*, 2006
- *Africa and America in The Sixties: A Decade That Changed The Nation and The Destiny of A Continent*, 2006
- *Relations Between Africans, African Americans and Afro-Caribbeans: Tensions, Indifference and Harmony*, 2007
- *Investment Opportunities and Private Sector Growth in Africa*, 2007
- *Kenya: Identity of A Nation*, 2007
- *South Africa in Contemporary Times*, 2008
- *South Africa and Its People*, 2008
- *African Immigrants in South Africa*, 2008
- *The Union of Tanganyika and Zanzibar: Product of The Cold War?*, 2008
- *Ethnicity and National Identity in Uganda: The Land and Its People*, 2009
- *My Life as an African: Autobiographical Writings*, 2009
- *Uganda: The Land and Its People*, 2009
- *Botswana Since Independence*, 2009
- *Congo in The Sixties*, 2009

- *A Profile of African Countries*, 2009
- *Africans and African Americans: Complex Relations - Prospects and Challenges*, 2009
- *Africa 1960 - 1970: Chronicle and Analysis*, 2009
- *Nyerere and Africa: End of an Era*, Fifth Edition, 2010
- *Zambia: Life in an African Country*, 2010
- *Belize and Its Identity: A Multicultural Perspective*, 2010
- *Ethnic Diversity and Integration in The Gambia: The Land, The People and The Culture*, 2010
- *Zambia: The Land and Its People*, 2010
- *Belize and Its People: Life in A Multicultural Society*, 2010
- *The Gambia and Its People: Ethnic Identities and Cultural Integration in Africa*, 2010
- *South Africa as a Multi-Ethnic Society*, 2010
- *Life in Kenya: The Land and The People, Modern and Traditional Ways*, 2010
- *Botswana: Profile of A Nation*, 2010
- *Uganda: Cultures and Customs and National Identity*, 2011
- *Burundi: The Hutu and The Tutsi: Cauldron of Conflict and Quest for Dynamic Compromise*, 2012
- *Identity Politics and Ethnic Conflicts in Rwanda and Burundi: A Comparative Study*, 2012
- *The People of Uganda: A Social Perspective*, 2012
- *Uganda: A Nation in Transition: Post-colonial Analysis*, 2012
- *Obote to Museveni: Political Transformation in Uganda Since Independence*, 2012
- *Uganda Since The Seventies*, 2012
- *Civil Wars in Rwanda and Burundi: Conflict Resolution in Africa*, 2013
- *Peace and Stability in Rwanda and Burundi: The Road Not Taken*, 2013
- *Africa at the End of the Twentieth Century: What Lies Ahead*, 2013
- *Statecraft and Nation Building in Africa: A Post-colonial Study*, 2014

- *Africa in The Sixties*, 2014
- *Remembering The Sixties: A Look at Africa*, 2014
- *Restructuring The African State and Quest for Regional Integration: New Approaches*, 2014
- *Africa 1960 – 1970: Chronicle and Analysis*, Revised Edition, 2014
- *Post-colonial Africa: A General Study*, 2014
- *British Honduras to Belize: Transformation of a Nation*, 2014
- *Why Tanganyika united with Zanzibar to form Tanzania*, 2014
- *Congo in The Sixties*, Revised Edition, 2014
- *The People of Kenya and Uganda*, 2014
- *Namibia: Conquest to Independence: Formation of a Nation*, 2015
- *Western Involvement in Nkrumah's Downfall*, 2015
- *Africa: Dawn of a New Era*, 2015
- *The Union of Tanganyika and Zanzibar: Formation of Tanzania and its Challenges*, 2016
- *The People of Ghana: Ethnic Diversity and National Unity*, 2017

References

1. Godfrey Mwakikagile, *Life in Tanganyika in The Fifties*, ISBN 9789987160129, New Africa Press, Dar es Salaam, Tanzania, 2009, p. 19. See also, G. Mwakikagile, *My Life as an African: Autobiographical Writings*, ISBN 9789987160051, New Africa Press, Dar es Salaam, Tanzania, 2009, p. 21.

2. *Life in Tanganyika in The Fifties*, p. 20; *My Life as an African*, p. 367; *The London Review of Politics, Society, Literature, Art & Science, Volume 9*, 24 September 1864, p. 341: "To open up this central African plateau to a legitimate and profitable trade with England and to European colonization is the leading feature of Dr.

Livingstone's scheme." See also Philemon A.K. Mushi, *History and Development of Education in Tanzania*, ISBN 9789976604948, Dar es Salaam University Press,Dar es Salaam, Tanzania, 2009, p. 64; Bella Walters, *Zambia in Pictures*, Lerner Publishing Group, September 2008, p. 77; Joseph F. Conley, *Drumbeats That Changed The World: A History of The Regions and Beyond Missionary Union and the West Indies Mission, 1873 – 1999*, ISBN 087808603-X,William Carey Library, Pasadena, California, 2000, p. 60; A. T. Dalfovo, et al.,eds., *The Foundations of Social Life: Ugandan Philosophical Studies*,ISBN 1565180070, The Council for Research in Values and Philosophy, Washington, D.C., 1992, p. 110.
3. *Life in Tanganyika in The Fifties*, p. 21-22. See also *My Life as an African*, p. 23; *Life in Tanganyika in The Fifties*, p. 58.
4. *My Life as an African*, p. 87.
5. *Life in Tanganyika in The Fifties*, pp. 44, 77, 122; *My Life as an African*, pp. 47, 48, 78, 89, 92, 117, 119, 138, 154, 172, 175; *Tanzania under Mwalimu Nyerere: Reflections on an African Statesman*, ISBN 9780980253498, New Africa Press, Pretoria, South Africa, 2006, pp. 15 – 16.
6. "Newsman Leaves for America," *Daily News*, Dar es Salaam, Tanzania, 7 November 1972, p. 3; *Life in Tanganyika in The Fifties*, pp. 122 – 123; *My Life as an African*, p. 176.
7. *My Life as an African*, pp 89 – 90; "Newsman Leaves for America," *Daily News*, Dar es Salaam, Tanzania, 7 November 1972, p. 3; *Life in Tanganyika in The Fifties*, p. 56.
8. "Newsman Leaves for America," *Daily News*, Dar es Salaam, Tanzania, 7 November 1972, p. 3; *Life in Tanganyika in The Fifties*, p. 123; *My Life as an African*, p. 90.
9. Wayne State University Alumni, 1975; *My Life as an African*, pp. 76, 86, 120, 140, 164, 188, 190, 192, 246,

250, 266, 281; Godfrey Mwakikagile, *Nyerere and Africa: End of an Era*, ISBN 0980253411, Fifth Edition, New Africa Press, 2010, Pretoria, South Africa, pp. 86, 491, 509-511, 658, 664-665.

10. *My Life as an African*, pp. 306, 328; *Nyerere and Africa*, p. 649.

11. "Former CUNA (Credit Union National Association) chairman Ken Marin dies," *Credit Union Times*, Hoboken, New Jersey, January 8, 2008. See also *My Life as an African*, p. 306; *Nyerere and Africa*, p. 649, 664.

12. *My Life as an African*, p. 328. *Nyerere and Africa*, p. 664; "Former CUNA (Credit Union National Association) chairman Ken Marin dies," *Credit Union Times*, Hoboken, New Jersey, January 8, 2008;*Credit Union Times*, December 4, 2012.

13. Godfrey Mwakikagile, *Economic Development in Africa*, ISBN 978-1560727088, Nova Science Publishers, Inc. Huntington, New York, June 1999.

14. Godfrey Mwakikagile, *Nyerere and Africa: End of an Era*, Fifth Edition, ISBN 0980253411, New Africa Press, Pretoria, South Africa, 2010; Fumbuka Ng'wanakilala, "Three Years After Mwalimu Nyerere: Nyerere: True Pan-Africanist, Advocate of Unity," *Daily News*, Special Edition, Dar es Salaam, Tanzania, Monday, October 14, 2002, p. 19.

15. F. Ng'wanakilala, "Three Years After Mwalimu Nyerere: Nyerere: True Pan-Africanist, Advocate of Unity," *Daily News*, Special Edition, Dar es Salaam, Tanzania, Monday, October 14, 2002, p. 19; A.B. Assensoh, review of *Nyerere and Africa: End of an Era*, in *African Studies Review*, Journal of African Studies Association; Kofi Akosah-Sarpong, "Nyerere's Vision," in *West Africa*, 25 November - 1 December 2002, p. 41.

16. David Simon, ed., *Fifty Key Thinkers on Development: Routledge Key Guides*, Routledge, Taylor & Francis Group, London, New York, 2005.

17. amazon.com, Barnes & Noble and other book sellers.

18. Kofi Akosah-Sarpong, "Nyerere's Vision," in *West Africa*, 25 November - 1 December 2002, p. 41; K. Akosah-Sarpong, "Back to The Roots," in *West Africa*, 21–27 January 2002, p. 43.
19. F. Ng'wanakilala, "Nyerere: True pan-Africanist, advocate of unity," in "Three Years After Mwalimu Nyerere, " in the *Daily News*, Dar es Salaam, Tanzania, Monday, October 14, 2002, p. 19.
20. Godfrey Mwakikagile quoted by South African Deputy President Phumzile Mlambo-Ngcuka in "Address Delivered by the Deputy President, Ms. Phumzile Mlambo-Ngcuka at the Third Annual Julius Nyerere Memorial Lecture at the University of the Western Cape, South Africa." Issued by the Presidency through the Ministry of Foreign Affairs, Pretoria, South Africa, 6 September 2006.
21. Kofi Akosah-Sarpong, "Back to The Roots," in *West Africa*, 21–27 January 2002, p. 43.
22. Godfrey Mwakikagile, *Africa and The West*, ISBN 9781560728405, Huntington, New York, 2001, pp. 1–46, and 201-218.
23. Godfrey Mwakikagile, *Nyerere and Africa: End of an Era*, ISBN 0980253411, Fifth Edition, New Africa Press, 2010, Pretoria, South Africa. For Mwakikagile's Pan-Africanist views and perspectives, see also Professor Eric Edi of Temple University, in his paper, "Pan-West Africanism and Political Instability: Perspectives and Reflections," in which he cites Godfrey Mwakikagile's books, *Military Coups in West Africa Since The Sixties* and *The Modern African State: Quest for Transformation*.
24. Kwesi Johnson-Taylor, "Author, a shrewd intellectual in defence of liberation icons," book review of *Nyerere and Africa: End of an Era*, amazon.com, February 21, 2006.
25. *Nyerere and Africa: End of an Era*.
26. Godfrey Mwakikagile, *Africa After Independence: Realities of Nationhood*, ISBN 9789987160143, New

Africa Press, Dar es Salaam, Tanzania, 2006, pp. 86, 91, 168-171; Godfrey Mwakikagile, *Africa 1960 - 1970: Chronicle and Analysis*, ISBN 9789987160075, New Africa Press, Dar es Salaam, Tanzania,2009, p. 510; Roger Pfister, *Apartheid South Africa and African States: From Pariah to Middle Power, 1961 – 1994*, ISBN 1850436258, International Library of African Studies 14, Tauris Academic Studies, an imprint of I.B. Tauris & Co. Ltd., London, New York, 2005, p. 40; Joseph Hanlon, *Beggar Your Neighbours: Apartheid Power in Southern Africa*, ISBN 0852553072, James Currey Ltd., London, UK, and Indiana University Press, Bloomington, Indiana, USA, 1986, p. 237; Mwesiga Baregu and Christopher Landsberg, eds., *From Cape to Congo: Southern Africa's Evolving Security Challenges*, ISBN 1588261026; ISBN 1588261271, Lynne Rienner Publishers, Inc., London, UK, and Boulder, Colorado, USA, 2003.

27. Jorge Castaneda, *Companero: The Life and Death of Che Guevara*, ISBN 9780679759409, Alfred A. Knopf, Inc., New York, 1998, p. 277; *Nyerere and Africa: End of an Era*, pp. 156, 158, 737.

28. In May 1963, the Organisation of African Unity (OAU) was founded in Addis Ababa, Ethiopia. The OAU chose Tanzania to be the headquarters of the African liberation movements under the auspices of the OAU Liberation Committee which was based in Tanzania's capital Dar es Salaam.

29. *Nyerere and Africa: End of an Era*, pp. 209, 223, 224, 252, 254, 255, 404, 487-489, 503.

30. *Life in Tanganyika in The Fifties*, pp. 92 – 93. See also *Nyerere and Africa: End of an Era*, pp. 10 – 12, 65, 314, 363, 375, 484.

31. *Nyerere and Africa: End of an Era*, pp. 224, 487-488; "Newsman Leaves for America," *Daily News*, Dar es Salaam, Tanzania, 7 November 1972, p. 3.

32. *Nyerere and Africa: End of an Era*, pp. 360, 486. See also, "Brendon Grimshaw Dead," *Seychelles Nation*,

Victoria, Seychelles, Thursday, 7 July 2012; "Brendon Grimshaw is dead," *Daily News*, Dar es Salaam, Tanzania, 7 July 2012.

33. "President Mourns David Martin," *The Herald*, Harare, Zimbabwe, 22 August 2007; "David Martin (April 1936 - August 2007) – 40 years of service to African liberation," Southern African Research and Documentation Centre (SARDC), Harare, Zimbabwe.

34. "Martin - Man of Many Talents," *The Herald*, Harare, Zimbabwe, 24 August 2007.

35. "Martin Laid to Rest," *The Herald*, Harare, Zimbabwe, 25 August 2007.

36. *Nyerere and Africa: End of an Era*, pp. 486, 500, 569; *My Life as an African: Autobiographical Writings*, pp. 89, 156, 176, 375-376, 378.

37. *Nyerere and Africa: End of an Era*; Godfrey Mwakikagile, *Africa after Independence: Realities of Nationhood*, ISBN 9789987160143, New Africa Press, Dar es Salaam, Tanzania, 2006; *The Modern African State: Quest for Transformation*, ISBN 9781560729365, Nova Science Publishers, Inc., Huntington, New York, 2001; *Military Coups in West Africa Since The Sixties*, ISBN 9781560729457, Nova Science Publishers, Inc., Huntington, New York, 2001; *Africa is in A Mess: What Went Wrong and What Should Be Done*, ISBN 0980253470, New Africa Press, Dar es Salaam, Tanzania, 2006.

38. *Africa is in A Mess: What Went Wrong and What Should Be Done*, ISBN 0980253470, New Africa Press, Dar es Salaam, Tanzania, 2006; *Africa After Independence: Realities of Nationhood*, ISBN 9789987160143, New Africa Press, Dar es Salaam, Tanzania, 2006; *The Modern African State: Quest for Transformation*, ISBN 9781560729365, Nova Science Publishers, Inc., Huntington, New York, 2001;*Military Coups in West Africa Since the Sixties*, ISBN 9781560729457, Huntington, New York, 2001; *Military*

Coups in West Africa Since the Sixties, ISBN 9781560729457, Huntington, New York, 2001. George B. N. Ayittey, *Africa Betrayed*, Palgrave Macmillan, New York, ISBN 9780312104009, 1993, p. 294.

39. Kwesi Johnson-Taylor, "Author, a shrewd intellectual in defence of liberation icons," in his review of Godfrey Mwakikagile's book, Nyerere and Africa: End of an Era, on amazon.com, February 21, 2006.

40. *Life in Tanganyika in The Fifties*, pp. 7 – 8.

41. *Life in Tanganyika in The Fifties*, pp. 31 – 32. See also *Africa is in A Mess* and *Africa and The West*.

42. Ronald Taylor-Lewis, in his review of Godfrey Mwakikagile, *The Modern African State: Quest for Transformation*, in *Mano Vision*, London, Issue 23, October 2001, pp. 34 – 35. See also Professor Catherine S.M. Duggan, Department of Political Science, Stanford University, in her paper, "Do Different Coups Have Different Implications for Investment? Some Intuitions and A Test With A New Set of Data," in which she cites Godfrey Mwakikagile on fundamental changes in African countries. See also Godfrey Mwakikagile, cited in Christopher E. Miller, *A Glossary of Terms and Concepts in Peace and Conflict Studies*, p. 87; and in Gabi Hesselbein, Frederick Golooba-Mutebi, and James Putzel, "Economic and Political Foundations of State-Making in Africa: Understanding State Reconstruction," *Working Paper No. 3*, 2006.

43. *The Modern African State: Quest for Transformation*, op.cit.; Wole Soyinka, *The Open Sore of a Continent: A Personal Narrative of The Nigerian Crisis*, Oxford University Press, 1997; Chinua Achebe, *The Trouble with Nigeria*, Fourth Dimension Publishing Co., Enugu, Nigeria, 2000.

44. Henry Augustine Brown-Acquaye, *African Developments in Doldrums*, ArtHouse, 2008, p. 81; M.I.S. Gassama, in *West Africa*, March 21–27, 1994; G. B.N. Ayittey, *Africa Betrayed*, p. 295; Peter Anassi,*Corruption*

in Africa: The Kenyan Experience, Trafford Publishing, Victoria, British Columbia, Canada, 2006, p. 209.

45. Ibid. See also Ismail Rashid, a Sierra Leonian in exile in Canada, in the *New African*, London, May 1992, p. 10; Rashid Ismail in G.B.N. Ayittey, *Africa Betrayed*, op.cit., p. 295. See also George B.N. Ayittey, *Africa in Chaos: A Comparative History*, Palgrave Macmillan, 1997; Wole Soyinka, in a speech at Wellesley College, Massachusetts, quoted by Zia Jaffrey, "The Writer in Exile as 'Opposition Diplomat,'" in the *International Herald Tribune*, May 2, 1997, p. 24; *Africa is in A Mess*, pp. 63 – 64; Peter Anassi, *Corruption in Africa: The Kenyan Experience*, p. 209; Peter Anyang' Nyong'o, in *Popular Struggles for Democracy in Africa* (London: Zed Books, 1987), pp. 14 – 25.

46. Ibid. Alfred A.R. Latigo, *The Best Options for Africa: 11 Political, Economic and Divine Principles*, Trafford Publishing, Victoria, BC, Canada, 2010, pp. 114 – 115; Senyo B-S.K. Adjibolosoo, *The Human Factor in Developing Africa*, Praeger Publishers, Westport, Connecticut, USA, 1995, p. 64; John Mukum Mbaku, *Institutions and Development in Africa*, Africa World Press, 2004. p. 236.

47. Dr. Kenday Samuel Kamara of Walden University in his abstract, "Considering the Enormity of Africa's Problems, is Re-Colonization an Option?" in which he cites Godfrey Mwakikagile's *Africa is in A Mess* and related works by other African leading academic authors including Professor Ali Mazrui, and Professor George Ayittey's *Africa in Chaos*. See Mwakikagile's book on the subject, *Africa is in A Mess: What Went Wrong and What Should Be Done*. See also Tunde Obadina, "The Myth of Neo-Colonialism," in *Africa Economic Analysis*, 2000; and Timothy Murithi, in his book, *The African Union: Pan-Africanism, Peacebuilding and Development*.

48. Professor Sabelo J. Ndlovu-Gatsheni, a Zimbambwean teaching international studies at Monash University, South

Africa campus, in his abstract, "Gods of Development, Demons of Underdevelopment and Western Salvation: A Critique of Development Discourse as a Sequel to the CODESRIA and OSSREA International Conferences on Development in Africa," June 2006. Professor Ndlovu-Gatsheni advances the same argument Godfrey Mwakikagile does and cites Mwakikagile's work, *Africa is in A Mess*, to support his thesis. See also Floyd Shivambu, "Floyd's Perspectives: Societal Tribalism in South Africa," September 1, 2005, who cites Godfrey Mwakikagile's *Ethnic Politics in Kenya and Nigeria*, in his condemnation of tribalism in post-apartheid South Africa; Mary Elizabeth Flournoy of Agnes Scott College, in her paper, "Nigeria: Bounded by Ropes of Oil," citing Godfrey Mwakikagile's writings including *Ethnic Politics in Kenya and Nigeria*; Professor Eric Edi of Temple University, in his paper, "Pan West Africanism and Political Instability: Perspectives and Reflections," in which he cites Godfrey Mwakikagile's books, *Military Coups in West Africa Since The Sixties* and *The Modern African State: Quest for Transformation*.

49. Professor Claude E. Welch, Jr., in *African Studies Review*, Vol. 45, No. 3, December 2002, pp. 124–125; and *Ethnic Politics in Kenya and Nigeria*, reviewed by Nigerian Professor Khadijat K. Rashid of Gallaudet University, Washington, D.C. In *African Studies Review*, Vol. 46, No. 2, September 2003, pp. 92 – 98).

50. Ibid.

51. Godfrey Mwakikagile in *Expo Times*, Freetown, Sierra Leone, and in *The Mirror*, Harare, Zimbabwe, 2002.

Godfrey Mwakikagile:
Born in Tanganyika

From Godfrey Mwakikagile, *Life in Tanganyika in The Fifties*

THE period during which I was born witnessed some of the most important events and changes in the history Tanganyika, the land of my birth, and indeed of the entire African continent. It was the dawn of a new era.

It was only a few years after the end of the Second World War in which many Africans, including two of my uncles, fought and in which many of them died; fortunately, both of my uncles survived and returned safely to Tanganyika.

It was also a period of political ferment in which the campaign for independence started in earnest in Tanganyika, the largest British possession in East Africa, and in other colonies on the continent.

I was born at 6 a.m. on Tuesday, 4 October 1949, in Kigoma, a port on Lake Tanganyika in what was then the Western Province in western Tanganyika. It was during British colonial rule and Tanganyika in those days had seven provinces: Western, Central, Lake, Northern, Coast, Southern and the Southern Highlands. The capital of the Western Province was Tabora.

My parents came from Rungwe District in the Southern Highlands. Rungwe District is in the Great Rift Valley and is ringed by misty blue mountains and is home to the Nyakyusa, my ethnic group, who today are one of the largest in Tanzania with more than one million people.

My father worked as a medical assistant during British colonial rule and that is how he and my mother ended up in Kigoma. Before I was born, my parents also lived in other parts of Tanganyika where my father worked. They lived in Handeni, Amani, Muheza, and Kilosa. They were also in Tanga for some time.

I am the first-born in my family. I was born in a hospital in Kigoma.

I don't know if my father worked at that hospital and I don't even remember whether or not my parents told me where he worked when I was born. But I do know that it was he who filled out my birth certificate. And it was he who always reminded me of my birthday every morning when I was growing up that October 4_{th} was my birthday. My mother also reminded me of that, but not as much as my father did and was not as punctual. As soon as I woke up, my father would remind me if it was my birthday.

He was one of the few Africans in Tanganyika in those days who had secondary school education. He went to Malangali Secondary School in Iringa where he completed standard ten and excelled in school. He was also head prefect at Malangali. And he would have gone to Tabora High School but couldn't because of family obligations. Instead, he went to Muhimbili National Hospital in Dar es Salaam in the mid-1940s for medical training and qualified as a medical assistant.

The hospital was then known as Sewa Haji and was later renamed Princess Margaret Hospital. It has always been the country's only national hospital and was renamed Muhimbili National Hospital after independence.

My father's assignment to Kigoma after working elsewhere in Tanganyika turned out to be one of the most important events in my life because that is where I was born. And it will always remain an important part of my life as my birth place more than anything else.

Unfortunately, in all the years I lived in Tanganyika, later Tanzania, I never got the chance to visit Kigoma as a youngster or as an adult. And I still haven't unto this day.

My parents never went back to Kigoma and I did not get the chance to go there even when I worked as a news reporter in Tanzania.

But I have two very important items with me which always remind me of Kigoma as my birth place.

One is my photograph taken when I was one year and three months old. It also has my father's handwriting on it in black ink, still legible 57 years later which was my age when I was working on the second edition of this book in 2007. He wrote in English: "Fifteen months old."

In this photograph, I'm standing looking at the camera, chubby and wide-eyed, and he's holding my right hand in front of the house in which we lived. It was a wooden house with a grass-thatched roof.

When I look at that picture, I can see how much I have changed through the years. I look chubby when I was a baby less than two years old, yet when I was growing up, I never gained much weight and was always slim. Many people said I was skinny. I thought my weight was in proportion to my frame. And I have always been that way, slim.

Another item I cherish so much is my birth certificate which my father gave me when I became a teenager and was attending Mpuguso Middle School in Rungwe District in the Southern Highlands from 1961 to 1964.

Also on my birth certificate are reminders of two other important historical events in my life: when I was baptised, by whom, and in what church.

I was baptised by Reverend Frank McGorlick on 25 December 1949, on Christmas day, two months and three weeks after I was born. My birth certificate also bears his name in his own handwriting. It was issued by CMS, the Church Missionary Society, which did a lot of missionary work spreading Christianity in Tanganyika and in many other parts of Africa.

Reverend McGorlick came from Victoria, Australia. Decades later, I was able to get in touch with his wife Barbara in Australia who told me that they lived in Tanganyika, later Tanzania, until the early 1990s and that her husband died in 1993. I got in touch with her in 2005, as I did with their son Richard who also lived in Victoria, Australia. He grew up in Tanganyika, later Tanzania, as did the other children.

I remember when I was growing up that my parents used to tell me I was baptised as a CMS member. That was also the church my parents attended when they lived in Kigoma even before I was born until they returned to Rungwe District years later as members of the Moravian Church which was well-established in that district. They were members of the same church before they left Rungwe District.

The Moravian Church in Rungwe District was established in the late 1880s by the Germans who were also the first colonial rulers of Tanganyika, while CMS was British in origin.

The Church Missionary Society (CMS) was founded in 1799 by a group of activist evangelical Christians. One of the founders was William Wilberforce, a prominent leader of the movement which was launched to abolish slavery. He was asked to be the first president of this missionary organisation but declined to take the offer and instead became its vice president. CMS was also supported by another prominent abolitionist, Dr. David Livingstone of the London Missionary Society, who was Scottish himself like Reverend McGorlick who baptised me.

Years later, when I became familiar with some Scottish names, I came to the conclusion that the minister who baptized me, Reverend McGorlick, was probably Scottish.

And I was right. Before I found out about him, I didn't know if he spent the rest of his life in Tanganyika, later Tanzania, or "returned to Britain" since I assumed that's where he came from. I was wrong. But there is no question that he left an indelible mark on me as the one who baptised me.

The Church Missionary Society of Australia effectively dates from 1916 when the individual CMS associations in the Australian states were amalgamated into a national organisation. CMS had sent missionaries to many countries by this time, including China, India, Palestine and Iran, but by 1927 they had particular interest in North Australia and Tanganyika.

After I was born in Kigoma, my parents moved to Ujiji which is only a few miles away. It was there, in that very small yet famous place, where my sister Maria was born a year-and-half after I was. She was born in April 1951.

It was also in Ujiji where Henry Morton Stanley uttered those famous words on 10 November 1871 when he found the famous Scottish missionary doctor and explorer: "Dr. Livingstone, I presume?"

Dr. Livingstone had been missing for three years and the Royal Geographical Society sponsored an expedition to look for him in Africa.

Although I never got the chance to visit Kigoma and see the place of my birth, my sister Maria ended up living in Kigoma years later with her husband who was sent by his church to work there as a Seventh-Day Adventist pastor while she worked as a nurse. And I have always been interested in learning as much as I can about Kigoma - as well as other parts of the country - not only because it is my birth place but also because it is an integral part of my home country Tanzania. But because it is my birth place, there is no question that I have special interest in Kigoma in a way I don't in other parts of the country.

And it has an interesting history. For example, not many people in Tanzania know that Kigoma was once a part of the Belgian colony of Ruanda-Urundi. Had it remained under Belgian control, my history would probably have been different. My father would never have been sent by the British colonial government to work in Kigoma, since it would not have been a part of their territory of Tanganyika. I would not have been born in Kigoma, or I may not even have been born at all!

But obviously, that was not my destiny. And Kigoma always brings back memories of my childhood in the fifties because that is where it all began, this short journey of mine into this world where we are mere mortals and which reminds me of one song by Jim Reeves, also sung by others, I used to listen to when I was a teenager in Tanzania in the sixties: "This world is not my home, I'm just passing through, my treasures are laid up, somewhere beyond the blue..."

But short as our presence is, in this world, we have to make the best of it. And in my case, my early life in Tanganyika played a critical role in determining what type of person I came to be years later. It is this land which I love from the very depth of my being, heart and soul. And it is this land that I will always love for the rest of my life.

It was in Tanganyika where I was born, and it was in Tanganyika where I was brought up. And it reminds me of another song we sang in Kiswahili in school and sometimes during national celebrations: *Tanganyika, Tanganyika, nakupenda kwa moyo wote*. In English it means: "Tanganyika, Tanganyika, I love you with all my heart."

It was also in Tanganyika where I spent one of the most important decades in my life and in the history of the country: the fifties. The fifties were my formative years. They were also the years when Tanganyika began its peaceful transition from colonial status to independence.

I witnessed some of those events during the transitional period especially in the late fifties. But I was still too young to understand exactly what they meant. I looked at things from a child's perspective, and simply having fun - chasing grasshoppers and butterflies - was more important to me than politics. And that is what I remember the most.

Even if they told me, I don't know if I would have been able to fully understand what was meant by *siasa*, which is a Swahili word meaning politics. And when I saw white people as child in the mid- and late-fifties, I saw them just as people. Yes, they looked different in terms of skin colour, but I still saw them as people nonetheless; and not as rulers or anything else.

Difference in skin colour meant absolutely nothing to me and other children in terms of an individual's worth as a human being, although even at that young age we noticed that white people had material things we didn't have. But we did not associate that with power or skin colour.

If someone tried to explain to me and other children the connection between skin colour and wealth or social status, we would have been confused. We just didn't understand why white people had things we didn't have, or why they lived in better houses than we did. Colonialism meant nothing to us at that age when we were under 10 years old.

And I had no reason to ask why white people were there, in Tanganyika, or where they came from, or why they had a different complexion. After all, there were Arabs and Indians in Tanganyika who also had a light complexion and even some Africans who had a light brown complexion.

Even my own mother had a light brown complexion. So did my brothers, some of my sisters, cousins, uncles and aunts; not white-looking or light-complexioned like the Indians and the Arabs we saw around when we were growing up but not dark-skinned either. Still, all that meant nothing to me.

I even remember my mother telling me when I was a young teenager in the early sixties that when we lived in

Mbeya around 1953 and 1954, a British couple used to give me some cake and sweets and other things now and then whenever we passed by their house. And that only reinforced - even if not consciously - whatever notions I had, as a child, of a colour-blind society; which was, of course, not entirely the case as older people of all races knew very well. As a colony, Tanganyika was a colour-conscious society. Yet to a child, such colour-consciousness meant something different, if anything at all, even though it was a fact of life for all of us since our status was defined by racial identity.

Still, in spite of all that, there were people of all races who got along very well. They got along very well at work; many white families and their African servants were on very good terms and even their children played together, especially when house maids took their children with them to work or if they lived on the same premises although under separate roofs. A house maid is called *yaya* in Kiswahili.

Sometimes good relations between Africans and whites went beyond accepted norms. There were those who even ate and drank together, although usually in private, and whites who did that would normally avoid doing so in front of other whites. They did not want to be seen getting too friendly with Africans who were by colonial definition no more than servants of whites. And they did not want to be alienated from the white settler community of which they were an integral part simply because they wanted to be friends with Africans and people of other races.

Yet, there were those who defied convention. They were not the majority but they did exist, although no one cannot be sure how many in terms of numbers or percentage. For example, I remember my mother telling me in the late fifties and early sixties that there was a British couple who wanted to take me with them to Britain as a child to provide me with education and told my father that they would bring me back to Tanganyika every year on holidays but I would have the benefit of excellent education in the UK beginning at a very early age. She said my father seriously considered doing that, but she was strenuously opposed to the idea saying I was too young to go so far away.

They knew my father very well. They also knew my mother but they dealt with my father more than they did with my mother. Language was also a barrier on my mother's part. She did not know English like my father did. He spoke English fluently and even taught me the language at home when I first started learning English in 1961 at the age of 11. And that gave me an advantage over other pupils.

I don't remember exactly where or when this took place. But I know it was in the early fifties, either in Morogoro in the Coast Province or in Mbeya in the Southern Highlands when my parents and the British couple discussed the possibility of my going to school in Britain at a very early age under their guardianship.

And there was something about this British couple which stayed in my mind through the years, especially when I was growing up in Kyimbila in Rungwe District in the Southern Highlands about four miles from Tukuyu.

Their interest in my education showed that there were ordinary whites in Tanganyika, who were not colonial administrators but simply ordinary people who lived and worked there, who were concerned about the well-being of Africans yet couldn't do anything to improve the situation because they did not have the power or the means to do so. It was probably only a minority of them but there were such people.

In fact, some of them never left Africa. They stayed in Tanganyika even after independence because it was their home even if they were not born there, although some of them were, or they moved to other parts of Africa, mainly South Africa. Some also moved to what was then Southern Rhodesia and a few to Kenya. Their heart was, and still is, in Africa.

And when I was writing this book while living in the United States, I got in touch with some ex-Tanganyikan Britons and other whites living in different parts of the world including Britain, Australia and the United States who still had relatives or friends living in Tanzania and involved in various activities, including philanthropic work, together with black Africans. They told me that their relatives and friends never left Tanganyika after the country won independence.

Even some of those who left Tanganyika after independence *still* maintained strong ties with the country and were involved in various activities helping the people in different parts of what is now Tanzania today. As Marion Gough stated in her email to me from England on 17 January 2006:

> Tanganyika was my home and is still very much in my blood. I try to get back as much as I can and am in the process of fund raising to help the building of an Orphanage.
>
> I have sent two shipments of text books, papers and pens to two different schools, together with several computers (used). I had such a happy, if not, lonely, childhood that I feel I must return the privilege.

And as she stated in another email on 21 January 2006:

> Jambo Godfrey,
>
> I am raising funds for the building of an Orphanage in Mufindi and going to get all the info ready to contact big companies to see if they would be willing to help, after a little research of course. If you know of any that are sympathetic to Africa please give me a nod. The Charity in USA is called Mufindi Orphans.
>
> It is going to be built by the Foxes. Geoff Fox (father) lives in Mufindi and has done so for 40 years. He has four sons and each helps run the company and safari camps in Ruaha, Mikumi and Katavi ,also a Highland lodge in Mufindi. They look after several villages by employing a lot of staff and they grow their own food for the camps, use local craftsmen and materials for the camps.
>
> Bruce lives in Gloucester which is 1/2 hour away from me and we

keep in close touch. Great family so enthusiastic for Africa. Bruce has stopped a lot of poaching and is also fighting to keep the Ruaha River flowing as a lot of water has been taken off for the rice fields! Therefore a lot of the wetlands has been destroyed which makes the land flood instead of sinking into the water table.

Sorry could go on for ever, will close here before I get carried away.

Hope the pics don't come out too big.

Take care,

Marion

I, of course, almost left Tanganyika myself even before independence when I was still a child.

Had I left with the British couple and gone to school in Britain at so early an age when I was under 10 years old, my life would probably have taken a different turn and I don't know where I would have ended up eventually. But it was not meant to be. Instead, I remained and grew up in Tanganyika although I did not stay there. As fate would have it, I ended up in the United States after spending my first 23 years of my life in Tanganyika, later Tanzania. But that is another story.

Yet when I look back at all those years since my childhood in Kigoma and Ujiji in western Tanganyika, I know - and I am glad - that I was exposed to other people and other cultures when I was growing up and in such a way that I ended up being what I am today as an open-minded person tolerant of other people's views and values as well as beliefs as long as they don't interfere with my well-being. As the saying goes, the right to swing your arm ends where my nose begins.

But it was with the innocence of a child that I looked at the world, and it was with this kind of innocence that I left Kigoma with my parents when my father was transferred to Morogoro in the Coast Province in the early fifties.

Although I hardly remember Kigoma to enable me to compare the life there with the life in Morogoro, I know that Morogoro was different. It was in the Coast Province with a strong influence of Islamic culture and only about 120 miles from Dar es Salaam, the capital, from where almost everything new started before spreading to other parts of the country.

By remarkable contrast, Kigoma was far in the hinterland - it's still there, of course, just as Morogoro is where it was back then - and being a port on Lake Tanganyika, it was linked to what was then the Belgian Congo just across the lake and played a major role as a hub of activity in the cross-cultural interaction between Congo and Tanganyika as much as it still does today.

It was also in Kigoma where Che Guevara had a supply base during his mission to the Congo in the mid-sixties and to where he sought sanctuary after his mission failed.

Although it was far from the coast, Kigoma was linked to Dar es Salaam by a railway which ran - and still runs - across the country from east to west forming the main artery of the railway network in what was then Tanganyika and which is now Tanzania. Although sparsely populated, Tanzania is a large country, bigger than Nigeria in terms of area, and Kigoma is more than 700 miles from Dar es Salaam.

While my memories of Kigoma are virtually none since I was only a baby under three years old when I was there, my recollections of some of the events in Morogoro are vivid mainly because of the "traumatic" experiences I had as a child in that "coastal" town.

It was also in Morogoro where my brother Lawrence was born in September 1952. He was the third-born but, tragically, he died in August 2005 in Mbeya. Coincidentally, it was also in Mbeya where my sister Gwangu was born in 1954 when we lived there after leaving Morogoro. She was the fourth-born. But her life also ended in tragedy. She died in Rungwe District in July 2004. And my mother died at home in our village of

Mpumbuli, Kyimbila, in November 2006 about one month before her 77th birthday.

All these tragedies were compounded by the fact that they occurred when I was far away in the United States.

And whenever I think about my siblings who passed away, I also remember them in terms of the fifties. We all had our beginning in the early fifties, although I was born two months before the beginning of the decade in which both of them were born.

But it was in the early fifties that I really became aware of my existence in this world and when my personality started to be formed.

And it was in Morogoro where my memories of the fifties started to crystallize and reflect some of the most vivid images of my life which I clearly remember even today.

My Early Years: Growing up in Colonial Tanganyika

Life in Tanganyika in the fifties meant different things to different people - African, European, Arab, and Asian (mostly Indian and Pakistani), the four main racial categories in the country. But it had one thing in common. Life was simpler, and the people, friendlier. There was less crime in those days, far less than what you see today.

But it was also colonial life, although sometimes barely perceptible. To children like me under 10 years old, it meant very little in terms of racial domination. Life went on as usual as if all the people got along just fine. And they did on many occasions but not all.

Even for those who got along just fine, it was still colonial rule. We all lived in a tiered society, racially stratified, with whites on top, Asians and Arabs in the middle constituting some kind of buffer zone, and blacks at the bottom.

It was a heap of vast black masses at the bottom. And they are the ones who propped up this lopsided structure with their cheap labour made even more abundant because of their numerical preponderance in a country that was overwhelmingly black.

Yet, in spite of all the interdependence, with Europeans and Asians - and sometimes Arabs - providing goods and services needed by a significant number of Africans especially those living in towns, and the cheap labour and raw materials provided by Africans to sustain the colonial system, there was little interaction among or between the races. The most that you could see was between Africans and Asians. And that was only during business transactions when Africans went to Indian shops in towns to buy the items they needed.

In the case of Tanganyika, the distance between the races, especially between Africans and Europeans, seemed to be even greater than in neighbouring Kenya because of the smaller number of the white settlers in the country. The distance was magnified even in terms of perception.

Whites were not only fewer in Tanganyika than in Kenya but were also less visible because of their smaller number, yet no less dominant as colonial rulers. But, the fewer they were, the farther they also were from Africans in terms of interaction, although that was not true in all cases. Still, it was extremely rare for Europeans and Asians to socialize with Africans. The races were in most cases far apart and preferred things to be that way.

However, there was one fundamental difference. The difference in this relationship was between the Europeans on the one hand and the Africans as well as the Asians and the Arabs on the other. And it had to do with power.

It was the Europeans who instituted the social hierarchy based on race and who sanctioned the asymmetrical relationship between the races to their advantage as the rulers of Tanganyika in order justify colonial rule. In that sense, the Asians and the Arabs were equally victims of racial domination by whites even if some of them did not think that they were being victimized like blacks.

But although there is no question that the Europeans were the rulers of a country that was overwhelmingly black African (there are also white Africans and Africans of Asian and Arab origin as well as others on the African continent), for many blacks, life went on as it did before the coming of the white man.

That was especially the case in the rural areas, including villages near towns and not only those far away from the urban centres, where the most visible alien intrusion in traditional life since the advent of colonial rule was the tax collector and sometimes, although rarely, a black policeman in khaki uniform and black boots coming on foot to make an arrest.

However, there was fundamental change in institutions of authority in the sense that an alien power had been imposed on us. All of us including traditional rulers became colonial subjects. African chiefs and other traditional rulers lost their power. They no longer had the same power they had before as the ultimate authority in their traditional societies.

Therefore the biggest change which took place when colonial rule was introduced was political. Africans lost power and independence. Attitudes towards life in general, and even towards traditional authority, also changed, although gradually, because of the dominant role European rulers played in the political arena. So it was a dramatic change when power shifted from Africans to Europeans.

Less perceptible were the changes which took place in other areas of life. One was the cultural arena.

Most of the people in the rural areas did not see themselves as victims of cultural imperialism in the same way the few educated Africans did. Their traditional way of life and values remained virtually intact unlike that of their brethren who lived in towns or those who acquired some education especially at the secondary school level and beyond.

The more education one had, the more acutely aware one became, of the racial disparities and introduction and sometimes imposition of alien values by Europeans.

But in many cases it was also far less of an imposition than a willingness by many Africans who had some education to accept European ways of life as some kind of achievement in life. In fact, a significant number of them saw it as a badge of honour to be Europeanized, live and act like Europeans.

It showed that they were now "civilized," or more "civilized" than their brethren - those who continued to live the traditional way of life in the villages and even in towns and also those who had less education.

Yet nationalist sentiments were strong especially among some politically conscious members of the African elite, although even they were not dismissive of all aspects of alien cultures including British in spite of their uncompromising stand in defence of the African traditional way of life. As Julius Nyerere said:

> A country which lacks its own culture is no more than a collection of people without the spirit which makes them a nation. Of all the crimes of colonialism there is none worse than the attempt to make us believe we had no indigenous culture of our own; or that what we did have was worthless...
>
> A nation which refuses to learn from foreign cultures is nothing but a nation of idiots and lunatics... But to learn from other cultures does not mean we should abandon our own.

Nyerere was quoted by Dr. Graham L. Mytton, former head of the BBC's International Broadcasting Audience Research (IBAR), in his book *Mass Communications in Africa*, and by Don Moore in his article, "Reaching the Villages: Radio in Tanzania," published in *The Journal of the North American Shortwave Association*.

And as one British official in Tanganyika admitted in 1955: "We ignore their tribal dances and try to give them cricket. I'ts awful." He was quoted by American journalist John Gunther in his book *Inside Africa*.

Gunther visited Tanganyika in 1954. Among the places he visited was the newly established radio station in Dar es Salaam.

The station was founded in 1951 in response to a proposal by a BBC official who felt that there was a need for such a station which should produce programmes for a native audience in Kiswahili. It was named the Dar es Salaam Broadcasting Station (DBS) and was later renamed the Tanganyika Broadcasting Service (TBS) and then the Tanganyika Broadcasting Corporation (TBC).

And as Sala Elise Patterson stated in a dissertation for a master's degree submitted to the School for Oriental and African Studies at the University of London entitled, "State Control, Broadcasting and National Development," focusing on Tanzania as a case study :

> Radio broadcasting began in Tanganyika in July 1951 in an unused attic of a house in Dar es Salaam. Aimed at city residents, the unit was called the Dar es Salaam Broadcasting Station (DBS).
>
> One year later the colonial government invested 10,000 GBP to upgrade the radio service realizing the importance of broadcasting in the territory to further the colonial process. Another 55,000 GBP was invested from the colonial fund in 1954.
>
> Then on May 8, 1956, the colonial authorities inaugurated the new and improved Tanganyika Broadcasting Service (TBS) with a 20-kilowatt transmitter that increased broadcasting capability to reach as far as Johannesburg.
>
> In July of the same year, the government consolidated their national broadcasting and established the Tanganyika Broadcasting Corporation (TBC) officially as an independent broadcasting body that took over the functions of the TBS.
>
> The colonial government closely monitored programming and the Governor had absolute power to prohibit the broadcast of any programme deemed inappropriate.

When Gunther visited the station in 1954, he was highly impressed by the staff's performance. It was a professional operation totally staffed by native Africans, in spite of the fact that the station had started, as Gunther wrote, "with little more equipment than a microphone and a blanket hung over a wall." It became so successful that it served as a model for broadcasting services in many other British colonies in Africa and elsewhere.

I remember listening to TBC when I was growing up in Rungwe District in the Southern Highlands in the 1950s and early sixties. And I still remember the names of some of the radio announcers, mainly David Wakati and Eli Mboto. Although the reception was poor most of the time, we still were able to listen to the news and to a variety of music, mostly Swahili and Congolese, broadcast from Dar es Salaam more than 300 miles away.

At first, there was not much interest in establishing a radio station because of the relatively small European population in Tanganyika, unlike in neighbouring Kenya where there was a significant number of white settlers. The British government did not encourage its citizens to emigrate and settle in Tanganyika mainly because the territory was not a typical British colony like Kenya but a UN trusteeship territory under British tutelage only for a limited, though not specified, period of time after which the country would become independent.

There were, however, some parts of Tanganyika which attracted a significant number of white settlers. For example, even before the British took over Tanganyika from the Germans after World War I, Lushoto in the Usambara mountains in the northeastern part of the country was a kind of "winter capital" for the Germans.

But, in spite of the relatively small number of whites in Tanganyika, there was an obvious need for a radio station for the indigenous population, although the broadcasts had a short radius and were initially limited to Dar es Salaam, the capital, which itself had Africans in the majority.

Even in the capital Dar es Salaam, European influence on the lives of most Africans was limited when compared to what happened in Nairobi, Kenya's capital, and elsewhere in Kenya especially in the "White Highlands" in the Central Province which had the largest number of white settlers in the country including Boers from South Africa. In fact, it was Boers who founded one of Kenya's most well-known towns, Eldoret.

In the case of Tanganyika, British cultural influence was very limited in terms of everyday life and only had significant impact on the elite. The most visible change in the African way of life was in the towns which were the administrative centres for the colonial rulers. That is where the District Commissioner, whom we simply called DC, and his white staff worked and lived if the town was the district headquarters. If the town was the capital of a province, you had the provincial commissioner, known as PC, as the head.

That is where you would see the colonial rulers and other whites, working and living there, although in some parts of the rural areas, there were also whites who owned farms and hired black labourers to work on coffee and tea plantations and other large farms.

In Tanganyika, white settlers could be found in places such as Lushoto in the Usambara mountains in the northeastern part of the country where they owned coffee farms and also a school exclusively for white children known as Lushoto Prep School; in Arusha in northern Tanganyika where they also had large farms and a school for white children called Arusha School; in Moshi near the slopes of Mount Kilimanjaro of majestic splendour where they also had a primary school exclusively for white children; and in the Southern Highlands Province where they also built the most prestigious school for white students in the whole country called St. Michael's and St. George's School in Iringa District near the town of Iringa, and another one in the town of Mbeya known as Mbeya

School in the same province.

Mbeya School, which is in my home region, was established in 1942 in buildings which were once a German School. It was closed in 1963 as an exclusively European school and became a secondary school for students of all races after Tanganyika won independence. But it became almost exclusively black after students of other races sought education elsewhere.

Besides the German School which became Mbeya School, another European school which was founded in Tanganyika to educate pupils of the same national origin was the Greek School in Moshi where there was a number of Greek farmers and other Greeks engaged in different pursuits.

The school also served Greek children from Arusha which also had a significant number of Greek settlers. As Gregory Emmanuel whose family settled in Tanganyika stated in his article "Grandfather Gregory Emmanuel 'Nisiotis' (1875 - 1977)":

> A large number of Greeks, many from Tenedos, came to Tanganyika, where Greeks became the second largest expatriate European community (Germans being the largest group).
> In both Moshi and Arusha there were thriving Greek communities and the need arose for a Greek school.
> As the house at Lambo was vacant, Grandfather leased it to the Greek community and it became the first Greek school in East Africa. It was a boarding school and was the first school attended by my father, Costas. (He told me that a student who sleepwalked was taken during the night by a leopard.)

Coincidentally, another school, Kongwa School, which was open to white children of all nationalities started as a primary school on 4 October 1948, exactly one year before I was born on 4 October 1949.

It evolved from the abortive groundnut scheme funded by the British Overseas Food Corporation at Kongwa.

After the groundnut scheme failed and was abandoned

in 1954, its buildings were converted into a secondary school, upgraded from a primary school. Then in 1958, the students at Kongwa School were transferred to a new school in Iringa, St. Michael's and St. George's.

All the European schools in Tanganyika were co-educational, attended by white children and students of all ages depending on the kind of school they went to. For example, St. Michael's and St. George's was a secondary school. And it was highly competitive with a reputation for academic excellence.

Many of its former students became very successful in life in different parts of the world, including Tanganyika itself, which became Tanzania, and have been holding reunions now and then to renew ties and reminisce on life in Tanganyika in those days.

In many ways, they were the good old days. Life was also much safer and simpler, and the people a lot friendlier than they are nowadays when everybody is busy fending for himself, with a large number of individuals preying on others in different ways besides robbery.

Although I did not attend St. Michael's and St. George's School after independence, there are many things which the former students and I agree on in terms of how life was in school and in Tanganyika in general in those days.

And we have another thing in common. They went to school in the same province where I come from: the Southern Highlands.

Even after independence, St. Michael's and St. George's stood out among all the schools in Tanzania. It had students up to Form VI (standard 14) and was renamed Mkwawa High School and admitted students of all races, which was not the case before Tanganyika became independent in 1961.

It was in the area of education where the colonial authorities instituted some of the most rigid structures of racial separation in the country.

They sanctioned inequality in the allocation of funds and provision of facilities including teachers which ensured that the children of the white settlers would get the best education and enjoy a privileged life style at the expense of Africans and, to a smaller degree, Asians whose status was no better than that of the Africans as colonial subjects; although they were treated better than Africans in many cases.

Arabs had their own Koranic schools and were not really an integral part of the mainstream in terms of formal education in the Western intellectual tradition.

But the bottom line was that even if the Asians - as well as the Arabs - were treated better than the Africans, they were still colonial subjects, therefore not equal to whites. And provision of separate educational facilities and funds affected their lives as well; although even in this case they were favoured by the colonial government when compared with Africans. As David Nettelbeck states in "Educational Separatism and the 1950s" in his book, *A History of Arusha School*:

> Because of the Government's lack of resources and unwillingness to take a strong initiative in educational provision, and in pursuance of the G.I.A. policy, there grew up three racially distinct systems of African, Asian and European education with each of the three subdivided into state controlled, state aided, and wholly private schools.
>
> In the African sector for example in 1937, there were 9,500 pupils in Government schools, 19,500 in aided schools and 100,000 in private schools. These latter were often sub-standard bush schools, and catechetical centres or Koranic schools along the coast. It was not until 1955 that the Government required these kinds of schools to be registered.
>
> In the same year, there were 985 places in Government schools for Indian children and another 3,318 in grant aided schools. The Indian community were quick to take advantage of the G.I.A. system and fulfil the requirements thus only 320 of their children were that year in private schools.
>
> For the European community in the 1930s, the Government made direct provision in three ways. Arusha School, primarily for boarders,

opened in 1934; a correspondence course was based in Dar es Salaam; and there was also a junior primary school in Dar es Salaam. The enrolment figures in 1937 show 59 children in the latter two, and 60 pupils at Arusha School.

There were in addition 704 grant-aided places for European children, a significant proportion of these being in national community schools for the Dutch, German and Greek children. Another 15 places were in a private school. The above figures are taken from the enrolment statistics 1931 - 1948 in Appendix G.

There is another way of looking at these statistics and that is to see the percentage of children being educated from each community. Listowell states that in 1933, 51% of the European children, 49% of the Asian and 2% of the African were at school.

By 1945 7.5%, of the African children attended school though few got beyond the fourth primary grade and none could attempt the entrance exam for tertiary study at Makerere in Uganda. By 1959, 40% of African children attended at least the first four years of primary education, and in 1961, 55% of the age group entered the first primary grade.

The present Government of Nyerere aims at universal primary education by 1980. (The comparative cost per head of population has been referred to above and is detailed in Appendix J.)

In 1930 an Education Tax was introduced with the primary object of affording security to the Government for the repayment of loans made to non-African communities. In 1932 the Indian and European communities were taxed for their education on a poll Tax basis and, in addition, fees were charged at their schools. Nevertheless the Government was making a far more generous per capita provision for European and Indian children than it was for African children.

The table in Appendix J shows the total expenditure for each community and the per capita cost from 1931 - 1937. Also the table in Appendix K shows that in 1955/56, 33.7% of the money spent by the Government on European education was collected in fees, 15.4% came from the European Education Tax and 49.1% from Central Revenue. In 1959 the central revenue provided for European Education an amount equivalent to 1% of the total territorial expenditure.

In 1956, £3,618,555 held by the Custodian of Enemy Property from funds collected from confiscated properties during the Second World War was distributed equally between the Tanganyika Higher Education Trust Fund for establishing tertiary education facilities, St Michael's and St George's School, a lavish secondary school for European children at Iringa, Indian education, and African education.

This 4 way split seem superficially fair but as President Nyerere has pointed out, the allocation on a per capita basis was equivalent to shs- 720/- to each European, shs. 200/- to each Asian and shs. 2/- to each African.

In 1948 and 1949, the three existing education systems described above were formalized by two ordinances, the Non-Native Education Ordinance and the Non-Native Education Tax Ordinance. This legislation brought into being an Indian Education Authority and a European Education Authority, each composed of representatives of the communities they were to serve.

They were responsible for the development and general over-sight of the systems, and for managing the education funds according to the budget approved by the Legislative Council.

There was also an Advisory Committee for Other (non-native) Education, which included Goan, Mauritian, Seychellois, Anglo-Indian, and Ceylonese children.

What began in 1948 as a very minor offshoot of basic Government responsibility for the development of the country with only 8,000 Asian and 300 European children, had become by 1961 a major concern catering for 28,000 Asian and 2,500 European children.

The three educational systems established along racial lines for Europeans, Indians and Africans - in descending order in terms of quality - were formalized in the 1940s and 1950s. And they mirrored the racial hierarchy in colonial Tanganyika instituted by the British colonial rulers. They were abolished in January 1962, soon after the country won independence on 9 December 1961, and all schools in Tanganyika were opened to students of all races.

Although the British constituted the largest group of whites during colonial rule, the white settler community in Tanganyika was a constellation of nationalities. It included many other whites such as Greeks, Germans, Italians, Afrikaners, Jews, Poles, Swedes, Danes, Russians, and Lithuanians. And that is not an exhaustive list. The white settler community was in some ways a microcosm of Europe.

There were even a few Americans in Tanganyika; for example, the first owner of the New Arusha Hotel, Kenyon Painter, a millionaire banker from Ohio. He went to

Tanganyika for the first time in 1907 and started building the New Arusha Hotel in 1927. It was completed in the same year.

The hotel was formally opened in January 1928 and the opening ball - in December 1927 - was attended by the Prince of Wales, Edward VIII.

Painter continued to live in the United States but he made several hunting trips to Tanganyika, especially Arusha. He died in 1940.

Before he arrived, there was only one tiny hotel in Arusha owned by a Jewish couple, Jane and Goodall Bloom, and they named the hotel, Bloom's, and it was the first Arusha Hotel. That's why when Kenyon Painter built his hotel, he called it the New Arusha Hotel.

Kenyon Painter bought 11,000 acres of land near the town of Arusha and he played a major role in establishing coffee farms in the region. He also built the first post office in Arusha, a church, a hospital, and a coffee research centre at Tengeru, 16 miles from Arusha.

The New Arusha Hotel became a historic landmark and a centre of social activity for many people including Hollywood stars such as John Wayne whose famous movie, "Hatari," which means danger in Kiswahili, was filmed in Arusha in 1962. There was also a sign in front of the New Arusha Hotel which said:

THIS SPOT IS EXACTLY HALF WAY BETWEEN THE CAPE AND CAIRO AND THE EXACT CENTRE OF KENYA, UGANDA, AND TANGANYIKA.

Arusha also was, and still is, one of the famous towns on what is known as The Great North Road from C to C, that is, from Cape Town to Cairo. And as someone described the two main hotels in the town of Arusha and the town itself in 1957:

Also in the main street were Arusha's two famous hotels.

The New Arusha displayed a board announcing that it was exactly midway between Cape Town and Cairo, and the Safari Hotel boasted an unusual copper topped bar to which a baby elephant had been led in for a drink in a recent Hollywood film Hatari (Danger).

Mount Meru overlooked the pretty garden town beyond the golf course and the main road to Nairobi to the north.

The streets in the residential areas were lined with purple jacarandas and the well kept gardens displayed a profusion of tropical zinnias, petunias and marigolds mixed with the roses, hollyhocks, ferns and carnations of England.

At 5000 feet above sea level, the climate was perfect after the sultry heat of the coast and the early mornings were a delight with dew-dappled lawns, mists and a nip in the air, mingled with the fragrant scent of cedar hedges.

It was the kind of climate which attracted many whites to the region. Today Arusha is the headquarters of the East African Community (EAC) comprising Kenya, Uganda, Tanzania, Rwanda and Burundi and is virtually the capital of East Africa and of the proposed East African Federation to be formed by 2013, if at all.

Other whites who lived in Arusha included Germans, Greeks, South Africans, Italians, and the British. They had farms around Arusha and some of them had small businesses in town.

Some of the crops grown in this fertile region included cereals, cherries, apples, citrus, coffee, cocoa, vanilla, and rubber. They were grown mostly by the Germans but other Europeans participated as well.

At the beginning of World War II, there were about 3,000 Germans and Italians living in Tanganyika. That was out of a total population of about 8,000 whites in the country. During the war itself, there were about 3,000 Italians including those who were held as prisoners of war in camps in Tanganyika; 9,000 Poles, 500 Greeks, and 180 Cypriot Jews, among many others.

According to the British Foreign and Commonwealth Office, the total number of Italians who were interned in

Tanganyika, mainly in Arusha and Tabora, and in Uganda and Southern Rhodesia during World War II was almost 15,000. The number given in May 1945 was 14,900.

Many whites came to live in Tanganyika after the Second World War. Also after Germany was defeated in World War I, she lost her colony of German East Africa which became Tanganyika, taken over by the British, and Ruanda-Urundi, by the Belgians. After the British took over the colony, they also used it for detaining prisoners of war (POWs) who included Germans and their allies.

Many of them ended up staying in Tanganyika. The Italians, for example, did not have any historical connection to Tanganyika like the Germans who were the first colonial rulers did, but they settled in the country in significant numbers. Most of them had been preceded earlier by a group of Italian missionaries as far back as the 1920s.

The Italians who were interned in Tanganyika during World War II were sent back to Italy after the war ended but many of them returned because they liked living there. They also felt that Tanganyika had better prospects for them than Italy did.

Many of them were craftsmen and worked in technical fields and in construction and knew that their skills were in great in demand in an underdeveloped colonial territory like Tanganyika. In fact, some of them had done the same kind of work when they in internment camps in Tanganyika.

The situation got even much better for them and the other prisoners of war or detainees in Tanganyika after 1947 when the property which had been confiscated from foreigners including some Italians by the "Custodian of the Enemy Properties," in essence the British colonial government itself, was returned to them.

Therefore the 1950s was a period when Tanganyika witnessed the arrival of a significant number of Italians who came to settle in the country in addition to the ones who were already there.

Some of them were employed on farms, for example on sisal plantations in Morogoro in the Coast Province, on tobacco farms in Iringa in the Southern Highlands, and in the cultivation of coffee and pyrethrum in Arusha and Moshi in the Nothern Province.

Other Italians went to work in the mines, mostly gold. They went to Geita in the Lake Province where they worked for the Gold Mining Company, in Musoma where they were employed by Tangold Company, and in the diamond mines of Mwadui in Shinyanga where they worked for the Williamson Diamonds Ltd. of Mwadui. There were, of course, people of other nationalities as well working in these mines, including the British and Afrikaners.

It was also during the same period that another development took place which improved prospects for a number of Italians seeking employment in Tanganyika in the 1950s.

Two projects were launched under the direction of the M. Gonella Company based in Nairobi. These were the construction of some oil depots at Kurasini in Dar es Salaam and of the first sewerage system also in Dar es Salaam, the country's capital in the Coast Province.

An average of about 200 Italians came to Tanganyika every year in the fifties to live or seek employment. The number may have been small but when looked at in the larger context of all the immigrants who came to Tanganyika in those years, we see that the figure was not really that small and Italy was one of the main countries of origin of the immigrants who settled in Tanganyika in the 1950s.

In 1952, a census was done and it showed that there were 17,885 Europeans living in Tanganyika. A total of 12,395, or 69.3 percent of the white population in the country, were British. Greeks were the second largest group with 1,292 people, followed by the Italians with

1,071; the Dutch, with 515; the Germans, 499; the Swiss, 496; and the Americans, with 331.

Other sources arrive at pretty much the same figure showing that the population of white settlers in Tanganyika in the fifties was much closer to 20,000. That was about a third of those in Kenya.

Some cited a higher figure. For example, *Time* magazine, in one of its 1965 editions stated: "Tanzania, which as Tanganyika once had 22,700 whites, now has 17,000."

But all these settlers had one thing in common. They were white and therefore members of the white settler community. Although they settled in significant numbers in only a few parts of Tanganyika, the areas where they settled were mostly in the fertile and cooler regions at high altitudes with temperatures most whites were comfortable with. There were, however, also significant numbers of whites in Dar es Salaam in the Coast Province because it was the capital and commercial centre of colonial Tanganyika.

Other whites were spread throughout the country living in different places such as Lindi, Nachingwea, Masasi and Mtwara in the Southern Province and other parts of the region; Kilosa in the Coast Province; Dodoma in the Central Province; Tabora in the Western Province; Mwanza and Bukoba in the Lake Province and other parts of Tanganyika.

Yet, even in areas with significant numbers of whites such as the Southern Highlands which were "extensively" occupied by the British, there was little interaction with Africans besides servants, farm labourers and house boys and maids, whose relationship with whites was defined by their subordinate status. There was also some interaction of the master-servant type in towns as well where whites lived and worked.

And the relationship couldn't be anything but that in a colony and racially stratified society dominated by

Europeans even if most Africans in Tanganyika rarely saw a white person in their lives or at least during the period of colonial rule. Most of them lived in villages and spent their entire lives without going into towns where whites were.

And even when they went into towns to buy and sell things, they did not always see white people, although many of them did on a number of occasions now and then in their lives.

I remember when I was growing up in Rungwe District in Mpumbuli Village, Kyimbila, about four miles from the town of Tukuyu which was the district headquarters, I rarely saw whites when I went into town. That was in the late fifties when I was under 10 years old and quite often ventured into town, walking or sometimes catching the bus.

The only time we saw quite a few whites was when they played golf and tennis in the town of Tukuyu. I remember when we passed by as children, they now and then gave us tennis balls which we used to play with as soccer, popularly known as football. And it was the right size of "football", or "soccer ball," for us as little boys between 6 and 9 years old.

To us the whites, who were mostly British, were friendly and we saw them simply as white people who were in town playing golf and tennis. Politics was the last thing on our minds. We did not have the slightest idea of what was going on. We didn't even know why they came to Tanganyika all the way from Europe.

Even our knowledge of geography was very limited at that age. To us, our home district was the entire world. We couldn't envision anything beyond the misty blue mountains which form a ring around Rungwe District in the Great Rift Valley. Next to that, as our world, after we grew a little older and learnt more about geography, was our province, the Southern Highlands Province; and then Tanganyika, our country.

We hardly knew about the rest of East Africa when we were six and seven years old and did not even know much about the neighbouring countries of Nyasaland and Northern Rhodesia which border our region.

We did not learn that in standard one and standard two until later when we were in standard three and standard four. And why whites were in Tanganyika, and when they came to Tanganyika and to Africa in general, was in the realm of history and politics far beyond our knowledge at that age.

The whites who came to Tukuyu to play golf came from Mbeya, about 45 miles away. Some even came from Northern Rhodesia, which is Zambia today. And there were, of course, those who lived in Tukuyu, although not many. From what I remember, it was only a few of them who lived in the town of Tukuyu.

The town was first built by the Germans, the first colonial rulers, and was named Neu Langenburg. They are the ones who first made it the headquarters of Rungwe District. The town was destroyed twice by earthquakes, first in 1910, and again in 1919, but was rebuilt by the British after they took control of Tanganyika after the end of the First World War. And it is still the headquarters of Rungwe District today.

Among the whites whom I remember when I was growing up in Rungwe District in the late fifties were the District Commissioner (DC), the most powerful man in the town of Tukuyu and in the whole district of no fewer than 300,000 people during that period; the manager of Shell BP petrol station, a British like the DC, also in the town of Tukuyu where my father once worked under him as an assistant manager in the late fifties, and about whom I have more to say elsewhere in the book; and the manager of Kyimbila Tea Estate and his wife, both British, about a mile-and-a- half from our house whom I also address in another chapter in this book.

He and his wife lived on the premises at Kyimbila next

to Kyimbila Moravian Church of which my family and I were members and whose pastor, Asegelile Mwankemwa, was my mother's uncle. He is also the one who helped raise my mother and her brothers after their parents died. My grandmother, my mother's mother, was his sister.

I don't remember any of the names of the whites I just mentioned except one, although when we were in primary school - I went to Kyimbila Primary School from 1956 to 1959 about two miles from Tukuyu and two miles from our home - we knew the name of the district commissioner (DC) of Rungwe District.

But I do remember the name of one provincial commissioner, Mr. J.T.A. Pearce. He was PC in the late 1950s and lived in Mbeya which was then the capital of the Southern Highlands Province. The former capital was Iringa but it was moved to Mbeya, although I don't remember exactly when; it was sometime in the late fifties, I believe.

The most visible symbol of colonial authority I remember when I was eight and nine years old in the late fifties was a wooden sign on the outskirts of the town of Tukuyu which said, "Native Authority." I remember it very well, almost 50 years later, and even exactly where it was. It was a white sign with black capital letters.

It was on the right-hand side of the road right at the foot of a small hill when on the way to Tukuyu, and on the left on my way home; on the same road that went all the way to Kyela, a town near the border with Nyasaland. It was very close to a junction where there was an Anglican Church. The other road led to a place called Makandana which was only about a mile from the town of Tukuyu.

I did not know what kind of sign it was - for direction, warning, or what - and it meant absolutely nothing to me. I had not even started learning English during that time, until later when I went to Mpuguso Middle School. It was a boarding school. I first went there in 1961, the same year I started learning English. I was 11 years and three months old when I started learning the language in January.

I was a day student from 1961 to 1962 before I was enrolled as a boarder in 1963. It was an all-boys school with a reputation for rigorous intellectual discipline and was one of the best middle schools in the Southern Highlands Province and in the whole country. It was also one of the oldest.

Among its alumni was Jeremiah Kasambala, son of a chief from the area who later became one of the first cabinet members under Nyerere when Tanganyika won independence. Another cabinet member, David Mwakyusa who once was a professor of medicine and President Nyerere's personal physician, was also a product of Mpuguso Middle School. He served as minister of health under President Jakaya Kikwete, Tanzania's fourth president since independence.

Other alumni through the years included doctors, lawyers and academics; and a general in the Tanzania People's Defence Forces (TPDF), my first cousin Owen Rhodfrey Mwambapa, who also became head of the Tanzania Military Academy, an officers' training school in Monduli, northern Tanzania, whose students came from other parts of Africa as well.

Another cousin of mine, Oscar Mwamwaja, who became one of Tanzania's first airline pilots, was also a product of Mpuguso Middle School.

And it was not until a few years later after I was at Mpuguso Middle School that I understood what that (Native Authority) sign meant after I learned some English, and even much later before I understood its political significance as a demarcation line between the colonizer and colonized.

It symbolised colonial power enforced by indirect rule, a system of administration first introduced by Lord Lugard in Northern Nigeria under which the colonial government ruled vast expanses of territory through native rulers including chiefs in my home district of Rungwe.

The town of Tukuyu was under direct rule by the district commissioner (DC), and the rest of the district under indirect rule through native authority; hence the sign, "Native Authority," showing where direct rule ended and where indirect rule began. Africans and Indian shopkeepers who lived in the town of Tukuyu were under direct rule of the white colonial administrators who also lived there.

But if the colonial authorities felt that direct intervention was warranted, they did not hesitate to exercise their power.

I remember one tragic incident in the late fifties when two Nyakyusa chiefs and their people in Kyela were involved in a bloody conflict, the exact nature of which I never understood; some said the conflict was over land, which seemed to be a plausible explanation, given the scarcity of land in Rungwe District of which Kyela was then an integral part; today Kyela is a separate district and has been one for years.

When the conflict erupted, an urgent message was sent to Mbeya, the provincial capital, and within the same day, the colonial authorities dispatched a contingent of Field Force Units (FFU) to stop the fighting. The FFUs, which still exist in Tanzania today, specialize in riot control and in stopping other violent conflicts and have a reputation for being tough and using weapons when necessary.

It was one of those instances during my life time when the British invoked *Pax Britannica* in the quest for peace under the Union Jack in their colony of Tanganyika. The FFU riot policemen were black but their officers white.

There were other whites I remember in Rungwe District including missionaries; for example, Catholic priests at Kisa Catholic Mission about five miles from our home. They used to walk most of the time all the way from Kisa to Tukuyu and back. I remember they were dressed in black robes.

There was also another white man whom I remember

very well. He used to drive down the road near our house on his way to Ilima coal mine and back to Tukuyu and Mbeya. They said he was the owner of the coal mine which was about 15 miles from our home and the Nyakyusa called him Tojilwe, obviously a corruption of his name, whatever it was; today, it sounds like Trujillo or Torrijos to me.

He could have been Spanish, I don't know, if his name was indeed Trujillo or Torrijos, what my fellow Nyakyusas called Tojilwe.

The mine was almost mid-way between Tukuyu and Kyela, a town near the Tanzania-Malawi border, and the road goes all the way to Malawi, which was then Nyasaland in those days.

Although Tojiliwe was in charge of the Ilima coal mine which was about 15 miles from our home in Mpumbuli village in the area of Kyimbila, and the people who did all the hard work were Africans, to him they were just that, coal miners.

His relationship with the coal miners was basically no different from the relationship other whites had with Africans in general. Few whites interacted with Africans on personal basis. Africans were no more than colonial subjects under the imperial flag fluttering under the tropical sun.

The interaction was minimal for racial and cultural reasons, as well as for reasons of personal taste probably on both sides. Africans who may have wanted to associate with whites - usually for social status more than anything else as members of "civilized" society which by colonial definition meant white - were inhibited in their desire by their well-founded fear and suspicion that they would not be accepted, let alone as equals, by a people who were their masters as colonial rulers and many of whom probably considered them to be inferior; while some whites, on the other hand, did not want to mingle with blacks because they did not consider them to be their equal in any conceivable way including mental capacity.

Africans dealt mostly with Indians who owned shops where African customers bought a variety of items such as clothes, soap, cooking oil, salt and sugar. And they communicated very well. I remember many Indians in Tukuyu who spoke Kinyakyusa, our "tribal" language, with their customers. And some of them knew the language very well.

Although many Africans probably did not notice or feel the colonial presence and white domination did not have a direct impact on their lives everyday, there were those who were acutely aware of the disparities in life among the races purely along racial lines. They knew the disparities or inequities were not merely accidental but a product of deliberate decisions by the colonial rulers who instituted a system of racial hierarchy to maintain colonial rule.

What set them apart from the other Africans besides their political consciousness was education. They were mostly educated, with secondary school education or higher and sometimes even less, and they worked directly under the supervision of whites especially in towns. And they are the ones who led the struggle for independence, not only in Tanganyika but in other African countries as well.

There was another politically conscious class of Africans who constituted a critical mass during the struggle for independence. These were the workers in towns. They formed trade unions demanding better wages and conditions at work which eventually led to demands for political equality and representation at the local and national levels.

Most of them were not educated in the traditional sense. They never got the chance to go to school, although a significant number of them did and had at least primary school education enabling them to read and write as well as count. But because they worked directly under whites, they became very much aware of the difference in living conditions among the races and they were among some of the most politically conscious people in Tanganyika and in all the other colonies across the continent.

Their consciousness was best demonstrated on a number of occasions when they went on strike to force the colonial authorities to meet their demands, a strategy which helped galvanize the independence movement.

In fact, the labour union leaders became some of the most prominent leaders in the independence struggle. For example, Rashid Mfaume Kawawa, a prominent labour union leader in Tanganyika, became prime minister and later vice president of Tanganyika and later of Tanzania. And in Kenya, Tom Mboya, another highly influential labour union leader, became the most prominent national leader after President Jomo Kenyatta and his heir apparent. He also held senior cabinet posts including the ministry of economic planning and development until his assassination in July 1969 at the age of 39.

I remember there were even songs by Kenyan musicians played on the radio, the Tanganyika Broadcasting Corporation, which in those days we simply called TBC, in the late fifties about Tom Mboya when he was one of the brightest stars on the Kenyan political scene even before independence.

In the case of Tanganyika, the late fifties were a turning point in the independence struggle, as much as they were for neighbouring Kenya, and witnessed among other things the departure of one of the last two governors of this vast country, the largest among the East African British colonies.

I witnessed some of those events, although I was only 8 and 9 years old.

I remember when Sir Edward Francis Twining, one of the last two governors of Tanganyika, came to Tukuyu in 1958. It was a farewell visit.

He was the governor from 18 June 1949 (about four

months before I was born) to June 1958. He was succeeded by Sir Richard Gordon Turnbull who was the last governor of Tanganyika from 15 July 1958 until independence day on 9 December 1961. Twining died in June 1967, and Turnbull in December 1998.

I remember the day Governor Twining came to Tukuyu in 1958 to say good-bye. I was about eight-and-a-half years old. It was a bright, sunny day, in the afternoon. I was then a pupil in standard three at Kyimbila Primary School about two miles from Tukuyu and our head teacher made arrangements for us to go and see the governor. So we were in school only half of the day and we walked the two miles to the town of Tukuyu to see the governor for the last time; it was also the first time most of us saw him on that day.

I even remember his attire. He was dressed in white. He also had on a white hat and white gloves. And Nyakyusa dancers performed the traditional dance called *mang'oma* in farewell to him.

There were also many whites on the scene. Some had accompanied him from Dar es Salaam and Mbeya and others simply came to see him. Also on the scene was the Provincial Commissioner (PC) of the Southern Highlands Province from Mbeya, the provincial capital, and the District Commissioner (DC) of Rungwe District who lived right there in Tukuyu, the district headquarters.

I remember it was a festive occasion. People were in jovial mood. Politics seemed to be the last thing on their minds, as the dancers swayed and swivelled to the rhythm and drum-beat of *mang'oma*, the most popular Nyakyusa traditional dance.

And the others who were there joyously clapped their hands for the governor when he climbed up the steps of the Barclays Bank building from where he waved to the crowd, smiling.

I remember the area well. The Clock Tower and the golf course were only a few yards away on the right hand-side when you faced the Barclays Bank Building.

Although I was too young to know what was going on in the country in terms of politics and the campaign for independence under the leadership of the Tanganyika African National Union (TANU) whose charismatic leader, Julius Nyerere, electrified his audiences by his mere presence even before he spoke whenever he campaigned in different parts of Tanganyika, I was still able to tell that there was no hostility of any kind towards the governor and other whites on the part of the Africans who were there on that day.

And that seemed to be the case even during the campaign for independence itself. There were no attacks on the British and other whites, and the people of all races seemed to get along just fine even if they did not mingle. The campaign for independence was peaceful and was waged along constitutional lines.

When reflecting on the transition from colonial rule to independence, Nyerere himself said that Tanganyika won independence by peaceful means, and there was no hostility towards whites even after the country won independence. As he stated in parliament during a debate on the citizenship bill when a few members wanted only black Africans to be citizens after Tanganyika became independent, as reported in the *Tanganyika National Assembly Debates* (Hansard), in October 1961 less than two months before the country won independence from Britain:

> If we in Tanganyika are going to divorce citizenship from loyalty and marry it to colour, it won't stop there...until you break up the country....They are preaching discrimination as a religion to us. And they stand like Hitlers and begin to glorify race. We glorify human beings, not colour.

Nyerere was furious when he heard a few members of the National Assembly speaking against citizenship for whites, Indians, Arabs and others. He was known to be very calm, tolerant and kind but he lost his temper during the course of the debate and accused them of racism and talking rubbish and behaving like Nazis.

Earlier as a little boy, before Nyerere gave that speech in the National Assembly in October 1961, I witnessed an event which embodied his vision of a multiracial society.

The reception the governor, Sir Edward Twining, was given by Africans and other people on that day in Tukuyu in 1958 during his last visit there was in many ways highly indicative of how things were going to be after Tanganyika won independence: people of different races and ethnic groups living and working together in harmony without hate and fear of each other or one another in the best interest of the country and for the sake of peace and stability enjoyed by all.

Governor Edward Twining's farewell visit marked the beginning of the end of British colonial rule in Tanganyika.

But, at that tender age, little did I or any of the other children – including many adults – know that independence was only three-and-a-half years away after 42 years of British colonial rule.

The Sixties

From Godfrey Mwakikagile, *Africa and America in The Sixties*, First Edition, New Africa Press, 2006.

Acknowledgements

WRITING about the sixties has been a personal odyssey for me.

I grew up in the sixties. I was ten years old at the dawn of the decade and the euphoric - and turbulent - sixties were an integral part of my life. And they always will be.

Therefore I write from personal experience. Much of what I have written in this book is what I knew, and even experienced, when I was growing up in the sixties.

But a lot of it also comes from other sources I have cited to complement my work. And for that I am very grateful to all the individuals and institutions whose material I have used in this study to help me look at the sixties from a better perspective I otherwise would not have.

I am also grateful to the people of my generation and others who were there in those days for inspiring this work. It was, in many ways, a collective experience. And it is, indeed, a decade to remember.

Godfrey Mwakikagile
Wednesday, 27th September 2006.

Introduction

IT WAS a decade of triumph and tragedy, of wars and assassinations, and much more. It was also the dawn of a new era for both Africa and America.

In Africa, we witnessed the end of colonial rule. In America, legal segregation was consigned to the dustbin of history following the triumph of the civil rights movement.

For us in Africa, the sixties ushered in the dawn of a new era in more than one way. While we celebrated the end of colonial rule, we also witnessed wars in the Congo which became the bleeding heart of Africa; and in Nigeria where a civil war became the bloodiest conflict in modern African history threatening the survival of Africa's most populous nation and one of the richest.

The Nigerian civil war was also one of the bloodiest in modern world history. And there were other conflicts on the continent.

But while the end of colonial rule signalled the dawn of a new era of independence under which we would be masters of our own destiny, the democracy we were supposed to enjoy was compromised by the emergence of a new phenomenon on the African political landscape: military coups which led to the institutionalization of militocracy, and dictatorship even under civilian rule, as the most powerful institution in most countries on the continent for almost three decades well into the nineties.

We also had a rude awakening to the harsh realities of nationhood, as we struggled to build our nations and consolidate our independence.

In America, around the same time, the nation's commitment to democracy and racial equality was severely tested in the streets and in the courts as the civil rights movement gained momentum throughout the decade, reaching its peak in 1968 with the passage of one of the most important civil rights laws in the country's history: the Opening Housing Act. Two others had been passed earlier, the Civil Rights Act of 1964, and the Voting Rights Act of 1965. Together they constituted the most comprehensive civil rights legislation in the nation's history.

The triumph of the civil rights movement coincided with the achievement of independence in Africa. By 1968, most African countries had won independence. The countries which had not won freedom by then included South Africa, the bastion of white rule and supremacy on the continent; the British colony of Rhodesia; the Portuguese colonies of Angola, Mozambique, Guinea-Bissau and Cape Verde, Sao Tome and Principe; and the Seychelles, the Comoros, and French Somaliland which became Djibouti.

It was a decade of triumph and tragedy, of hope and despair. In America, it was also the decade of the Vietnam war which bitterly divided the nation; of the counterculture, and much more. But above all, it was a decade of optimism.

In Africa, we were highly optimistic of the future after we won independence. And in America, many people saw the triumph of the civil rights movement as the dawn of a new era for the nation in which people would "not be judged by the colour of their skin but by the content of their character," to quote Dr. Martin Luther King.

And from a personal perspective, the sixties were for me a period of political awakening as I followed the struggle for independence and other political developments in Africa and for racial equality in the United States. I grew up in the sixties. I was then in my teens.

When our country, what was then Tanganyika, won independence from Britain at midnight on 9 December 1961, I was 12 years old. I was born at 6 a.m. on Tuesday, 4 October 1949, in the town of Kigoma, a port on Lake Tanganyika in western Tanganyika which for decades especially after independence has been a haven for refugees from neighbouring Congo, Rwanda and Burundi.

I was baptised Godfrey on Christmas day, 25 December 1949, as a member of the Church Missionary Society (CMS) but grew up as a member of the Moravian Church in my home district of Rungwe where German missionaries established themselves in the 1880s.

Twelve years after being baptised, I witnessed the end of British colonial rule and the birth of a new nation, Tanganyika, the first in East Africa to attain sovereign status.

One of my mother's elder brothers, uncle Johan Chonde Mwambapa who was a primary school teacher, took me on his bicycle to see fireworks and witness the lowering of the Union Jack at midnight at a soccer stadium in Tukuyu, four miles away from our home.

The town was founded in the 1890s by the German colonial rulers who preceded the British and named it Neu Langenburg. It was destroyed by an earthquake in 1910, and again by another earthquake in 1919, but was rebuilt by the Germans and the British.

The town was renamed Tukuyu after German East Africa -*Deutsch Ostafrika* - became a British colony called Tanganyika following the end of World War I.

Throughout colonial rule, German and British, the small town was and still is the capital of Rungwe District, my home, in the Southern Highlands of Tanzania in Mbeya Region in the southwestern part of the country on the border with Malawi, formerly Nyasaland, and Zambia, formerly Northern Rhodesia.

Rungwe District lies in the Great Rift Valley and is ringed by misty blue mountains except the southern part which is bordered by Lake Nyasa, also known as Lake Malawi.

In Tanzania, we still call it Lake Nyasa as it was during colonial rule because part of the lake belongs to Tanzania. The border runs in the middle of the lake and was established before 1914 between the British colony of Nyasaland and German East Africa (Tanganyika). It was never changed or disputed by the British who ruled both Tanganyika and Nyasaland which was renamed Malawi after independence, although they put the lake under the jurisdiction of Nyasaland for administrative purposes since there was no separate administration for the Tanganyika portion.

And since the boundary between the two countries was established by two colonial powers, Germany and Britain, Britain alone had no legal authority to redraw the map and change the border. They were in control of both countries after the end of World War I and they knew the boundary that was agreed upon by both Germany and Britain ran in the middle of the lake.

It's the government of Malawi under President Kamuzu Banda which renamed the lake, Lake Malawi, contending that the entire lake belongs to Malawi. Tanzania contends otherwise and has done so since colonial times. The lake belongs to both Tanzania and Malawi and to Mozambique as well.

Colonial rule caused a lot of problems for us and this is just one of them. Before colonial rule, the people on both sides shared the lake without any problems. There was no such thing as German East Africa (Tanganyika) or British Nyasaland. There was just Africa, and Africans, free to migrate anywhere and share the resources – including fish in Lake Nyasa – without hindrance or being accused of taking what did not belong to you. It belonged to all of us.

And unfortunately, when colonial rule ended, many of the problems which had been caused by colonialism remained with us – including border disputes.

As I witnessed the end of colonial rule on 9 December 1961, little did I realise that I would be living in a new country only about two-and-a-half years later. It was the new nation of Tanzania formed after Tanganyika united with Zanzibar on 26 April 1964. The new country was called the United Republic of Tanganyika and Zanzibar and was renamed Tanzania on October 29 the same year.

The leader of the newly independent country was Julius Nyerere. When he led Tanganyika to independence in 1961, he was 39 and the youngest leader in the world. He became the country's first prime minister.

On 9 December 1962 on the country's first independence anniversary, Tanganyika became a republic. And Julius Nyerere became president.

A towering intellectual yet a humble leader committed to equality for everybody, especially to the well-being of the masses probably more than anybody else, he tried to transform Tanzania into a classless socialist society, although not with much success, and even sent his children to local schools instead of sending them overseas as was the case with many other leaders and other highly privileged members of society across the continent.

I went to school with his eldest son, Andrew. And he lived in the same student hostel with the rest of us when we were at Tambaza High School in Dar es Salaam where I completed standard 14, or Form VI, which would be equivalent to the 14th grade in the United States had the American school system been structured to go that far before one goes to college or university.

More than 30 years later, Andrew contributed generously towards completion of a project I was working on and which had direct bearing on his family. I wrote a book about his father, President Nyerere, entitled *Nyerere and Africa: End of An Era*, and he answered all the questions I asked him and helped me with other things. He also wrote quite a few comments on different subjects which I included in the second edition of the book published in January 2005. The book has now gone through four editions.

And a strange coincidence occurred when I started writing this book: *Africa and America in The Sixties: A Decade That Changed The Nation and The Destiny of A Continent*. Just one day after I started writing the book, I learnt that one of my former colleagues at the *Daily News* in Dar es Salaam, Tanzania, in the early seventies had died. His name was Stanley Kamana.

He was the first journalist with whom I covered President Nyerere for the first time not long before I started working full-time as a reporter at the *Daily News* which was Tanzania's largest and oldest newspaper and one of the four largest and most influential in East Africa together with the *Daily Nation* and the *East African Standard*, both Kenyan newspapers based in Nairobi; and the *Uganda Argus*, based in Kampala, Uganda.

A veteran journalist since the late sixties, Stanley Kamana was one of the best and most seasoned news reporters and political commentators Tanzania has ever produced and will be sorely missed.

I read the news of his death in a Tanzanian newspaper on the Internet when I was in the United States. The story was published in the *Guardian*, Dar es Salaam, Tanzania, 13 October 2005, with the headline, "Kamana Laid to Rest":

"Hundreds of people attended the burial ceremony of veteran journalist, the late Stanley Kamana, yesterday at Kinondoni cemetery in Dar es Salaam.

Relatives, friends, and journalists from various media houses had earlier tearfully paid his body the last respects at his house in Tandika, Dar es Salaam.

The IPP (a Tanzania media company) Executive Chairman Reginald Mengi, former Prime Minister Joseph Sinde Warioba, Habari Corporation Chairman, Jenerali Ulimwengu, CCM Union presidential candidate Jakaya Kikwete (now president of Tanzania), NCCR-Mageuzi presidential candidate Sengondo Mvungi, were among the many dignitaries who attended the burial ceremony.

James Mpinga representing the staff from the IPP said the death of Kamana was a hard blow to the media fraternity: 'He was a hard working man. I don't think that his gap will be easily replaced. His contribution was of great impact on the development of the country.'

Reverend Samson Kameeta of the Tanzania Assemblies of God (TAG), Tandika Mabatini Parish, in his sermon, told the mourners that they should invest in the kingdom of God by committing good deeds.

Many people described Kamana as a man of the people.

He left behind six children and a widow Zakia Kamana.

Kamana died of a heart attack at Temeke Municipal Hospital in Dar es Salaam last Thursday aged 58. Until his death, he was working for IPP Media as a sub-editor."

Kamana was one of the reporters with whom I worked closely at the *Daily News*, as I did with many others.

But long before I became a news reporter, I had other career ambitions which had nothing to do with journalism.

I wanted to be a doctor but changed my mind when our American Peace Corps biology teacher at Songea Secondary School, Mrs. Gallagher whose husband taught history at the same school, showed us how to dissect a frog.

That was in 1968 when I was in standard 12, my final year, before I went to Tambaza High School (standard 13 and standard 14, usually known as Form V and Form VI) after passing the dreaded final exams taken by all the students in all the three East African countries of Kenya, Uganda and Tanzania. We took the same exams, on the same day, throughout East Africa.

I also wanted to be a lawyer and then a writer, goals I felt I could easily achieve now that we had won independence from Britain and would be masters of our own destiny, especially with the free education for everybody provided under the leadership of President Julius Nyerere all the way to university. Medical service was also free for everybody under Nyerere as were other social services.

I was 13 years old when our country became a republic on 9 December 1962, and had no idea where I was headed in life. Ten years later, I ended up in the United States as a student after working as a news reporter at the country's largest newspaper, the *Daily News*, formerly the *Standard*, and briefly as an information officer at the Ministry of Information and Broadcasting in the nation's capital Dar es Salaam.

President Nyerere became our editor-in-chief after the *Standard* was nationalized in 1970 and renamed *Daily News*. But he did not serve in any executive capacity and played only a ceremonial role as the head of this government-owned newspaper and public institution.

The executive role was played by our managing editor, Sammy Mdee, who later became President Nyerere's press secretary. He was succeeded by Benjamin Mkapa, whom we simply called Ben Mkapa. Mkapa also became President Nyerere's press secretary and held other high government positions through the years, including ambassadorial and ministerial posts. He once served as Tanzania's ambassador to the United States in the eighties and later became Tanzania's minister of foreign affairs.

When I left for the United States, Mkapa was our editor at the *Daily News*. And it was he who helped me to go to school in the United States. He later became president of Tanzania and served two five year-terms from

1995 to 2005.

I left Tanzania for the United States on a flight from Dar es Salaam to London around 8 a.m. on Friday, 3 November 1972, and arrived in New York around 4 p.m. the next day. It was the first time I had set foot on American soil. I was 23 years and exactly one month old when I landed in New York on November 4th.

I have lived in the United States since then and longer than I did in Africa, which partly explains why I have decided to write about America during her turbulent years in the sixties.

But I have done so mainly from an African perspective and in relation to the events which unfolded in Africa during the same period where comparative analysis is warranted in the study of the events on both sides of the Atlantic during those tempestuous times.

When I first arrived in America, Dr. Martin Luther King had been assassinated only four years earlier in April 1968; the civil rights movement reached its peak in the same year when Congress passed the Fair Housing - also known as the Open Housing - Act of 1968; and memories of riots in more than 120 cities across the nation which had been sparked by King's assassination were still fresh in the minds of most people, including my sponsors in Detroit where I attended Wayne State University.

I was sponsored by the Pan-African Congress-USA, an organization founded in 1970 by a group of African Americans in that city to forge and strengthen ties between Africa and Black America, among other things. Sponsoring African students was one of the ways of achieving this goal.

The first student to be sponsored was Kojo Yankah. He attended Wayne State University during the same time I did and later the University of Michigan. He returned to Ghana after finishing school.

We arrived in America as students at a time when the

country was still going through dramatic changes as a result of the civil rights movement and the reaction to the racial injustices black Americans had been subjected to for centuries. Many of them, especially the young, had reacted by rioting in the sixties.

Detroit itself had been the scene of some of the worst riots in the nation's history which erupted in 1967 soon after Newark exploded only a few days earlier, and not long after Watts went up in flames in 1965. It was badly scarred and gutted buildings were a common sight in many parts of the city including the area where I lived, not far from 12th Street where the riots started.

In 1975, 12th Street was renamed Rosa Parks in honour of "the mother of the civil rights movement" whom I had the chance to meet in the same year, together with US Congressman Charles Diggs from Detroit, at an African event at Wayne State University where a member of the Pan-African Congress, the organization which sponsored me, showed a documentary he had filmed in Angola showing the brutalities perpetrated by the Portuguese colonial forces against innocent civilians in villages during the liberation struggle.

The film had many gruesome scenes, including gaping wounds, I will never forget. One old man had virtually been scalped. Others were burnt with napalm.

And there was much more that we saw in that documentary.

Rosa Parks, her husband Raymond, and her mother Leona McCauley moved from Montgomery, Alabama, to Detroit in 1957 at the urging of Rosa's younger brother Sylvester and amidst death threats - they also lost their jobs - because of her refusal to give up a seat to a white man on a city bus on 1 December 1955; an act that precipitated the modern civil rights movement but whose spirit had been harboured in the hearts and minds of most blacks across the nation for years.

Her courageous act also catapulted a little known

Baptist minister, Dr. Martin Luther King, into the spotlight after she and others sought some help from him.

Dr. King was her pastor at the Dexter Avenue Baptist Church and was new in Montgomery. Only 26 years old, he was chosen to lead the Montgomery Improvement Association, a new organization formed to direct the nascent civil rights struggle in that city.

It included a bus boycott by blacks because of the city's refusal to treat them as full citizens with the same rights as whites to whom they were routinely forced to give up their seats on the city buses; an act of injustice and humiliation they could no longer tolerate. The boycott lasted for 381 days.

In December 1956, one year after the boycott started, the United States Supreme Court outlawed segregation on city buses, declaring it unconstitutional. The ruling gave momentum to the battle against segregation laws which were enforced throughout the southern states in public accommodations and businesses.

Rosa Parks died years later at her home in Detroit on Monday, 24 October 2005, at the age of 92 and was buried in the same city. Her husband Raymond also died in Detroit before her in 1977. Her mother also died before her in Detroit. And both were buried in the same city.

Rosa Parks' long life and commitment to racial equality and dignity remained a source of inspiration to many people of all races who continued to carry on the struggle for justice across America and elsewhere. It is a struggle I have witnessed through the years.

For more than 30 years, I have been an integral part of American life and have had the opportunity to observe and study events in this country just like millions of other people have and continue to do; but with one exception in my case and of many others whose background is similar to mine as an African. I also look at those events from an African perspective. It is a perspective that goes way back to the sixties. And I have seen a lot as a part of that history myself as an observer and as a participant like millions of others.

Africa at The Dawn of The Decade

THE YEAR 1960 stands out in the history of Africa in one fundamental respect. It was the year in which the largest number of African countries won independence, a feat that was not duplicated in any of the following years.

A total of 17 African countries won independence in 1960. Almost all of them were former French colonies with the exception of Nigeria which was once a British colony and won independence on 1 October 1960.

But they were not the first countries on the continent to emerge from colonial rule. They had been preceded by Egypt which won independence from Britain in 1922; Libya from Italy in 1951; Morocco and Tunisia from France in 1956; Sudan from Britain and Egypt also in 1956; and by Ghana and Guinea.

Ghana became the first country in black Africa to emerge from colonial rule. Formerly known as the Gold Coast, Ghana won independence from Britain on 6 March 1957 under the leadership of Kwame Nkrumah. And Guinea under Sekou Toure became the first French colony in sub-Saharan Africa to win independence on 2 October 1958.

Guinea made a dramatic entry into the community of free nations which angered the former colonial power, France, similar to what happened in the Congo when

Prime Minister Patrice Lumumba gave a fiery speech on independence day denouncing Belgian colonial rule which the Belgian king at the ceremony tried to portray as benevolent to Africans.

Although he was the prime minister and the country's elected leader chosen by parliament of several parties to be the head of government, Lumumba had not even been scheduled to speak on that day - President Joseph Kasavubu was - and many observers say his fiery speech sealed his fate which ended in his brutal assassination only a few month later. As he stated in his speech in Congo's capital, Leopoldville, on June 30, 1960:

"Men and women of the Congo,

Victorious fighters for independence, today victorious, I greet you in the name of the Congolese Government.

All of you, my friends, who have fought tirelessly at our sides, I ask you to make this June 30, 1960, an illustrious date that you will keep indelibly engraved in your hearts, a date of significance of which you will teach to your children, so that they will make known to their sons and to their grandchildren the glorious history of our fight for liberty.

For this independence of the Congo, even as it is celebrated today with Belgium, a friendly country with whom we deal as equal to equal, no Congolese worthy of the name will ever be able to forget that is was by fighting that it has been won [applause], a day-to-day fight, an ardent and idealistic fight, a fight in which we were spared neither deprivation nor suffering, and for which we gave our strength and our blood.

We are proud of this struggle, of tears, of fire, and of blood, to the depths of our being, for it was a noble and just struggle, and indispensable to put an end to the humiliating slavery which was imposed upon us by force.

This was our fate for eighty years of a colonial regime;

our wounds are too fresh and too painful still for us to drive them from our memory. We have known harassing work, exacted in exchange for salaries which did not permit us to eat enough to drive away hunger, or to clothe ourselves, or to house ourselves decently, or to raise our children as creatures dear to us.

We have known ironies, insults, blows that we endured morning, noon, and evening, because we are Negroes. Who will forget that to a black one said *tu*, certainly not as to a friend, but because the more honourable *vous* was reserved for whites alone?

We have seen our lands seized in the name of allegedly legal laws which in fact recognized only that might is right.

We have seen that the law was not the same for a white and for a black, accommodating for the first, cruel and inhuman for the other.

We have witnessed atrocious sufferings of those condemned for their political opinions or religious beliefs; exiled in their own country, their fate truly worse than death itself.

We have seen that in the towns there were magnificent houses for the whites and crumbling shanties for the blacks, that a black was not admitted in the motion-picture houses, in the restaurants, in the stores of the Europeans; that a black travelled in the holds, at the feet of the whites in their luxury cabins.

Who will ever forget the massacres where so many of our brothers perished, the cells into which those who refused to submit to a regime of oppression and exploitation were thrown? [applause]

All that, my brothers, we have endured.

But we, whom the vote of your elected representatives have given the right to direct our dear country, we who have suffered in our body and in our heart from colonial oppression, we tell you very loud, all that is henceforth ended.

The Republic of the Congo has been proclaimed, and our country is now in the hands of its own children.

Together, my brothers, my sisters, we are going to begin a new struggle, a sublime struggle, which will lead our country to peace, prosperity, and greatness.

Together, we are going to establish social justice and make sure everyone has just remuneration for his labour [applause].

We are going to show the world what the black man can do when he works in freedom, and we are going to make of the Congo the centre of the sun's radiance for all of Africa.

We are going to keep watch over the lands of our country so that they truly profit her children. We are going to restore ancient laws and make new ones which will be just and noble.

We are going to put an end to suppression of free thought and see to it that all our citizens enjoy to the full the fundamental liberties foreseen in the Declaration of the Rights of Man [applause].

We are going to do away with all discrimination of every variety and assure for each and all the position to which human dignity, work, and dedication entitles him.

We are going to rule not by the peace of guns and bayonets but by a peace of the heart and the will [applause].

And for all that, dear fellow countrymen, be sure that we will count not only on our enormous strength and immense riches but on the assistance of numerous foreign countries whose collaboration we will accept if it is offered freely and with no attempt to impose on us an alien culture of no matter what nature [applause].

In this domain, Belgium, at last accepting the flow of history, has not tried to oppose our independence and is ready to give us their aid and their friendship, and a treaty has just been signed between our two countries, equal and independent. On our side, while we stay vigilant, we shall respect our obligations, given freely.

Thus, in the interior and the exterior, the new Congo, our dear Republic that my government will create, will be a rich, free, and prosperous country. But so that we will reach this aim without delay, I ask all of you, legislators and citizens, to help me with all your strength.

I ask all of you to forget your tribal quarrels. They exhaust us. They risk making us despised abroad.

I ask the parliamentary minority to help my Government through a constructive opposition and to limit themselves strictly to legal and democratic channels.

I ask all of you not to shrink before any sacrifice in order to achieve the success of our huge undertaking.

In conclusion, I ask you unconditionally to respect the life and the property of your fellow citizens and of foreigners living in our country. If the conduct of these foreigners leaves something to be desired, our justice will be prompt in expelling them from the territory of the Republic; if, on the contrary, their conduct is good, they must be left in peace, for they also are working for our country's prosperity.

The Congo's independence marks a decisive step towards the liberation of the entire African continent [applause].

Sire, Excellencies, Mesdames, Messieurs, my dear fellow countrymen, my brothers of race, my brothers of struggle-- this is what I wanted to tell you in the name of the Government on this magnificent day of our complete independence.

Our government, strong, national, popular, will be the health of our country.

I call on all Congolese citizens, men, women and children, to set themselves resolutely to the task of creating a prosperous national economy which will assure our economic independence.

Glory to the fighters for national liberation!

Long live independence and African unity!

Long live the independent and sovereign Congo!"

Lumumba's militancy had been preceded elsewhere, in Guinea, under another fiery and uncompromising African nationalist Ahmed Sekou Toure. Both were dynamic leaders but it was Ahmed Sekou Toure's militancy which became one of the most prominent features in the early years of the African independence struggle when he defied French wishes and refused to keep his country in the French community in 1958, about two years before Lumumba led Congo to independence on June 30, 1960.

Sekou Toure's militancy started early in his life. He did not go far in school in terms of formal education but was well-read and very knowledgeable like a number of other African leaders who also never got the chance to go to college.

Zambian president, Kenneth Kaunda, was one of them. He completed standard six, what Americans call sixth grade, and worked as a school teacher before entering politics.

Yet he successfully led his country to independence and was one of the most prominent, and most knowledgeable, leaders in post-colonial Africa. Sekou Toure was another one among several.

Born in 1922 of peasant origin like most of his contemporaries including the majority of African leaders, Sekou Toure received primary school education but was expelled from a trade school for leading a food strike when he was only 15 years old.

A firebrand, he became actively involved in trade union activities and rose to prominence as a national leader of the African trade-union federation he formed after breaking away from the Communist French trade-union confederation.

Sekou Toure also formed the Democratic Party of Guinea. His party lost the 1954 elections which were rigged against him by the French colonial authorities. But in 1957, he won complete control of the Guinea National Assembly, clearing the way for him to lead his country to independence.

In the referendum of September 1958, he won endorsement - by an overwhelming majority - of his position for immediate independence and led Guinea to become the first African French colony to emerge from colonial rule; and by doing so, helped blaze the trail for African emancipation together with Kwame Nkrumah who, only the year before in 1957, became the first black African leader to lead his country to independence.

The independence struggle which had already been going for many years in different parts of Africa was finally beginning to bear fruit, with the sixties being the most important years in the history of African decolonization.

But with decolonization came problems as was tragically demonstrated by the events in the Congo when the country descended into chaos only eleven days after country won independence from Belgium, tirggered by the secession of Katanga Province under the leadership of Moise Tshombe backed by Western interests.

Therefore, while 1960 was hailed as the dawn of a new era for Africa when 17 countries on the continent won independence in that year, it was also a sign and a warning of things yet to come and about which African countries could do very little to avert the catastrophes that befell the continent in subsequent years.

Some of those events were linked to or influenced by what was going on in the United States during that period. The Congo crisis was one of those events in which the United States was actively involved in pursuit of its national and geopolitical interests as the main rival of the Soviet Union in Africa and other parts of the Third World.

Another event was the civil rights movement in the United States which had a lot in common with the African independence struggle.

As we look at the chronology of the main events on the African continent through the years, we see that Africa has come a long way since the sixties. And she still has a long way to go in terms of achieving the goals she set out to achieve at the dawn of independence in the 1960s.

We also going to look at some of the major events in the United States in the 1960s, especially when they complement our analysis of what took place on the African continent during those years.

But we are also going to look at the events which unfolded in the United States during the turbulent sixties on their own merit even if they are not in any way linked or related to any of the events which took place in Africa during the same period since this work is a study of both - Africa and America - and what happened in both places in what is probably one of the most important decades in the history of the world since the end of World War II.

The Sixties and Seventies

From Godfrey Mwakikagile, *Tanzania under Mwalimu Nyerere: Reflections on an African Statesman*, New Africa Press, 2006:

Tanganyika after Independence

TANGANYIKA was the first country to win independence in East Africa. It was followed by Uganda in October 1962, and by Kenya in December 1963. On May 31, 1962, the government of Tanganyika announced that the country would become a republic in December that year and continue to be a member of the Commonwealth.

It became a republic on December 9, 1962, on the first independence anniversary, and Julius Nyerere who had served as prime minister until then became the country's first president.

A new constitution was adopted and was in many ways similar to that of Ghana under Kwame Nkrumah whom Nyerere admired. In fact, in the first official portrait after independence, Nyerere and some of his cabinet members wore Kente cloth like Nkrumah, his ideological compatriot, and his colleagues did and just like many other Ghanaians still do.

The new constitution of Tanganyika after

independence outlawed strikes and greatly increased presidential powers. A preventive detention act aimed at curbing subversive activities had been passed by parliament a few months earlier in the same year, 1962, and greatly enhanced the authority of the government in many areas, although it was viewed with apprehension by some people as an oppressive instrument.

To consolidate national unity, parliament passed a law in 1965 and made Tanganyika a *de jure* one-party state; the year before, in 1964, Ghana also became a one-party socialist state after a controversial referendum and Nkrumah was declared life president, something Nyerere refused to accept when some members of parliament proposed that he should be made life president.

Even before 1965, Tanganyika had been operating as a *de facto* one-party state because it had no opposition in parliament following the devastating defeat of the radical African National Congress (ANC), the main opposition party, in previous elections. The African National Congress was led by Zuberi Mtemvu who left TANU to form the opposition party in pursuit of Africanization which, according to his definition, would virtually exclude non-blacks from the new dispensation as equal members of society.

Soon after independence, Tanganyika faced serious problems in many areas – economic development, education, medical services, civil service, communications and transport, among others – because it did not have enough qualified people to provide much-needed high-level manpower for the young nation. When it won independence, it had only 120 university graduates, among whom were two engineers, two lawyers, and 12 doctors in a country bigger than Nigeria in terms of area, or the size of Texas, Oklahoma and West Virginia combined.

Tanzania is one of the 10 largest countries in Africa in terms of area and population; yet one of the poorest even in Africa itself, and one of the 25 poorest in the world, with a population of about 40 million people in 2006 roughly the same as Canada's.

To solve some of the country's problems, Nyerere instituted a self-help programme and preached self-reliance as national policy under which people volunteered to build roads, bridges, schools, clinics and work on other projects to develop the nation. Teams of volunteers worked across the country and succeeded in completing many of these projects.

The campaign also included adult literacy. People who could read and write volunteered to teach others. The adult literacy campaign was so successful that within a few years, Tanganyika, later Tanzania, had the highest literacy rate in Africa and one of the highest in the world, over 90 percent. Yet it remained poor, very poor.

To tackle poverty, Nyerere introduced the policy of *ujamaa*, a Kiswahili word which means familyhood. It was a policy of socialism with a human face, unlike that of the Marxist brand.

People established communal villages to work on communal farms and other projects but without much success. It was, in fact, a disaster in economic terms and retarded Tanzania's economic growth for more than a decade since its introduction in 1967.

But it also had notable success in many areas. People lived closer together, making it easier for the government to provide them with social services including clinics and schools. The people also built primary schools in their own areas and other facilities which could not have been built had they lived miles apart before *ujamaa* was introduced.

The policy also help to instill egalitarian values and ideals which played a critical role in keeping the people united without accentuating cleavages so typical of capitalist societies which propagate elitism as a virtue, leading some people to feel that they are better than others.

Without such egalitarianism achieved under *ujamaa*,

Tanzania would not be what it is today as a stable, peaceful country where the majority of the people treat each other as brothers and sisters on equal basis in spite of grinding poverty among millions of them. Under Nyerere, ostentatious display of wealth was shunned and even despised. And everything possible was done to reduce the gap between the rich and the poor.

I remember how life was under Nyerere. All of us were involved in development projects, one way or another, sometimes working without being paid. People worked as volunteers on many public projects including farming, the mainstay of the economy. Others were involved in adult education, teaching adults in towns and villages how to read and write. And those of us who had just finished secondary school or high school went into National Service which was mandatory for us in order to participate in development projects instead of simply waiting to get office jobs or go for further education.

We were not paid when we were in National Service. But we were provided with all the basic necessities - food, shelter and clothing. Our induction into National Service was one of the most successful policies which fostered egalitarian values among the elite, including us, many of whom felt they were better than the poor and illiterate peasants and workers, the very same people who paid for our education with their tax money.

I went to Ruvu National Service in January 1971, about 25 miles from Dar es Salaam, and underwent rigorous training which included military training. Other trainees included volunteers from different parts of the country. Most of the volunteers had very little formal education or none. Yet we lived together in the same tents and ate together at the same table without discrimination.

I remember there were some young men and women, fresh from secondary school and high school, who felt that they were better than the illiterate volunteers. They also resented the fact that our participation in National Service was mandatory. But they were a minority. The majority of us accepted the poor and illiterate young men and women from the rural areas as equal to us and we worked together on different projects without any problems.

From Ruvu, I was sent to Bulombora National Service camp in Bukoba district in northwestern Tanzania for further training. The camp was located very close to the shores of Lake Victoria, only a few minutes' walk.

Altogether, the training in National Service camps lasted for six months.

After that I went to Dar es Salaam to work for the ministry of information and broadcasting as an information officer in July 1971 and then went back to the *Daily News*,where I had worked before. I stayed at the ministry of information and broadcasting only for a short time.

Our participation in National Service continued after we left the training camps. We were required to wear National Service uniforms at work, and a large chunk of our salaries, I think about 40 to 60 percent, was deducted to go towards national development projects as mandated by the government.

It was a two-year programme, from the time we first went in, and it taught us discipline and helped instill in us not only egalitarian values but a strong sense of patriotism. We already loved our country. But we were at the same time constantly reminded that there were enemies within, working with enemies outside, to try to destroy our country, sabotage our economy and independence, and we should always be on guard against such fifth columnists. "Be vigilant," we were always reminded in speeches and patriotic songs.

Some of the patriotic songs we sang in National Service training camps concerned apartheid South Africa and other white minority regimes in southern Africa and in Portuguese Guinea in West Africa. They were pretty violent songs, ready to irrigate our land with the blood of the enemy, reminding ourselves that we were on the frontline of the African liberation struggle and should be ready to defend our country, anytime, and at any cost, and be prepared to fight alongside our brothers and sisters still suffering under colonialism and racial oppression anywhere on the continent.

And all that had to do with the leadership of President Julius Nyerere as a staunch Pan-Africanist and strong advocate of African unity who took an uncompromising stand on those issues. And he remained that way until his death.

Apartheid South Africa was the primary target as the most powerful white minority regime on the continent and as the most stubborn. And it evoked some of the strongest feelings among us because of the diabolical nature of the regime and its abominable institution of apartheid.

The Portuguese colonial rulers in Mozambique, our neighbour on the southern border, were not saints, either, and triggered an equally hostile response from us; our anger fuelled by attacks on our country including aerial bombings and planting of deadly mines on our soil by the Portuguese colonial forces because of our uncompromising support for the liberation struggle in Mozambique led by FRELIMO – a Portuguese acronym for Front for the Liberation of Mozambique – waging guerrilla warfare against the colonial forces.

All this was done because of Nyerere's strong commitment to the liberation of Africa and to the independence of Tanganyika, later Tanzania, as a self-reliant nation whose prosperity depended on the people themselves: us.

His Pan-African commitment galvanized him into action probably more than anything else. As he stated in an interview with the *New Internationalist*:

"I have always said that I was African first and socialist second. I would rather see a free and united

Africa before a fragmented socialist Africa."[1]

The humiliation of Africa by our European conquerors also played a major role in shaping his attitude towards them. As he told Rolf Italiaander, the author of *The New African Leaders* (1961), "I have learned to be a moderate through observing the inflexible behaviour of the Europeans."[2]

He made those remarks shortly before independence and they defined his policies after we won independence when he welcomed Europeans and others to stay and live on the basis of equality with us. Jomo Kenyatta expressed similar sentiments shortly after he came out of prison in 1961 but in more strident a tone. As he stated on October 14th the same year:

"Non-Africans who still want to be called 'Bwana' should pack up and go, but others who are prepared to live under our flag are invited to remain."[3]

On January 28, 1962, Kenyatta went a little further, with the stipulation that it is non-Africans who now had to learn to call Africans, "Bwana." The literal translation of "Bwana" is "Mister." But it has deeper meaning, implying "Sir," and someone above you, our European conquerors, for example, in our case.

And that is exactly what Jomo Kenyatta meant when he said on that day in January that Europeans and other non-Africans should not only stop expecting to be called "Bwana" by Africans but should, from now on, learn to call Africans "Bwana." As he put it:

"I want Europeans, Asians and Arabs to learn to call Africans 'Bwana.' Those who agree to do so are free to stay."[4]

Nyerere argued along similar lines saying the first

thing we got when we won independence was dignity. But he also warned against retaliation by Africans now that we were free. It was obvious that many of them including some leaders were in a vindictive mood. As he stated:

"Many of the leaders suffered from discrimination themselves, and some have been unable to achieve that degree of objectivity which would enable them to direct their hatred towards discrimination itself instead of at the racial group which the discriminators represented."[5]

He saw Europeans who remained in Tanganyika and other non-black citizens such as Arabs and Asians as an integral part of the nation not only in terms of equal rights but also in terms of participation in national development and in other areas of national life on equal basis; unlike in neighbouring Kenya where they were marginalized and relegated to the periphery of the mainstream after black Africans assumed power following independence. As the leader of Tanganyika, later Tanzania, Nyerere wanted to see the country develop but without compromising its independence and losing its African personality and culture by becoming a carbon copy of Europe.

Without development, nothing else - fighting poverty, ignorance and disease - could be achieved. And development demanded hard work and a lot of sacrifice; hence the Swahili slogan, *Uhuru na Kazi*, meaning Freedom and Work, Nyerere and other leaders used constantly to exhort us to achieve our nation's goals as one people regardless of race, tribe, colour, creed or national origin. We were all Tanganyikans, later Tanzanians, and we were all Africans. Indians were in India, Europeans in Europe. Those in Africa were African like us. And they still are.

But Nyerere also believed that the country could not develop if its economy and resources were controlled by foreigners. If they did, then they would continue to dictate policy to us as we also continued to delude ourselves into believing that we were truly independent and masters of our own destiny. We just couldn't be independent if our country was controlled by foreigners.

And no country can claim to be truly independent if its economy, not just its government, is controlled or dominated by others. In fact, you can't even have an independent government if you are not economically independent or are told what to do by outsiders. That is why in the mid-sixties Nyerere asked West Germany to withdraw all of its aid from Tanzania when it made such aid conditional. He could not accept anyone dictating terms to us. I remember that time. We lost the assistance that we needed but it was worth the sacrifice.

One of the main reasons Nyerere was able to get the support he needed to implement his policies was his determination to ensure mass participation in the political process from the grassroots level all the way to the top leaving out nobody. And this helped to make even the poorest, illiterate peasants in the remote interior feel that they were a part of the decision making process which affected their lives and that of the entire nation. Thus imbued with a sense of patriotism, millions across the country were prepared to make great sacrifices when asked to do so, or did so simply on their own when they felt that something had to be done in their communities or for the benefit of the country as a whole.

They came to embrace a national cause as their own and felt that whatever they did at the local level was also for the good of the country. And they did so because they sincerely believed that Nyerere who encouraged them to do so was deeply committed to their well-being and that of the entire nation. And he was.

The Tanganyika I knew after independence was one of extraordinary peace and tranquility in spite of poverty; and one of caring for the least endowed amongst us. I remember the free education, the free medical service, and the free transport we were provided with as students going to and coming from our boarding schools.

We did not pay one cent. For example, I remember the warrant we were given to go to Songea Secondary School and back home during holidays (vacation) in the months of June and December every year from 1965 to 1968. A warrant was a free bus ticket given collectively to a group of students going to the same destination. Those of us from Rungwe district were given one for the round trip to and from school, with one student being responsible for keeping it; students from Mtwara district were given theirs, as were the others.

If you went alone in one direction, you were also given yours. For example, I was given one when I travelled from Tukuyu to Dar es Salaam in 1969 to go to Tambaza High School and continued to get it until I finished Form VI, or standard 14, in 1970.

The first decade of independence under Nyerere was also noted for its euphoria and optimism among the people across the country. Most had not yet enjoyed the fruits of independence but there was a sense of hope and strong belief that we now at least had the freedom and opportunity to do what we wanted to do as a free people. That is something we had not been able to do before when we were under colonial rule.

Besides getting free medical service, many schools including the University of Dar es Salaam were also built during the first decade of independence in the sixties; universal primary education was vigorously pursued, and the people in villages and towns were brought into the political process to participate in decision making to ensure justice and equality for all on a scale unprecedented anywhere else in Africa. As Nyerere said back in the late 1950s about his commitment to equality:

"Our struggle has been, still is, and always will be a struggle for human rights....Our position is based on the belief in the equality of human beings, in their rights and their duties as citizens."[6]

Rights came with responsibilities, and responsibilities entailed discipline. I remember when President Nyerere visited our school, Songea Secondary School, one evening in 1966. He had been touring Songea district and came to speak to us before flying back to Dar es Salaam that night. He did not have much time and spoke for only a few minutes after he was introduced by our headmaster, Paul Mhaiki who, only a few years later, became head of adult education in Tanzania.

The one and only thing the president emphasized in his speech to us that evening was discipline. He told us, we could not succeed in school, or do anything else constructive or be productive in life, without discipline. And just before he left, he said, "You must have discipline. Always remember discipline." And he knew exactly what he was talking about, not only as the leader of our country but as a former secondary school teacher himself before he went into politics to lead Tanganyika to independence. As he once said, he was a teacher by choice and a politician by accident.

The first decade of independence for Tanganyika, later Tanzania, under President Nyerere witnessed some of the most dramatic changes in the direction of our country which had an impact beyond our borders. Probably the most memorable ones, and the most profound in terms of impact, were the adoption of the one-party system and the promulgation of socialist policies enunciated in the *Arusha Declaration* whose implementation led to nationalization of the country's major assets and to the establishment of *ujamaa* villages.

One interesting thing about the *Arusha Declaration* is that many people who criticized it had not even read the document; not only Tanzanians but others as well, including some African students from other parts of

Africa whom I went to school with at Wayne State University in the United States in the early and mid-seventies.

Because they did not like socialism and *ujamaa* villages, they automatically dismissed the *Arusha Declaration* as a deeply flawed document in all its aspects.

Some of them, if they get the chance to read this book, may have second thoughts after they read the Declaration reproduced in the book in its entirety.

Throughout the document, one theme constantly comes up. And that is Nyerere's deep concern for the well-being of the poor, the peasants and the workers, especially the peasants, who constitute the vast majority of the population of Tanzania and those of other African countries and others in the Third World.

The Arusha Declaration earned Nyerere a reputation as one of the most prominent socialist thinkers in the world and one of the most articulate spokesmen of the poor and the oppressed. It was also one of the most important political and economic documents to come out of the Third World.

In the context of Tanzania, it had far-reaching consequences. Almost everybody in Tanzania was affected by the *Arusha Declaration*. And its impact is still felt today even after it was abandoned and virtually repudiated in this era of globalisation and free market policies.

But the masses and the poor will always remember the *Arusha Declaration* as a political manifesto and an economic blueprint whose implementation enabled them to be accorded dignity as equal citizens entitled to the same rights as the rich; made it possible for them to get a lot of benefits including free education and free medical service provided by the government; and, in the case of workers in factories and elsewhere including government offices, they were guaranteed job security under the guidance of workers' committees – which monitored and sometimes even disciplined employers – without fear of being summarily dismissed or terminated without just cause.

In fact, in the late 1990s and beyond, many people demanded a return to the status quo ante when the *Arusha Declaration* was in force because of the neglect they now suffered in a free market economy.

The one-party system was also renounced after the adoption of capitalism. But, like the *Arusha Declaration*, it also played a critical role in maintaining national unity by instilling egalitarian ideals and providing equal access to the political process for all citizens under one umbrella which would have been impossible under divisive politics so typical of multiparty democracy in the African context where political parties are no more than interest groups formed on tribal and regional basis to promote the interests of their members and supporters at the expense of the nation.

Tanzania under Nyerere was spared the agony of civil wars and ethnic conflicts which have devastated many African countries because of the inclusive nature of the one-party system under his leadership.

After multiparty democracy was introduced in 1992, the country was rocked by violence a few years later, even if only on a limited scale, because of the partisan nature of the political parties appealing to ethnoregional allegiances to the detriment of national unity, peace and stability; with each striving to get the biggest chunk of the national pie.

In terms of social justice, it was a golden era under Nyerere. It is a by-gone era we will never see again.

Africa in The Nineties: End of the The Cold War and Transition to Democracy

THE collapse of the Soviet Union in the late eighties and early nineties marked the beginning of the end of the Cold War between the East and the West which started within two years after the end of World War II.

The world witnessed the end of communism in the Soviet Union itself and in other countries in Eastern Europe – as well as others elsewhere – and the renunciation of Marxism as a state ideology in some African countries which had adopted socialism in pursuit of economic development along Marxist-Leninist lines.

Tanzania, the only country which formulated and implemented African socialism as a state ideology, which was non-Marxist-Leninist, also abandoned its policy although the ideology was not officially renounced by the ruling party. But the party's decision to adopt free-market policies clearly marked the end of socialism, known as *ujamaa*, in Tanzania as official policy.

It was also the beginning of the end of autocratic rule and military dictatorship in Africa, although the transition was gradual. Only a handful of countries on the continent fully embraced democracy.

Even today, the people in most of the countries across Africa are still fighting for democracy, as the leaders continue to deny them freedom in order to perpetuate themselves in office. They have done so by carrying out what have come to be known as constitutional coups, changing constitutions to extend their rule. They remove term limits or add terms, effectively becoming life presidents. Rwanda and Uganda are some of the best examples where the leaders have amended constitutions to extend their tenure in office.

All this is can be traced to the decline of the post-colonial state that began in the late seventies. Authoritarianism which began in the euphoric sixties, as Africans celebrated the end of colonial rule and sometimes overlooked the emergence of the oppressive state as leaders consolidated power while justifying suppression of dissent for the sake of national unity, reached its peak in the seventies. It was also during that period when people across the continent began to notice that their leaders had in many cases failed to deliver on their promises.

Life was becoming harder and harder even for the elite who were supposed to play a critical role in helping governments implement policies to achieve economic development.

Even policies were, in many cases, deeply flawed in terms of formulation, focus and implementation – good intentions notwithstanding.

It was the beginning of the decline of the post-colonial state that was already structurally flawed because it was not structured to reflect African realities but was instead no more than an extension of the colonial order built on the imperial premise of ruling from the top, with decrees and other forms of administrative fiat, as the best way to govern and control the people.

The eighties witness a continuation of this decline and the institutionalisation of what came be known as failed states across the continent; what Jonathan Frimpont-

Ansah, a former senior official of the Bank of Ghana, described as vampire states. The very saviours of the people had become their predators.

African leaders turned to the outside world, instead of seeking solutions within, to seek relief and try to rejuvenate their economies which had literally collapsed through the years because of corruption and wrong policies. It was as if Africans had never had solutions to their own problems and had to beg outsiders to come in and help them solve those problems. Indigenous knowledge and institutions, partly destroyed by colonial rule, were despised even by Africans themselves. Critical analysis of the African condition in order to find solutions relevant to Africa was ignored.

It is worth remembering that Botswana, the only country on the continental mainland which has practised true democracy continuously since independence in 1965, has used traditional institutions to achieve this goal. It is also the most prosperous, economically, despite some setbacks now and then.

Tragically, for many countries on the continent, they have ignored traditional institutions in their modernisation process and in their quest for democracy. That has been the case since independence. They never looked inward to find solutions to their problems, except in very few cases such as Tanzania where Nyerere tried to build a modern nation on the basis of traditional values and principles which collectively constituted familyhood or *ujamaa*.

For the rest, everything had to be westernised or Europeanised.

But even Tanzania was caught in the same dilemma – the same predicament: independent yet dependent – when she was compelled to seek economic aid for her ailing economy, although the international financial institutions Africans turned to for help, as Nyerere himself said, were never intended to help African countries.

They were not structured to reflect African realities,

accommodate Africans or consult them on how the assistance they sought should be used. They were intended to help Western European countries rebuild their economies and recover from the damage they suffered in World War II.

They were later transformed into predatory institutions to exploit African countries and others in the Third World by providing loans which could never be repaid and which were never intended to help those countries develop.

Desperate for help, African countries became colonies again in the new imperial order known as globalisation dictated by the West whose members include Africa's former colonial masters.

The harsh reality is that Africa has never really been free; her political independence – what little she has – neuralised by her economic weakness.

Coinciding with the decline and in some cases the collapse of the post-colonial state across Africa was the demand for freedom.

It was a demand by the people for participation in government in order to make decisions for themselves and control their destiny instead of leaving it in the hands of politicians and bureaucrats who, through the years, had failed and refused to listen to them.

It was a demand for popular democracy by the masses who constitute the largest yet most neglected segment of the population in every country across the continent. Tragically, it is a demand that in many cases has gone unheeded through the years.

Leaders use all kinds of ways, especially by allowing limited freedom and co-opting the opposition and its ideas and policies, to perpetuate themselves in office. Power is concentrated in their hands, the opposition is subordinate to them, and true democracy remains a sham. As Professor Crawford Young states in his book, *The Postcolonial State in Africa: Fifty Years of Independence, 1960 – 2010*:

By the mid-1990s, the term 'semidemocracy' – or 'semiauthoritarianism' – had emerged to describe a system of rule whereby incumbents adapted to the new rules of the game by adopting the formalities of a liberalized polity but restricted their application to assure retention of power. Marina Ottaway defines such regimes as 'ambiguous systems' not easily classified as democratic or authoritarian.

William Case had earlier coined the phrase to capture the political essence of such durable Southeast Asian regimes as Malaysia, Singapore, and Thailand. Richard Joseph proposes a different metaphor, 'virtual democracy,' driven by the twin imperatives of retaining power and securing 'external presentability.' – Crawford Young, *The Postcolonial State in Africa: Fifty Years of Independence, 1960 – 2010*, Madison, Wisconsin, USA: University of Wisconsin Press, 2012, p. 28).

He goes on to state:

Such hybrids of democracy and authoritarianism appeared a durable regime type by the early twenty-first century; well over a third of African states fell in this category.

By 2004, eighteen rulers who held power on the eve of the democratic wave in 1988 were still in office. Opposition forces that sprang to life at the peak of the transition in 1990s over time became demoralized by their inability to oust such governments in countries like Gabon and Cameroon, among others....

Still, semidemocracy was in most respects a clear improvement on the patrimonial autocracy that preceded it. There was some opportunity for an opposition in the legislature or through a free media. Human rights groups organized and became forceful voices, linked to an international network that amplified their message. National and international nongovernmental organizations could take root and provide alternative forums and mechanisms for social action." – (Ibid., p. 29).

The end of apartheid in South Africa coincided with the wave of democratisation across the continent, partly facilitated by the collapse of the Soviet Union and the end of communism in almost all the countries where it was adopted as a national policy.

Also, the end of white minority rule in Namibia, which

was ruled by apartheid South Africa, and in South Africa itself, the citadel of white supremacy on the continent, coincided with the demand for truly representative government across Africa with an intensity that had never been witnessed before in the post-colonial era.

But it was a demand that was met with resistance from the authoritarian governments and entrenched dictatorships determined to maintain the status quo. However, the demand was relentless and despotic rulers such as Dr. Hastings Kamuzu Banda, life president of Malawi, were forced out of office in democratic elections which only a few years before would have been unthinkable.

The demand for democracy was a continental phenomenon. But the achievement was not; it was limited to only a few countries as the people in other parts of Africa continued to organise and mobilise forces to bring about fundamental change. It is a struggle that continues today.

There is a concerted effort by many leaders to reverse the achievements of the 1990s and return to the status quo ante of authoritarian rule.

Even in the few countries where democracy is being institutionalised, consolidation of power at the centre remains the norm. Leaders refuse to decentralise power and restructure let alone replace the highly centralised state despite its deficiencies as an oppressive apparatus.

But there is hope for Africa, clearly demonstrated by the ouster of a number of leaders who have been forced out of office by the people. The people are determined to be free. They are also determined to hold their leaders – including some of the most repressive regimes – accountable for their actions.

They have mobilised themselves into a potent force of popular resistance to corrupt, authoritarian rule to achieve democracy which cannot be complete until it is truly representative of the people all the way down to the grassroots level where they make decisions for themselves and decide what is best for them instead of leaders and bureaucrats in distant capitals doing that "in the name of the people."

This change, which started in the late 1980s and gained momentum in the 1990s and beyond, is unstoppable. That is the wave of the future for Africa in the twentieth-first century.

www.ingramcontent.com/pod-product-compliance
Lightning Source LLC
LaVergne TN
LVHW051823080426
835512LV00018B/2708